GREAT BATTLES

GREAT BATTLES

General Editor: Christer Jorgensen

Bath · New York · Singapore · Hong Kong · Cologne · Delhi · Melbourne

This edition published by Parragon in 2010

Parragon
Queen Street House
4 Queen Street
Bath BA1 1HE, UK

Copyright © Parragon Books Ltd 2007

Cover design by Ummagumma

All illustrations and maps © Art-Tech Ltd.

ISBN: 978-1-4454-1129-3

Editorial and design by
Amber Books Ltd
Bradley's Close
74–77 White Lion Street
London N1 9PF
United Kingdom
www.amberbooks.co.uk

Project Editor: Michael Spilling
Design: Hawes Design
Picture Research: Terry Forshaw
Text: Martin J. Dougherty, Michael E. Haskew,
Christer Jorgensen, Chris Mann, Chris McNab,
Michael Neiberg, and Michael Pavkovic

Printed in China

CONTENTS

INTRODUCTION

History is more than a simple collection of wars and battles. Yet some battles have altered the course of history and with it the fate of the human race. In this book a number of distinguished military historians have presented in a series of short, crisp chapters some 30 battles that were either decisive or great.

Is there a difference between greatness and decisiveness? Indeed there is. A battle can be famous without being decisive, a military landmark, or even important. It only needs to have the mark of greatness. To give an example: the Battle of Adrianople in 378, although a humiliating defeat for the Roman Empire (just like Cannae half a millennium earlier) the battle changed nothing. Even though the glorious edifice that was the Roman Empire was crumbling, it lingered on in the West for another century while the Eastern (Byzantine) Empire existed for another millennium. The German barbarians may have destroyed an army and slain an emperor, but they had only dented Roman might.

THE SCOTS GREYS' CHARGE into the center of the French line at Waterloo has gone down in the annals of great cavalry encounters. Waterloo was a great battle that ended Napoleon's chances of reestablishing himself as emperor of France.

GREAT BATTLES, GREAT CONSEQUENCES

Then what constitutes a decisive or great battle? Here one has to make use of speculation, so-called counterfactual history, in order to conjure up a vision of what the world would have looked like should an individual battle have turned out differently—in other words, if the defeated party had won the battle and then been able to exploit the resulting victory.

Had the Athenians lost the sea battle of Salamis the Persians would have been able to conquer Greece. As a collection of tributary states, the Greek nations would probably not have played their respective roles as incubators of western European civilizations. That civilization would have borne an imprint of Persian origins.

In 732 Charles Martel defeated the Arabs and as a consequence Islam was confined to the southwestern corner

of the European continent. Had Martel lost the battle then the strongest military feudal state in western Europe—the Kingdom of the Franks—would have been crushed and with it an embryonic Christian European civilization. Europe would have been a larger version of Muslim-dominated Al-Andalus (Spain).

Three hundred years later, the Battle of Hastings saw the Anglo-Saxons decisively defeated by Duke William of Normandy, giving birth, after another three hundred years, to an English (Anglo–Norman) national identity. Had Harold prevailed, the course of English history would have been different.

This single, decisive battle altered the course of history and made Anglo-Saxon England more European. Equally, had the Spanish Armada in 1588 swept the sea of Drake and Howard's fleets, combined with Parma's army in Flanders and landed on England's shores, then Britain would have been re-Catholicized. As a consequence, there would probably have been no British empire and the history of the world would have been altered irrevocably.

Two decisive battles from the American Civil War are also featured: Antietam and Gettysburg. Although both battles were technically "draws," these two epic encounters undermined the Confederacy's ability to wage war and contributed to the Union's victory over the Southern states.

Some of the major battles of the twentieth century are also featured. On the beaches of Normandy, the Allies sought to begin the liberation of Europe from the Nazis on June 6, 1944. The success or failure of the largest seaborne invasion in the history of warfare would define the future of Western Europe.

Yet a battle does not need to be decisive or even important from a military point of view to be a great battle. It simply needs to be great because of its commanders, the use of some new tactic, weaponry, or formations or it could—like Constantinople—have a vital symbolic value as the end of one era or the beginning of a new epoch. Greatness, like military glory, is fickle and fleeting and changes with time. But some of it endures down the centuries having become immortal as well as being touched by greatness and that is why we—both writers of great battles and the readers—continue to discuss, read, and write about such battles. Great battles endure because they have something more than most military encounters and therefore continue to keep us enthralled down the ages.

The authors of this volume of great battles sincerely hope that you the reader share our fascination for the great military battles of the past.

Christer Jorgensen, General Editor

ALTHOUGH ULTIMATELY achieving very little, the forceful charge of Pickett's Confederate infantry against the Union center at the Battle of Gettysburg in 1863 has gone down in military folklore for its dash and bravery.

A GERMAN OFFICER scans the horizon amid the rubble of Stalingrad, October 1942. The Battle of Stalingrad involved some of the most ferocious urban fighting ever seen in the history of warfare. The Soviet destruction of the German Sixth Army decisively turned the war on the Eastern Front.

THE AGE OF
THE SWORD

The individual warrior dominated much of warfare in the Ancient and Medieval eras, often fighting in massed, ill-disciplined hordes. It was the rise of Sparta in Ancient Greece that showed what a professional, disciplined force of heavily armed infantry could do in the face of superior numbers. This was brought to climactic fruition with Alexander the Great's seemingly invincible Macedonian phalanxes. Later, the Romans created the most complete, efficient professional army of the Ancient era: their use of well drilled, tightly packed infantry cohorts dominated the battlefields of Europe and the Mediterranean for centuries.

However, with the demise of the Roman empire, military technology and professionalism regressed—only the Normans and Byzantines kept the tradition of the professional soldier alive. Starting from the fourteenth century onward, during the High Middle Ages, professional armies again began to dominate the battlefield, and, as seen at Agincourt, such armies could decisively defeat a numerically superior foe.

THIS FIFTEENTH-CENTURY MANUSCRIPT ILLUSTRATION of the capture of Damietta (1219) in Egypt during the Fifth Crusade shows the very bloody and personal nature of hand-to-hand fighting with swords. The sword was the dominant sidearm until the development of arquebus and pistol in the sixteenth century.

MARATHON 490 B.C.E.

At Marathon, an outnumbered force of Greek hoplites seized a chance to defeat their Persian foes, exploiting their superior armor and discipline to win one of the most famous tactical victories of the Ancient World. It was, however, not the end of the Persian threat to the independent Greek city-states.

By 539 B.C.E. the Persians under Cyrus the Great had conquered much of Anatolia, including those Greeks living in Ionia on the coast. Initially, relations between the Persians and their Greek subjects were relatively cordial. Over the course of the next several decades a number of tensions emerged, which soured that relationship. The Persians impeded the Greeks' economic development with trade restrictions. Moreover, the autocratic Persians imposed puppet tyrants on the Ionian city-states—something antithetical to the independent-minded Greeks. In 499 B.C.E. the Ionians finally broke into open revolt against the Persians. Their leader, Aristagoras of Miletus sought aid from the states on the Greek mainland. His first

MARATHON FACTS

Who: Nearly 11,000 Athenians and Plataean hoplites, led on the day of the battle by the Athenian general Militiades, were opposed by a multi-ethnic Persian army numbering perhaps 25,000, under the command of the Persian Artaphernes and the Median noble Datis.

What: The Athenians weakened the center of their line and strengthened their wings, allowing the Persians to push through the center, only to be defeated on the flanks and have their center enveloped by the victorious wings of the Greek army.

Where: The Plain of Marathon, about 26 miles (41.8km) from Athens.

When: August 12, 490 B.C.E.

Why: The Persians wanted to attack Athens to punish the city for its support for the rebellion of the Ionian Greek cities.

Outcome: The Persians were driven from Greece for 10 years.

AT THE BATTLE OF MARATHON MILITIADES, *with 10,000 Athenian and 400 Plataean hoplites, defeated a Persian force nearly double their size, including 10,000 Immortals, proving the value of the phalanx infantry formation.*

attempt to secure allies was with Sparta. The Spartans had the best army in Greece and so were a good choice. Unfortunately, King Cleomenes did not see how sending forces to fight for the far-off Ionian Greeks was in the Spartans' interest and so declined to support the revolt. Aristagoras received a better reception at Athens. He made a speech to the Athenian assembly where he argued that the Persians were inferior to the Greeks in battle and that the wealth of the great empire would provide much loot for the victors. The assembly debated the issue and decided to send aid to their Ionian cousins—a squadron of 20 warships. The Greek armada put in at Ephesus where its troops were landed. The army proceeded to the Persian capital, Sardis, and the city was quickly taken and, with a Persian army approaching, burned to the ground. In a subsequent battle, the Greeks were defeated and the Athenians decided to return home. The revolt continued until 493 B.C.E. but the result was a foregone conclusion— the powerful and centralized Persian armed forces outclassed the individualistic Greek states in fighting a protracted war.

THE BATTLE OF MARATHON ended dramatically with the collapse of the Persian line and a flight to the beached Persian ships. Only seven of the Persian ships escaped capture. Herodotus numbered the Persian dead at 6,400.

Although the revolt had been successfully suppressed, the Persian Great King, Darius I, had learned about the participation of the Athenians and was livid. A story by Herodotus recounts how Darius had a slave tell him "Master, remember the Athenians" three times before dinner lest he forget to punish them for their interference. And so, in 492 B.C.E. Darius sent an expedition under his son-in-law Mardonius to do just that but hostile tribesmen in Thrace and bad weather off Mount Athos, necessitated the forces return home.

THE CAMPAIGN

But Darius was not going to give up on his plans for punishing the Athenians. Thus in the following year another expedition was being prepared. This would move across the Aegean to punish the Athenians and Eretrians, who had also supported the revolt, by burning their cities and enslaving the populations. This force would be totally transported by sea, thereby avoiding the problems that had beset Mardonius' expedition. The naval component of the expedition was composed of nearly 600 ships. Perhaps 200 of these were warships serving as the fleet's escort while the remaining 400 were transports that would carry the troops and their supplies. The transports included a number of specially designed horse transportation to carry the mounts for the Persian cavalry. The landing force numbered perhaps 25,000 fighting men including a small cavalry contingent, probably about 1,000 strong. This force was commanded by Darius' nephew Artaphernes and Datis, a nobleman of Median descent. Also present was Hippias, who had ruled Athens as a tyrant until he was expelled in 510 B.C.E. The Persians understood the fractious nature of politics in a Greek city-state and no doubt saw the potential of using Hippias to raise a fifth column within Athens itself.

The Persian fleet set sail from Tarsus and sailed westward. The armada put ashore at a number of islands along the way and reduced them either through the threat or the use of force. A major landing was made on the island of Euboea in order to attack the city of Eretria, singled out, along with Athens, by Darius for punishment on account of their role in supporting the Ionian revolt. The people of Eretria were in a quandary as to what to do in the face of such a powerful force.

Some were in favor of trying to hold the town while others argued for abandoning the city and continuing to fight from nearby hills. But before a decision could be made the town was handed over by a faction who had been bribed with Persian gold in exchange for opening the gates of the town to the enemy. The temples of the city were burned in retribution for the destruction at Sardis. From Euboea the Persians headed to Attica, landing at the plain of Marathon on August 5, nearly 26 miles (41.8km) from Athens. The landing spot was undoubtedly chosen in consultation with Hippias since it provided everything the Persians required, including a long beach where their ships could be brought ashore, an ample water supply, access to Athens, and room to maneuver, especially for their cavalry, should the Athenians choose to give battle there.

When the Athenians learned of the Persians' landing, they immediately sent for aid—the herald Phlippides' most famously ran 140 miles (225.3km) to Sparta. Unfortunately, the Spartans were not able to send help on account of a religious festival, the Carneia, which would not allow them to march until August 12. With this news, the Athenians debated their course of action. Some were in favor of preparing for a siege—although given Hippias' presence and the treachery at Eretria, this seemed rather risky. Others argued that it was imperative to keep the Persians penned in at Marathon and not allow them to reach the city. Included in this group was the general Miltiades. His opinion carried some weight since he had previous dealings with the Persians and had fought in the Ionian revolt. As a result, the Athenian army of nearly 10,000 hoplites, heavily armed infantry, marched out to Marathon. They were joined by a force of between 600 and 1,000 hoplites from the city of Plataea, a longtime ally of Athens.

DISPOSITIONS

The Persians hauled their ships ashore along a narrow strip of beach known as the Schoinia, beyond which lay an expanse of marsh. Beyond the marsh was a village with a large area of open ground that was near a spring and it is here the Persians seem to have made their main encampment because it would have provided them with water and fodder. The Athenians and their Plataean allies encamped at the southern edge of the Plain of Marathon north of a small marsh, the Brexisa, between some high ground and the sea. The Greeks protected their camp using fallen trees with specially sharpened branches.

THE BATTLE

The two armies faced each other for perhaps four days. Each side had good reason to wait. For the Athenians, each day that passed brought Spartan aid closer—with the end of the Carneia on August 12, the Spartans would be able to march to their aid arriving perhaps by the 15th. Moreover, given the large expanse of the Plain of Marathon, and the ability of the Persians to deploy and maneuver their cavalry there, it did not make tactical sense for the Greeks to march out of the favorable terrain near their fortified camp, which was situated between the sea and the hills. This would make the heavily armed hoplites, in their phalanx formation, a formidable force against the more lightly equipped Persians. For their part, the Persians also had reason to believe that

AN ACCURATE GREEK phalanx formation cannot be determined from ancient sources. This drawings shows one possibility, with the hoplon attached to the soldier's left arm and the spear held in both hands.

time was on their side, at least initially. As had occurred at Eretria, they hoped for help from within the city itself. In this case, they expected the supporters of Hippias to betray city to them, no doubt with the encouragement of Persian gold. The Persians were waiting for signal, a highly polished bronze shield would be flashed from Mount Pentele, which would indicate that all was ready.

While the details of the plan are not known, it seems clear that the Persians would embark the bulk of their troops on ships and sail to Athens while the Athenian forces were still at Marathon. Moreover, the Persians did not wish to assault the Athenians and Plataeans while in their strong position at the southern end of the plain since the terrain would nullify both their numerical advantage and the mobility of their cavalry.

By the evening of August 11, however, time was running out for the Persians. There had been no shield signal from the fifth column in Athens and the Spartan festival would be coming to an end shortly. That meant that the Athenians

GREEK HOPLITE

A typical hoplite of the Persian War era. His primary weapon was a long iron-headed spear, which could be between 6–10ft (2–3m) in length. It was usually held overarm in combat, and underarm when maneuvering. He also carried a short sword about 2ft (60cm) in length, made of iron with bronze fittings. The sword was used in both a cutting and thrusting motion. For protection he carries a hoplon (shield) made of wood with a bronze face and leather inner lining. The hoplon was secured to the hoplite's forearm by a band, and he held a grip in his left fist. His Corinthian helmet is topped with a plume of horsehair, which could be dyed for effect. His torso is protected by a cuirass of stiffened linen with metal scales added for greater protection. On his shins are molded bronze greaves, while simple leather sandals are worn on his feet.

RELIEF OF IMMORTALS *at the Apadana, Persepolis, Iran. The Immortals were an elite royal guard within the Achaemenid Persian army. Only ethnic Persians or Medeans could be members of the unit which, according to the Greek historian Herodotus, always numbered precisely 10,000 men.*

could expect Spartan reinforcements and the presence of such tough, well disciplined hoplites would dramatically transform the military balance on the Plain of Marathon. As a result, the Persians began to embark a part of their forces on the transports so they could sail for Athens the next morning while the remainder of their forces kept a watch on the Athenian and Plataean hoplites at Marathon. Even without the shield signal, the Persians could hope for help from within the city if the army were away.

This force was to be under the command of Datis and seems to have included the majority of the cavalry who would be very useful in making a dash for Athens once the task force made landfall at Phaleron Bay. Artaphernes would stay at Marathon and maintain a close blockade of the Athenian camp. He probably had about 15,000 men with him, almost exclusively infantry. Fortunately for the

CLASSIC HOPLITE HELMETS, *from left to right: a simple Corinthian helmet; the classic Corinthian design with long cheek pieces; a later Illyrian helmet; and a late Corinthian design with a space cut out for the wearer's ears to improve their hearing.*

Athenians, they were alerted to the Persian plan by some sympathetic Ionians who were serving with the Persians. They sent the famous message "the cavalry are away," which galvanized the resolve of the Athenian commanders to offer battle. Indeed, the 10 Athenian strategoi, generals elected from each of Athens' 10 tribal divisions, were deadlocked as to whether or not to stay put and fight, return to Athens (they, too, were mindful of treachery from within the city), or to offer battle, a course of action favored by Militiades.

Fortunately, the War Archon (a ceremonial position in which the holder can cast the deciding vote in the case of such a deadlock) supported staying at Marathon and advancing against the Persians. The decision was made to launch an attack at dawn. If they could quickly and decisively defeat Artaphernes' troops it would be possible to make a forced march along the coastal road to Athens and arrive before the Persian assault force.

The next morning saw the opposing forces arrayed for battle. Militiades, who understood Persian tactics, was in command that day, and deployed the Greek forces. He knew the Persians were likely to put their best troops in the center of their battle line and that the Persian numbers would make it likely that if he arrayed his phalanx eight-deep along the entire front, they would be outflanked. In order to prevent this he made the center of his line thinner, knowing that the Persians would initially have success there.

However, Militiades also knew that the wings of the Persian formation would be formed from lighter-armed and less enthusiastic levies and that the heavily armed wings of the Greek army would be victorious. He therefore ordered that the wings not pursue the defeated levies but once they had been driven off, to wheel inward on the Persian center. The right wing was under the command of the War Archon Callimachus and the left was formed by the Plataeans.

Artaphernes deployed his troops as Militiades had expected. His best troops, Iranian soldiers from the standing army and tough Saka mercenaries, formed the center of his formation with various levies, including unenthusiastic Ionian Greeks, on the flanks. In order to maintain his close

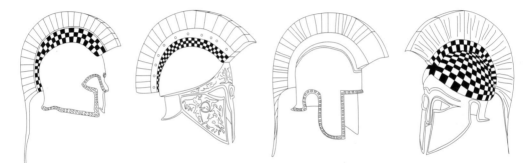

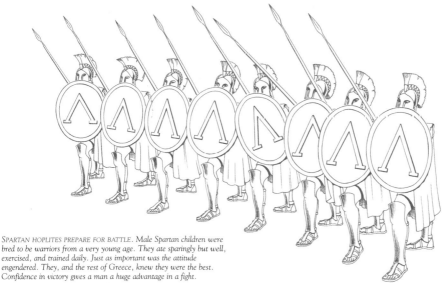

SPARTAN HOPLITES PREPARE FOR BATTLE. *Male Spartan children were bred to be warriors from a very young age. They ate sparingly but well, exercised, and trained daily. Just as important was the attitude engendered. They, and the rest of Greece, knew they were the best. Confidence in victory gives a man a huge advantage in a fight.*

blockade of the Athenian camp, he advanced to within eight stades, or 1 mile (1.6km), of the Greek positions.

The Greeks advanced from their camp toward the Persian lines. Herodotus recounts that they did so at the run, to reduce the considerable number of arrows that would be shot by the Persians, many of who carried bows. This is very unlikely since to run a mile in heavy hoplite armor would have been nearly impossible and unnecessary—the Athenians likely broke into a jog at about 150 yards (137m) —the range of a Persian bow. The battle lines engaged and

the Persians had the better of it in the center where the best of the Persian troops were posted and the Athenians were pushed back. On the wings, however, the levies were routed. Following their orders, the victorious Greeks wheeled in against the Persian center catching them in a double envelopment. A slaughter followed with 6,400 Persian casualties, mostly Iranian and Saka troops, and only 192 Athenians, including Callimachus, and a handful of Plataeans killed. The Greeks also captured seven Persian ships although the others escaped.

AFTERMATH

The Athenians, could not, however, rest after their victory. While one tribal division held the field, the remainder made a forced march back to Athens. They arrived in time to deter the Persians from landing and so Datis, now joined by Artaphernes' survivors, was forced to return home. While the Athenians and Plataeans had won a great victory, they had not really won the war.

The Persians returned home where, almost immediately, they undertook preparations for another campaign—although it would take 10 years, the Persians would return in force with any eye to conquering all of Greece, not just punishing the Athenians.

POPULAR MYTH HAS IT *that following the Greek victory at Marathon, the Athenian runner, Philippedes, delivered the news to the worried Athenians 26 miles (42km) away. The modern marathon race celebrates his feat.*

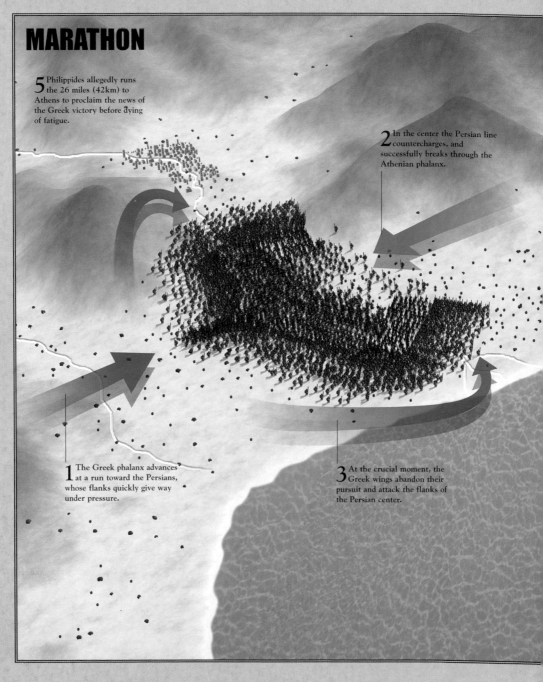

MARATHON

5 Philippides allegedly runs the 26 miles (42km) to Athens to proclaim the news of the Greek victory before dying of fatigue.

2 In the center the Persian line countercharges, and successfully breaks through the Athenian phalanx.

1 The Greek phalanx advances at a run toward the Persians, whose flanks quickly give way under pressure.

3 At the crucial moment, the Greek wings abandon their pursuit and attack the flanks of the Persian center.

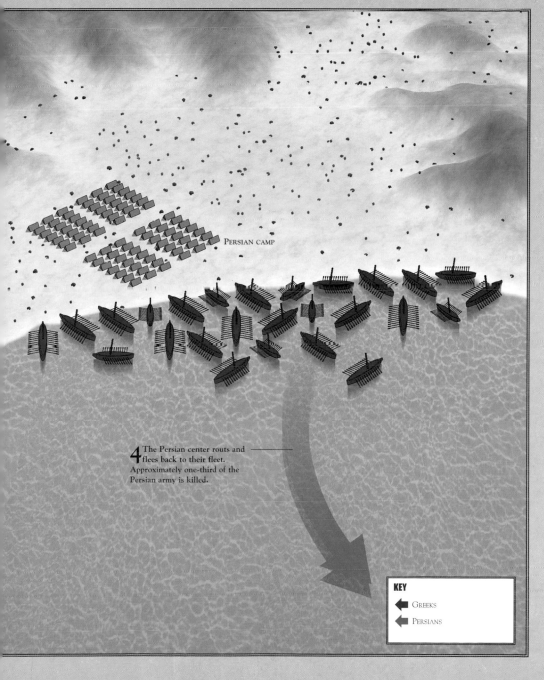

PERSIAN CAMP

4 The Persian center routs and flees back to their fleet. Approximately one-third of the Persian army is killed.

KEY

◀ GREEKS

◀ PERSIANS

SALAMIS   480 B.C.E.

On land and sea, the Persian Great King Xerxes moved with massive force against the Greek city-states, principally Athens and Sparta. At Thermopylae, a mere 300 Spartan hoplites sacrificed themselves to buy precious time. At Salamis, the Greeks inflicted a crushing naval defeat on the invaders and preserved the flower of Western culture.

During the fifth century B.C.E., the vast empire of Persia was at the height of its glory. The realm of King Darius I extended from the Caucasus to the Indian Ocean and from the shores of the Mediterranean Sea to the Indus River, and his subjects included a great diversity of peoples. Among these were the Ionian Greeks, who had settled on the western coast of Asia Minor. In 500 B.C.E., the Ionians rose in rebellion against Darius. They were defeated after six years of bitter fighting. The people of Athens had recognized their ancestral ties with the Ionians and burned the Persian city of Sardis. In 491 B.C.E., Darius sought to punish the Athenians for their interference in what he considered a domestic affair. His punitive expedition,

SALAMIS FACTS

Who: A combined Greek naval force under the Athenian Themistocles and numbering 300 triremes opposed 400 Persian triremes commanded by several admirals as Xerxes (d. 486 B.C.E.) watched from nearby heights seated on a golden throne.

What: The Persian fleet was routed and fled in confusion after being lured into shallow waters, surrounded and set upon by the rams of the Greek vessels.

Where: In the Saronic Gulf near the island of Salamis, west of modern Athens, Greece.

When: September 20, 480 B.C.E.

Why: The Persian Great King Xerxes intended to avenge the defeat of his father, Darius, at Marathon a decade earlier and extend his empire into Europe.

Outcome: The Persians suffered grievous losses and were compelled to withdraw. Greek civilization was preserved and continued to flourish.

GREEK STATES

PERSIAN EMPIRE

SALAMIS

SEA WARFARE in the Ancient world, as shown here in this nineteenth-century painting of the Battle of Salamis, was a chaotic, messy affair that was often decided by the judicious deployment of forces before the battle.

however, met with disaster on the plain of Marathon. Forced to drink the bitter dram of defeat, Darius died after a 36-year reign, his thirst for vengeance unquenched.

ENTER XERXES

When Xerxes, the son of Darius, ascended the throne of Persia, he did not initially embrace his father's quest for revenge. However, after crushing a revolt in Egypt, he called his advisors together to discuss another military move against Athens. "As you saw, Darius himself was making preparations for war against these men. But death prevented him from carrying out his purpose," Xerxes thundered. "I, therefore, on his behalf and for the benefit of all my subjects, will not rest until I have taken Athens and burnt it to the ground…. If we crush the Athenians and their neighbors in the Peloponnese, we shall so extend the empire of Persia that its boundaries will be God's own sky."

During an average lifetime, a citizen of Athens might have personally known such intellectual giants as Socrates, Aeschylus, Sophocles, Euripides, and Aristophanes. The heirs of Western culture in philosophy, medicine, mathematics, drama, and democracy owe their existence to such men. Athens and Sparta, the principal Greek city-states, had coexisted though their relations were strained at times. Facing a growing threat from the Persians, it was apparent to the Greeks that cooperation and mutual defense offered their only hope for survival. In 482 B.C.E., a rich vein of silver had been discovered in the mines at Laurium, near Athens. During the heated debate that swirled around the highest and best use for the new-found wealth, the voice of Themistocles was clear and persuasive. Athens must expand her navy to counter the threat of Persian invasion. Themistocles had undoubtedly considered that the Persians would require large numbers of ships to transport the necessities of war if they approached Greece once again. He was also aware of the fighting proficiency of the heavily armed Spartan hoplites on land.

THE CAMPAIGN

The Greek historian Herodotus wrote that the Persian army numbered five million men and that it drank rivers dry as it passed. A more realistic number would be approximately 500,000. The Persian fleet was said to consist of 1,207 triremes, so named because the vessels were powered by oarsmen in three rows. Early in the campaign, the Persians accomplished a pair of major engineering feats. They bridged the Hellespont, today known as the Dardanelles, with a pair of spans roughly 1,400 yards (1,280m) long. When a storm wrecked the first bridges, two replacements were constructed. The Persians also spent three years digging a canal 1.5 miles (2.4km) wide across an isthmus near

"THE SEA BATTLE OF SALAMIS"—a romantic depiction of the battle by German artist Wilhelm von Kaulbach (1804–74).

A GREEK BIREME *dating from the fifth century* B.C.E. *It has a prominent ram at its prow. Note the chair provided for the helmsman, who has two large paddles to act as a rudder.*

Mount Athos. Finally, 10 long years after its humiliating defeat at Marathon, the Persian army was again on the move toward Greece. A number of Greek cities pledged allegiance to Xerxes as his juggernaut advanced inexorably toward them. Athens and Sparta, however, remained defiant against overwhelming odds.

THERMOPYLAE

On August 18, the advancing Persians reached the pass at Thermopylae, through which the force had to move in order to reach Athens. The Persians drew up before the pass, which was barely 50ft (15m) wide and defended by 6,000 Spartan hoplites under the command of their king, Leonidas. Time after time, the Persians charged the Spartans, and each time they were repulsed with heavy losses. Even the "Immortals," the elite of the Persian army and well known for their dash and élan, failed to carry Thermopylae (which translates as "pass of the hot springs").

Some of the troops with Leonidas departed, and controversy persists as to whether the king dismissed them with contempt or withdrew them to fight another day. Whatever the truth, the end was nearing for the 300 Spartans who remained on the third day of the fight at Thermopylae. A Greek traitor named Ephialtes showed the Persians an alternate route over the mountains, which would allow them to attack the Spartans from the rear. Herodotus wrote that he committed the names of the 300 Spartans who stood their ground to memory "because they deserved to be remembered."

When one Spartan was told that the Persians would loose so many arrows that they would darken the sky, he replied, "This is pleasant news...for if the Persians hide the sun we shall have our battle in the shade." Killed to the last man, the Spartans claimed the lives of two of Xerxes'

brothers. Years after the battle, a plaque was erected to commemorate the stand of Leonidas and his men. It read: "Go tell the Spartans, you who read: We took their orders and are dead." The heroic Spartans of Thermopylae did not sacrifice themselves in vain. Their stand cost the Persians precious time, and a pair of violent storms sank more than 200 Persian ships. Themistocles, meanwhile, had led the Greek fleet to victory at the Gulf of Pagasae and Artemisium. When he received the news that the Persians had taken Thermopylae, Themistocles withdrew his fleet to the island of Salamis, which offered safe harbor.

DELAY AND DECEPTION

By the time the Persian army reached Athens, most of the citizenry had fled. Those who had not were put to the sword. The city, including the Acropolis, was looted and burned. Still, in order to win a decisive victory, Xerxes had to defeat the Greek army on land. To defeat the Greek army, his triremes had to be able to maneuver in safety. Therefore, a victory over the Greek fleet became an immediate necessity. As Themistocles had predicted years earlier, the decisive battle in the life of Athens, and indeed all of Greece, would take place at sea.

IT IS SAID THAT PERSIAN KING XERXES I (right) was so confident of victory he had a throne set up on the shore, to watch the battle in style and record the names of commanders who performed particularly well.

THE GREEKS CELEBRATE their victory over the Persian navy in the Battle of Salamis, which took place in the Gulf of Aegina near Athens, September 480 B.C.E. This painting was by nineteenth-century artist F. Cormon.

PERSIAN MARINE

At the Battle of Salamis, Xerxes relied heavily on marines, placing at least 30 on each vessel. At the heart of this decision was probably Persian distrust of sea power and failure to recognize the effectiveness of the ship itself as the primary weapon. Xerxes may also have distrusted his Egyptian, Phoenician, and Ionian Greek subjects who manned the ship, and sought to assure their loyalty with a strong Persian marine presence. Impressive as they appeared, the marines probably did more harm than good. They were so tightly packed on the ships they could not fight effectively and their lack of body armor and light weapons were no match for the Greeks.

As Xerxes neared the narrow isthmus which connects northern Greece with the Peloponnese, the Spartans and other Peloponnesians built a wall and other defensive positions. Themistocles then demonstrated his true military genius by sending a slave named Sicinnus to Xerxes with false information. Sicinnus gave Xerxes a report of dissent among the allied Greeks and noted that the morale of the Greek forces was waning. In fact, he said, the Greek commander himself was sympathetic to Xerxes and wished for a resounding Persian victory. Preventing the escape of the disorganized Greeks would ensure a triumph. Xerxes took the bait and weakened his force by sending a squadron of Egyptian vessels to cover potential escape routes.

DISPOSITIONS

Xerxes planned simply to overwhelm the 300 Greek triremes, which opposed his force of 400 vessels in the narrow waters around Salamis. Themistocles, however, had other ideas. He deployed his fleet with the Athenians and Corinthians on the left, the Aegenitans and Spartans on the right, hoping that the Persians would be drawn into the shallow and narrow waters near the Bay of Eleusis. As the Persians approached, most of the Greek triremes would be obscured from their view by a nearby island. In order to lure the Persians to their doom, Themistocles would order the 50 Corinthian triremes under his command to hoist their sails and feign retreat.

The Persian triremes, apparently constructed for combat on the open sea, would find maneuvering virtually impossible in the narrows. They were heavier than those of the Greeks and sat higher in the water while carrying up to 30 infantrymen or archers as opposed to 14 aboard the Greek vessels.

THE BATTLE

On the morning of September 20, 480 B.C.E., Xerxes ascended a golden throne on the heights above Salamis. The Greek oarsmen were reported to have sung a hymn to the god Apollo as they struck the Persian vanguard, overextended in its pursuit of the supposedly retreating Corinthians. When the commanders of the leading Persian ships realized they had fallen into a trap, they ordered a backwater. However, those vessels behind them had nowhere to go, throwing the fleet into confusion. The Persians' superior numbers had now become a hindrance rather than an advantage.

A line of Greek triremes moved in orderly fashion to encircle the confused enemy, and their bronze rams inflicted deadly punishment on the foundering Persian ships. Aeschylus, who is remembered as the father of literary tragedy, fought at both Marathon and Salamis. He described the scene as reminiscent of the mass netting and killing of fish on the shores of the Mediterranean. "At first the torrent of the Persians' fleet bore up," Aeschylus wrote. "But then with the press of the shipping hemmed there in the narrows, none could help another."

Standing off from the tangle of Persian with Persian, the Greeks struck virtually at will. Aeschylus related a grisly scene as if from the Persian perspective. "The hulls of our vessels rolled over and the sea was hidden from our sight, choked with wrecks and slaughtered men. The shores and reefs were strewn with corpses. In wild disorder every ship remaining in our fleet turned tail and fled. But the Greeks pursued us, and with oars or broken fragments of wreckage struck the survivors' heads as though they were tunneys and a haul of fish. Shrieks and groans rang across the water until nightfall hid us from them."

AFTERMATH

The Persian fleet was crippled at Salamis, losing 200 triremes, roughly half its strength, to a mere 40 for the Greeks. In the wake of the disaster, Xerxes had little choice but to retire to safety, lest the Greeks sail northward and destroy the bridges over the Hellespont, severing his overland supply route.

The Greeks did not immediately recognize the magnitude of their victory. There was still some fighting to be done. When Xerxes departed, he left a force of 300,000 soldiers under the command of Mardonius. The following spring, the Persians captured Athens once again, but that summer the combined armies of the Athenians and Spartans forced Mardonius northward, defeating him decisively at Plataea in September. During the same month, a Greek fleet commanded by Xanthippus defeated the Persians once again at Mycale.

Greece was at last free from the threat of Eastern domination. For half a century Athens maintained the strongest fleet in the Ancient World, while the army of Sparta was the preeminent force on land. Increasing rivalry and distrust eventually brought the two city-states to war with one another. Ironically, the names of Marathon, Thermopylae, and Salamis were remembered with reverence by both. It had been a time when Greek stood with Greek and these victories had shaped the course of human history.

SALAMIS

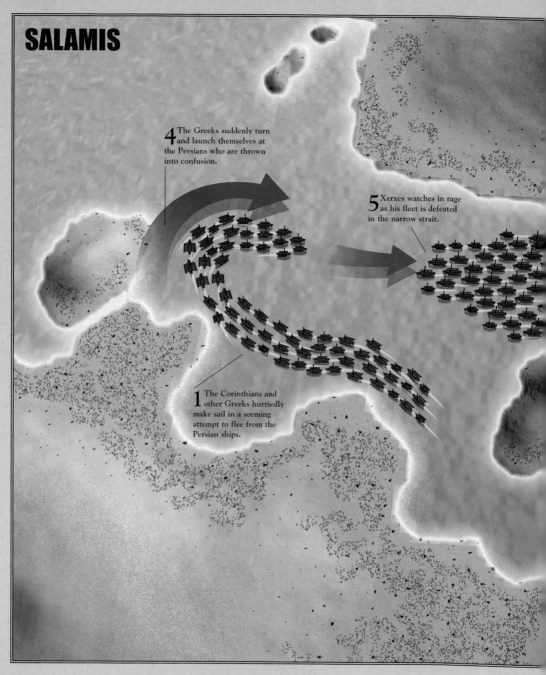

4 The Greeks suddenly turn and launch themselves at the Persians who are thrown into confusion.

5 Xerxes watches in rage as his fleet is defeated in the narrow strait.

1 The Corinthians and other Greeks hurriedly make sail in a seeming attempt to flee from the Persian ships.

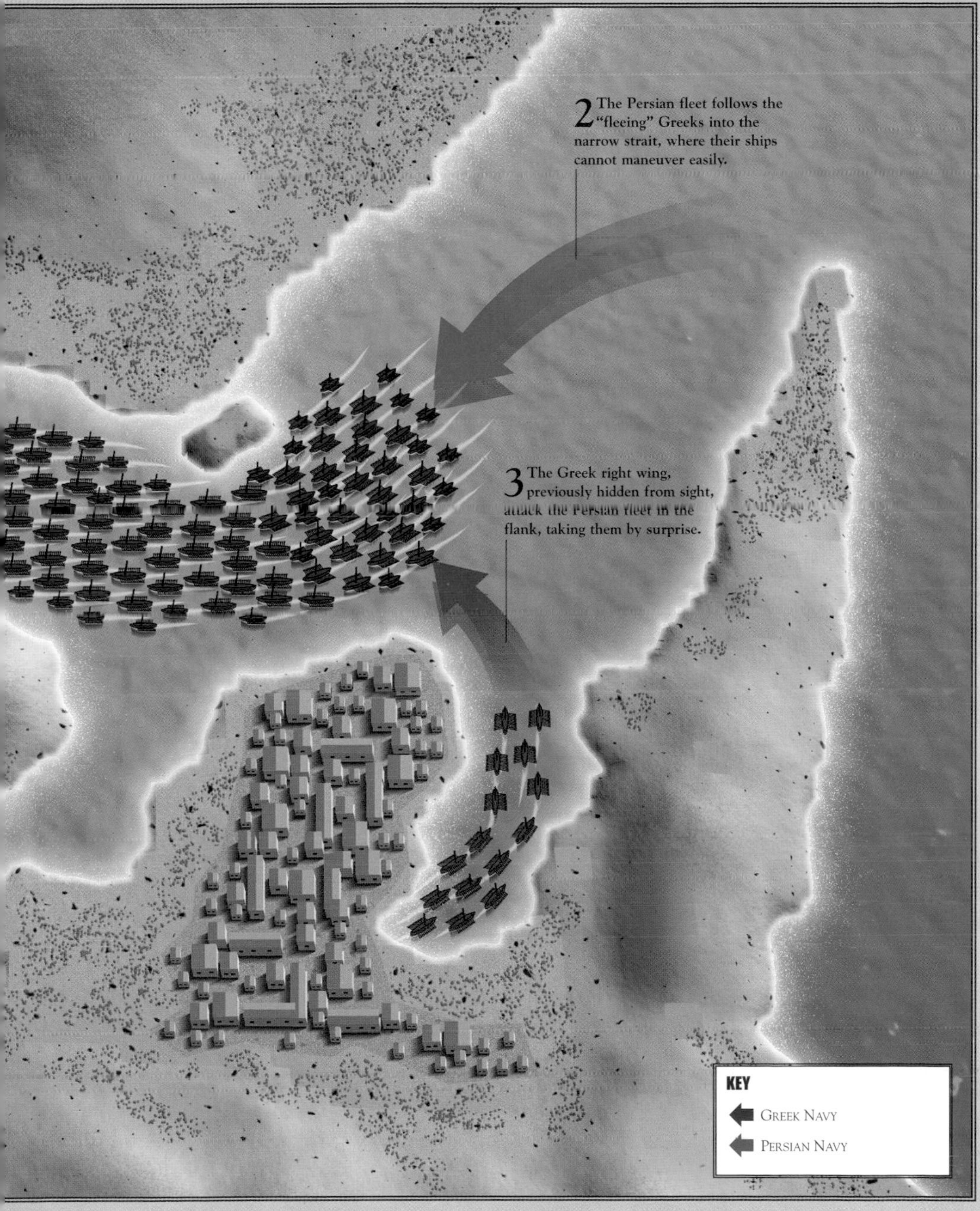

2 The Persian fleet follows the "fleeing" Greeks into the narrow strait, where their ships cannot maneuver easily.

3 The Greek right wing, previously hidden from sight, attack the Persian fleet in the flank, taking them by surprise.

KEY

← GREEK NAVY

← PERSIAN NAVY

GAUGAMELA 331 B.C.E.

Gaugamela was one of Alexander's greatest triumphs. Outnumbered five to one, the Macedonians outfought their Persian foes as Alexander out-generaled Darius, despite the Great King fighting on ground of his own choosing, specially prepared for special weapons such as scythed chariots and war elephants.

Alexander inherited more than a kingdom from his father, Philip II of Macedon. He inherited a powerful military instrument and the desire to use it. Philip had fought for many years to unify the kingdom of Macedon and impose his power over neighboring Greeks and barbarians. The army he forged to do it was the basis for Alexander's conquests. Had Philip not been assassinated at the age of 46, he and not Alexander might have made war upon great Persia.

Alexander was raised as a Greek prince should be, on heroic tales from the epic poetry of Homer. He was part of a culture that required great men to disregard personal danger and take risks for the sake of experience. He was also schooled by

GAUGAMELA FACTS

Who: Alexander the Great (356–323 B.C.E.) with 47,000 Greek/Macedonian troops vs. 240,000 Persians under the Great King Darius (reigned 336–330 B.C.E.).

What: Alexander used an oblique formation to break the Persian front, Darius fled and the Persian army then collapsed.

Where: Near Tel Gomel, in what is now northern Iraq.

When: October 1, 331 B.C.E.

Why: Alexander sought to finally defeat Darius in battle and complete his conquest of the Persian empire.

Outcome: Darius was murdered, possibly by his own generals. Alexander became master of Persia.

ALEXANDER LEADS HIS COMPANION CAVALRY *across the Granicus, seizing the initiative from the Persians. Like most successful military commanders, Alexander was no stranger to luck.*

27

nobility now had a requirement for military service and the army was a clear route to greatness. Philip lavished rewards on his officers and soldiers who distinguished themselves, and Alexander was not slow to notice the morale effects of his father's generosity.

Philip was murdered by one of his own bodyguards, and it is possible Alexander was behind the plot. There are other plausible explanations, and Alexander himself took the line that Persia was behind the murder of the king of Macedon. Alexander's succession was a typically messy business involving the murder or execution of potential rivals and enemies, and it had repercussions that lasted throughout Alexander's reign. He did not dwell over it, however, but immediately began his own campaign of conquest. Alexander's early campaigns were to subdue rebellions among tribles on his northern border and in Greece itself. As soon as he was able, he turned against Persia as he had always intended. A Macedonian force was already skirmishing in Persia, though little of importance had been achieved. In 334 B.C.E. Alexander reinforced this army and began his great campaign.

THE PERSIAN EMPIRE IN 334 B.C.E.

The Persian Empire was enormous, stretching all the way from the Mediterranean to the Indian Ocean. It was extremely wealthy but internally divided. The Persian Empire under Darius could field vast numbers of troops but these were drawn from many different regions and cultures. They had no common structure and in some cases spoke an entirely different language. Many of the troops of the empire were provided by subject peoples who resented their status and were not totally enthusiastic about fighting for their Great King. This created an additional problem—not only did Persia need to protect and control a huge area, some of the troops it fielded were not very reliable.

Some of Darius' troops were Greek mercenaries. This was common and often the mercenaries were more reliable than the forces of subject peoples that made up the great mass of Persian soldiery. These Greek mercenaries formed the backbone of the army that first opposed Alexander as he advanced into Asia Minor.

VICTORY AT THE GRANICUS

Alexander was an extremely aggressive commander who saw any sort of defensive preparation as a sign of weakness. He was therefore encouraged, rather than dismayed, when a Persian army drew up behind the Granicus River, forcing him to make an opposed crossing. Alexander declared that

Aristotle himself in matters of philosophy and science, and was a charming host to court guests even as a boy. Aristotle was appointed, to a great extent, to curb Alexander's rashness and aggression or at least temper it with more philosophical and civilized values. In this he was not entirely successful.

Alexander learned a great deal from his tutor and became a very erudite man, but he remained essentially the boy who wanted to be Hercules. Hercules was Alexander's inspiration; Homer's tales of his deeds inspired Alexander in general attitude and some specific instances. It is likely that Alexander saw himself as a modern-day version of the classic Greek heroes. In many ways this was true.

At the time Alexander inherited the kingdom of Macedon, Philip II had made it the dominant power in Greek affairs. Athens, Thebes, and even Sparta were eclipsed, and the Persians had been driven from Thrace. Alexander had been involved in some of the later campaigning and was making a name for himself as an aggressive, even reckless commander. Philip had also changed the nature of Macedonian society. The existing the Persians were not confident of victory and were counting on the steep riverbanks to break the force of his attack sufficiently for the Persian cavalry to defeat him. He hurled his cavalry across the river at the point where the enemy seemed strongest, and after a hard-fought mêlée was able to rout the Persian cavalry. The Persian second line, the Greek mercenaries, stood firm but were massacred.

The Granicus established the moral dominance of Alexander's army over his foes and forced Darius into an even more defensive mindset. Several cities of the region came over to Alexander and he was able to consolidate his conquest of the region without much interference. Only the fortified port of Halicarnassus put up much of a fight, and since no serious attempt to relieve it was made, the city eventually fell to Alexander's army.

Alexander's army was able to rapidly secure the whole region of Anatolia. The Persian army did not interfere, though local tribes caused some problems. Alexander advanced on Cilicia, from here he could strike either toward Egypt or directly at the Persian heartlands. Darius was finally forced to act.

Darius had assembled an army some 140,000 strong while Alexander was clearing his flank of holdout coastal cities and subduing hill barbarians. Alexander moved south into Syria to place his army across Darius' rear and Darius, entering Cilicia through mountain passes in the north, found himself positioned across Alexander's line of supply. Darius, still thinking defensively, chose a good position on the Pinarus River and awaited Alexander's next move. Alexander again interpreted this as a sign of nervousness and launched a head-on attack. Alexander fought on foot at the head of his infantry and, as at Granicus, defeated the Persian force at the critical point. The Persian army disintegrated and the Macedonians pursued the remnants with great vigor. Darius himself escaped, though his family were captured.

THE LULL

During the next two years Alexander, who now held half the Persian Empire, reduced pockets of resistance and eliminated the Persian fleet's Mediterranean bases. He cheekily seized Egypt, trusting to Darius' defensive mentality to prevent an attack on his rear while he was campaigning to the west.

By the summer of 331 B.C.E., Alexander was ready to complete his conquest of the Persian Empire. Vastly outnumbered and at the end of a long line of supply, he nevertheless decided that rather than accept Darius' offer to recognize his conquests he would stake all on an attempt to take the whole empire. This was Alexander's attitude in a nutshell—all or nothing. Advancing into Mesopotamia, the ancient cradle of civilization between the Tigris and Euphrates rivers, Alexander offered his challenge to Darius, King of Kings. Darius considered retreating further into his territory and perhaps scorching the earth behind him, but instead decided to give battle.

DARIUS' PREPARATIONS

Darius knew that Alexander would need to give battle as soon as he could since he was operating at the end of a long supply line and the Persians were not. He chose his ground near the modern city of Mosul in Iraq and made his preparations for battle. Darius was determined to give himself all the advantages, even though he commanded five

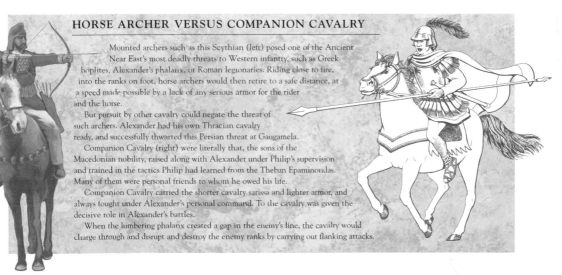

HORSE ARCHER VERSUS COMPANION CAVALRY

Mounted archers such as this Scythian (left) posed one of the Ancient Near East's most deadly threats to Western infantry, such as Greek hoplites, Alexander's phalanx, or Roman legionaries. Riding close to fire, into the ranks on foot, horse archers would then retire to a safe distance, at a speed made possible by a lack of any serious armor for the rider and the horse.

But pursuit by other cavalry could negate the threat of such archers. Alexander had his own Thracian cavalry ready, and successfully thwarted this Persian threat at Gaugamela.

Companion Cavalry (right) were literally that, the sons of the Macedonian nobility, raised along with Alexander under Philip's supervision and trained in the tactics Philip had learned from the Theban Epaminondas. Many of them were personal friends to whom he owed his life.

Companion Cavalry carried the shorter cavalry sarissa and lighter armor, and always fought under Alexander's personal command. To the cavalry was given the decisive role in Alexander's battles.

When the lumbering phalanx created a gap in the enemy's line, the cavalry would charge through and disrupt and destroy the enemy ranks by carrying out flanking attacks.

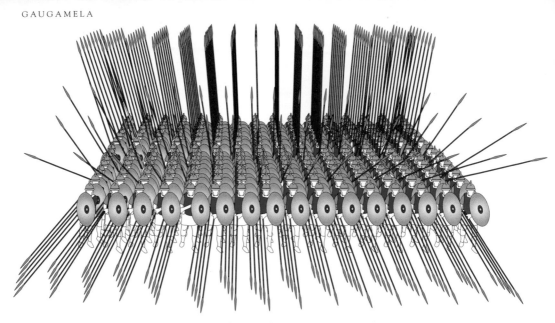

times as many troops as Alexander. He ordered the ground flattened and obstructions removed to allow his cavalry and scythed chariots the best possible run at the enemy.

Darius' initial attack would be made by his first line, which was composed mostly of cavalry with a few of the best Persian infantry units mixed in. Darius himself was in the center of the Persian line with his 10,000-strong personal

PAINTED IN 1673 by Charles Le Brun (1619–90)—a full 1,800 years after the battle—"The Battle of Gaugamela" (oil on canvas) is a highly romanticized depiction of the bloody confrontation between Darius's Persians and Alexander's Macedonians.

A FOREST OF SPEARS—a frontal view of a Macedonian speira, the unit making up the larger infantry phalanx. The ranks behind the front five would hold their counterweighted pikes aloft until required to fill a gap, and in the hope of deflecting incoming missiles.

guard, who were known to the Greeks as the Immortals. In front of them were arrayed some 200 scythed chariots. A second line, composed of enormous numbers of infantry, was positioned behind the first. Darius expected to be able to envelop both of Alexander's flanks with his vastly superior numbers and to crush his army from all sides. Alexander's line would be punctured and broken by the onslaught of

cavalry and chariots (and, according to some accounts) war elephants. The infantry would then advance to complete the victory. However, Alexander had other ideas.

BATTLE COMMENCES

To help protect his flanks from envelopment Alexander used a version of the oblique order of battle pioneered by the Thebans in 371 B.C.E. He positioned the units of his cavalry on the flanks with each one echeloned back from the last, creating "refused" flanks that required the enemy to move further if he wanted to engage them. His phalanx of well drilled Macedonian infantry was positioned in the center of the Greek line. A reserve phalanx formed Alexander's second line. Alexander's plan called for his left flank, under the veteran general Parmenio, to fight a holding action while Alexander led the right wing to victory. He was assisted in this by the Persians themselves, who sent their left-flank cavalry far around Alexander's right, opening up a gap in their line. The Macedonian army was drifting to the right. If Darius delayed too long his chariots might not gain the benefit of their prepared run. So the attack was launched. Darius' cavalry swept around the flanks of the Macedonian force as the chariots (and, in some accounts, 15 war elephants) made their initial frontal attack.

The Macedonian line was able to fend off the chariots and weather the initial onslaught, though some of the Persian cavalry were able to break through. They were engaged by the reserve phalanx and by light troops, which had been briefed for the task. Some Persians began rifling the Macedonians' baggage train. If they had turned on the rear of the outnumbered and embattled Macedonians they might have contributed to a victory. Instead they took themselves out of the battle when they were most needed. As he had planned, Alexander led his elite Companion Cavalry and supported forces against the Persian left. Exploiting the gap that was opening between the Persian left wing cavalry and the center, the Companions inflicted a savage blow on the forces in front of them. They were followed by a great wedge of infantry and light troops which fell on the disorganized Persians.

Fearing that he would be cut off, the commander of the Persian left wing, Bessus, began to retire, which eased the pressure on Alexander's refused far right flank. Meanwhile, Darius himself was feeling the pressure. If Alexander's all-conquering cavalry wheeled his way instead of savaging

Bessus, Darius himself might be surrounded and captured. Thoughts of previous defeats may have played heavily on the Persian emperor, for he, too, began to retreat. The withdrawal became a rout as Darius' bodyguards followed their leader in fleeing the field. Alexander was not able to pursue because the situation on his left was becoming desperate. Parmenio's forces were hard-pressed on the left but had done their job, tying down the Persians' force. Now Alexander fell upon the rear of the Persians engaging Parmenio, forcing them to retreat. The Persian right wing commander, Mazaeus, tried to conduct an orderly retreat but was vigorously attacked and his troops thrown into confusion.

This represented the end of organized Persian resistance at Gaugamela. The remaining Persian forces were scattered, chased off, or cut down and the baggage train was captured. Alexander began a three-day pursuit of Darius' surviving forces but was unable to catch his enemy, who regrouped much of his surviving cavalry and a few thousand infantry and made good his escape. Behind the fleeing Darius were left 40,000 dead Persian troops, 4,000 more as prisoners and the remainder of the army scattered about the countryside.

AFTERMATH

Gaugamela was a decisive defeat for Darius. He retained his crown and part of his army, but was unable to pose any challenge to Alexander, who pushed on into Persia itself. Taking Susa, he drove on to the capital Persepolis and made himself master of the Persian Empire in all but title. With Darius alive he could not claim the title.

Darius evaded capture, finally, reaching the friendly kingdom of Bactria where he was found dead, murdered. Finally, the Persians could surrender. Alexander was proclaimed "Great King" and added Persia to his growing empire. Alexander's reign would eventually extend to India.

GAUGAMELA

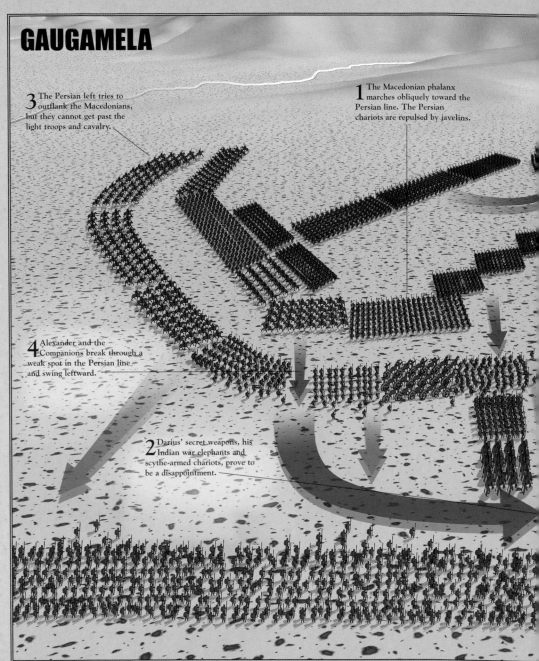

3 The Persian left tries to outflank the Macedonians, but they cannot get past the light troops and cavalry.

1 The Macedonian phalanx marches obliquely toward the Persian line. The Persian chariots are repulsed by javelins.

4 Alexander and the Companions break through a weak spot in the Persian line and swing leftward.

2 Darius' secret weapons, his Indian war elephants and scythe-armed chariots, prove to be a disappointment.

5 Some Persians break through the phalanx, but they head to the rear to attack the Macedonian baggage train.

6 The Greek left wing is hard-pressed by the Persian cavalry until Alexander appears in the latter's rear.

KEY
MACEDONIANS
PERSIANS

7 Darius, fearing for his safety, decides to flee from the battlefield, effectively giving the victory to Alexander.

CANNAE

216 B.C.E.

Hannibal's destruction of a Roman army at Cannae by a brilliant double envelopment provided a model for commanders for centuries to come. But even this, the third of his great tactical victories over the Roman Republic, did not end the Punic Wars.

After their defeat in the First Punic War (264–241 B.C.E.) the Carthaginians began trying to expand and develop possessions in Spain to make good territorial losses in Sicily and Sardinia. Much of this was carried out by the Barca family, especially Hamilcar, the distinguished young general of the first war with Rome and his son, Hannibal. Under the Barcas, the Carthaginians extracted the mineral and manpower resources that Spain had to offer them.

The Romans watched the Carthaginian subjugation of Spain with a certain amount of trepidation and so, in 226 B.C.E., a treaty was concluded that placed Spain south of the Ebro River in the Carthaginian sphere of influence and leaving the territory to the north in the Roman sphere. But the treaty was to be short-lived. By 221 B.C.E. the Carthaginian empire had (once again) become wealthy and rebuilt its

CANNAE FACTS

Who: Hannibal Barca (247–183 or 182 B.C.E.) with a Carthaginian army of 50,000 men faced the Roman consuls Paullus and Varro with an army of 86,000 men.

What: Hannibal made the most of his advantage in cavalry and planned a double envelopment of the Romans. He weakened his infantry center and strengthened his wings with good infantry and cavalry.

Where: At the mouth of the Aufidius River in Apulia, Italy.

When: August 2, 216 B.C.E.

Why: Hannibal had invaded Italy to weaken Rome by separating her from her Italian allies.

Outcome: The battle was a devastating tactical defeat for the Romans with more than 48,000 killed and 20,000 prisoners. Although the battle had a profound psychological effect on the Romans for centuries to come, the strategic advantages of Roman manpower and stalwart allies minimized the overall impact of the battle.

ROMAN REPUBLIC

ROME

CANNAE ✝

THIS NINETEENTH-CENTURY ILLUSTRATION shows Hannibal and his army stripping the defeated Romans of arms and armor after their victory at Cannae.

LEFT: THIS SPANISH CHIEFTAIN *wears a fine bronze helmet, the color of reddish brass, and a mail shirt. The links were very expensive because they were individually forged and riveted together. He rides a small horse. Modern research shows the lack of stirrups would not affect his ability to throw his spear or strike downward against infantry in a mêlée.*

HANNIBAL ENTERING A NORTHERN ITALIAN TOWN *on elephantback in triumph. Elephants had helped Hannibal in his crossing of the Alps, but once the Roman troops and cavalry became inured to these strange beasts, they were relatively ineffective on the battlefield.*

army, composed mainly of Carthage's Libyan subjects, Numidian mercenaries and levies from subject Spanish tribes. At this time, the Carthaginians, led by Hannibal, supported one of their allies against Saguntum, a town located south of the Ebro, and besieged and took the town in late 219 or early 218 B.C.E. Unfortunately, the Romans claimed a preexisting alliance with Saguntum and demanded that the Carthaginians desist and turn Hannibal over to them. The outraged

Carthaginians responded that they would do no such thing and so the Second Punic War began.

THE SECOND PUNIC WAR

Hannibal quickly took the offensive and launched an invasion of Italy with an army of 59,000 men including 9,000 cavalry. He moved quickly and thereby avoided Roman efforts to intercept him in Gaul. The swift passage of his army was not, however, without consequences and Hannibal entered Italy in November of 218 B.C.E. with a force that was greatly weakened by campaigning—only 6,000 cavalry and 20,000 infantry had survived the passage over the Alps. The Carthaginian strategy was for Hannibal to quickly seek battle and he won a cavalry skirmish at the Ticinus River and the Romans were forced to withdraw. The following month, Hannibal fought the set-piece battle of the war when he lured a Roman army across the Trebia River. Pinning the Romans with his infantry, Hannibal used his superior cavalry and a hidden force to attack the Romans in the flanks and rear respectively. The Romans were decisively routed, losing perhaps three-quarters of their 40,000 men as casualties or prisoners of war.

Hannibal was in control of northern Italy and in the spring of 217 B.C.E. began his march into central and then southern Italy. Although the Romans tried to keep Hannibal and his army contained in the north, he managed to slip by them. The Carthaginians were pursued by a Roman army and, along the shores of Lake Trasimene on June 21, Hannibal sprung an ambush on the Roman troops. Caught between the lake and the Carthaginians, the Roman army was smashed losing perhaps 15,000 men.

FABIUS MAXIMUS

Having suffered two major defeats, the Romans took the unusual step of suspending their constitution, under which the state and army were controlled by two annually elected consuls, and elected a dictator who would prosecute the war with supreme power for a period of six months. The man elected was Quintus Fabius Maximus. Fabius devised a strategy based upon the Romans avoiding battle with Hannibal while shadowing his army. This "Fabian Strategy" allowed the Romans to trade space for time while making it difficult for Hannibal to disperse his forces during the winter. Since the Romans and their allies controlled most of the towns, this posed some logistical difficulties on the Carthaginians. Hannibal had hoped that his victories would convince many of Rome's Italian allies to abandon her, but in fact most remained steadfast in their loyalty to the Romans. Moreover, time favored the Romans in that it allowed them and their allies to muster a large army from their significant reserves, estimated to be more than three-quarters of a million men. The Roman army was composed of citizen soldiers who were conscripted annually to train and prepare for the coming battle with the Carthaginians. The Romans followed Hannibal's army into Apulia, Samnium, and Campania. The strategy seemed to be working since Fabius' second-in-command was even able to inflict a defeat on the Carthaginians in a major skirmish while the latter were dispersed in order to forage. The Romans, however, were not happy with Fabius' strategy, especially since Hannibal had, on more than one occasion, been able to outmaneuver the Romans when they seemingly had him contained.

THE CAMPAIGN AND THE ARMIES

Although Fabius' term as dictator expired at the end of 217 B.C.E., his successors basically continued to avoid Hannibal, waiting for reinforcements to arrive under the new consuls for the year 216 B.C.E. The new consuls were Lucius Aemilius Paullus and Gaius Terentius Varro. Paullus was a man of some considerable military experience who had seen action fighting against the Illyrians and had held the

A Numidian light cavalryman from around 200 B.C.E. He is armed with a javelin and small shield. These horsemen were such good riders they had no need of a bridle to control the horse.

consulship on a previous occasion. He had even been awarded a triumph for the campaign. Varro was less experienced but was apparently a popular politician with much support amongst both the aristocracy and the common folk. The consuls, elected in March, had spent the spring raising additional troops and joined the army watching Hannibal in Apulia sometime in July. When they arrived, the army under their command was the largest the Romans had ever put in the field. It was composed of eight legions, 10,000 infantry and 2,400 cavalry, and an equal number of Italian allies, totaling 40,000 on foot and 3,600 on horses. About half of the Roman force probably had some experience but the remainder were freshly levied, modestly trained troops, who had not seen combat.

ROMAN LEGIONARY

Roman infantry knew what was expected of it and was given the means to fulfill the Republic's demands. The long hasta in this legionary's hand marks him as one of the *hastati*, the third line of the Roman legion that held the formation in place while the *principes* and *triarii* changed position in the front of the formation. His bronze helmet and greaves show more Greek influence than would those worn by his successors. A laminated scutum of wood and leather strips has not yet reached its full evolutionary weight of 16.5lb (7.5kg).

WARTS AND ALL, Republican heroes such as Publius Cornelius Scipio Africanus left accurate likenesses behind to inspire an admiring posterity. Hannibal's eventual destroyer had the war's long interval to study his opponent's tactics before taking the war to Carthage in a shattering assault.

Hannibal, meanwhile, had spent the winter at the town of Geronium where he remained until he could collect some of the local grain harvest. He then moved some 60 miles (97km) toward the town of Cannae near the mouth of the Aufidius River. Cannae was a Roman supply depot and allowed him to control Apulia via the Aufidius River valley. At this point the Carthaginian army numbered about 40,000 foot soldiers and 10,000 cavalry. About 16,000 of his infantry were veterans from the crossing of the Alps and subsequent victories, perhaps 10,000 of whom were Libyan and 6,000 Spaniards. Another 16,000 were Celts who had been recruited in northern Italy. The remaining infantry were light troops recruited from a variety of sources. Hannibal's cavalry consisted of perhaps 2,000 Spanish and 4,000 Celtic heavy cavalry and 4,000 Numidian light horse. By the end of July, the Romans had advanced on the

THE SITE OF THE BATTLE at Cannae today. Stand on the ridge above the river as Hannibal must have done and let your imagination conjure up the enthusiastic Romans rushing into the trap. If ghosts exist then surely, here, there must be many thousands.

Carthaginian army at Cannae. The Romans had been cautious in their advance, not wishing to repeat mistakes that had costly them dearly earlier in the conflict. By July 31, the Romans had encamped within view of the Carthaginian positions. The majority of the Roman forces were north of the Aufidius River, facing Hannibal's encampment, but a smaller force occupied a camp south of the river.

DISPOSITIONS

On August 1, Hannibal deployed his troops north of the river and offered battle to the Romans. The two consuls alternated command and on that day Paullus was in charge. He decided not to accept the offer of battle, probably because Hannibal had formed up north of the river and had positioned himself so that the terrain favored him and, most likely, his superiority in cavalry. On the next day, when Varro was in command, the Romans deployed their army, with the exception of 10,000 left to guard the main camp, south of the Aufidius, and offered battle. Hannibal obliged and both sides arrayed their battle lines.

The Romans arranged themselves according to their customary order of battle. Light infantry, known as velites, were arrayed before the main line. Behind them, legions and allies were deployed by companies known as maniples in three supporting lines. This formation was known as the acies triplex or triple battle line in which the maniples of each line were placed so that the maniples of the line behind could move up in support—this gave the acies triplex the appearance of a chess board. There was, however, one difference from a normal acies triplex in that the maniples were deployed in much deeper formations than was normal. One reason for this is that the Romans intended for the legions to have the depth to punch through the Carthaginian heavy infantry. Another factor may have been

DESPONDENCY IN ROME: after defeat at Cannae. Hannibal still did not feel strong enough to attempt to besiege Rome. So, a stalemate ensued in Italy and the seat of the war moved to Spain. It ended with the Roman invasion of Africa and the battle of Zama in 202 B.C.E.

the massive size of the Roman army at Cannae required deeper formations and a narrower frontage. The main infantry lines were protected by cavalry on the wings, the Roman horsemen on the right, and the allied Italian horse on the left. Roman commanders placed themselves with this cavalry: Paullus leading the Romans and Varro the Italians.

Hannibal arrayed his forces in such a way so as to maximize his advantages, especially his more numerous and better cavalry, while minimizing his weaknesses, in particular his overall numerical inferiority. He deployed his light infantry as a screen before his main battle line to counter the Roman velites. The center of his line was formed of alternating units of Spanish and Celtic infantry, probably hoping that the veteran Spaniards would stiffen the notoriously brittle Celts. Moreover these troops were placed in a concave formation so that the center of the line was closer to the enemy than those moving along the wings. On either side of the Spaniards and Celts, were the Libyan veterans, placed in deep columns. Protecting the left flank of the infantry line were the heavy cavalry, Celts, and Spaniards. The right flank was held by the nimble Numidian light cavalry who were experts at skirmish tactics. Hannibal placed himself in the center of his battle line leaving the cavalry wings to his subordinate commanders.

THE BATTLE

The battle began with a clash of the opposing light infantry, who engaged with missile weapons including javelins and slings. Neither side seems to have gained much of an advantage and as the opposing main battle lines approached one another the light infantry retired behind their respective heavy infantry. Meanwhile, on the flanks the Spanish and Celtic cavalry rushed forward to engage the Roman horsemen in close combat. On this flank the advantage lay with the Carthaginian troopers who were more numerous and probably more heavily armed, with more armor. The result was that the Roman cavalry were routed. Paullus was wounded and unhorsed in the fighting and eventually killed. On the other flank, the Numidians engaged the Italian troopers in a prolonged skirmish with neither side gaining the upper hand. Unfortunately for the Italians, the Celtic and Spanish horsemen, rather than continuing their pursuit of the Roman cavalry, rode across the rear of the Roman army and attacked the Italian horse in the flank as the latter were still engaged with the Numidians. This was too much for the Italians who broke and fled. The pursuit of the Italians was left to the Numidians while the Carthaginian heavy cavalry reformed in the rear of the Roman army.

As the cavalry battles were underway, the two infantry battle lines became engaged. In the initial combat the Romans began to gain the advantage. The exposed center of Celts and Spaniards was severely pressed by the Romans, especially as more Roman maniples moved in to attack the apex of the concave formation. Although these soldiers were hard pressed by the Romans, they did not break. At the same time, the veteran Libyan troops pushed forward until they were pressing on the flanks of the legionary battle line, which had pushed itself forward to attack the Celts and Spaniards. The result was a massive double envelopment of the Roman legions. As the Libyans attacked the flanks, the Roman formations could no longer maintain the momentum to drive back Spanish and Celtic infantry in the center. The near destruction of the Roman army was complete when the Spanish and Celtic heavy cavalry charged into its rear. The resultant casualties were staggering—the Romans listed around 48,000 killed including the Consul Paullus and more than 20,000 prisoners making Cannae one of the bloodiest defeats by a European army on a single day of battle.

AFTERMATH

Hannibal was unable to convince Rome's allies to desert her, leaving Rome with significant manpower resources. The Romans opened new theaters of operations in Spain and Africa that allowed them eventual victory.

CANNAE

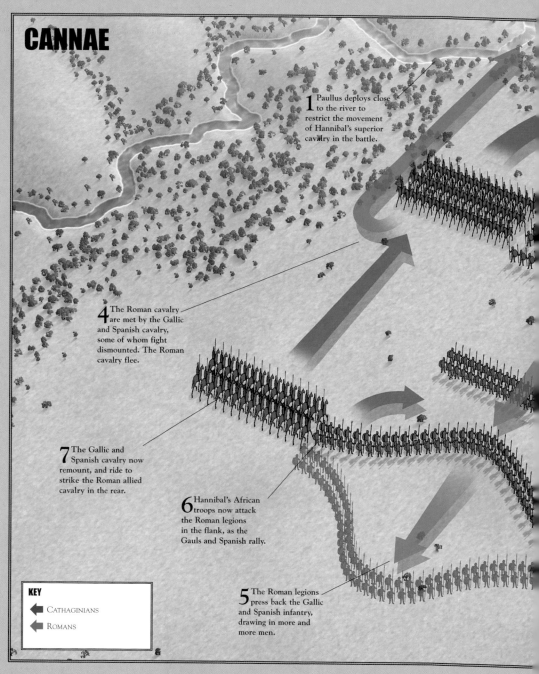

1 Paullus deploys close to the river to restrict the movement of Hannibal's superior cavalry in the battle.

4 The Roman cavalry are met by the Gallic and Spanish cavalry, some of whom fight dismounted. The Roman cavalry flee.

7 The Gallic and Spanish cavalry now remount, and ride to strike the Roman allied cavalry in the rear.

6 Hannibal's African troops now attack the Roman legions in the flank, as the Gauls and Spanish rally.

5 The Roman legions press back the Gallic and Spanish infantry, drawing in more and more men.

KEY

← CATHAGINIANS

← ROMANS

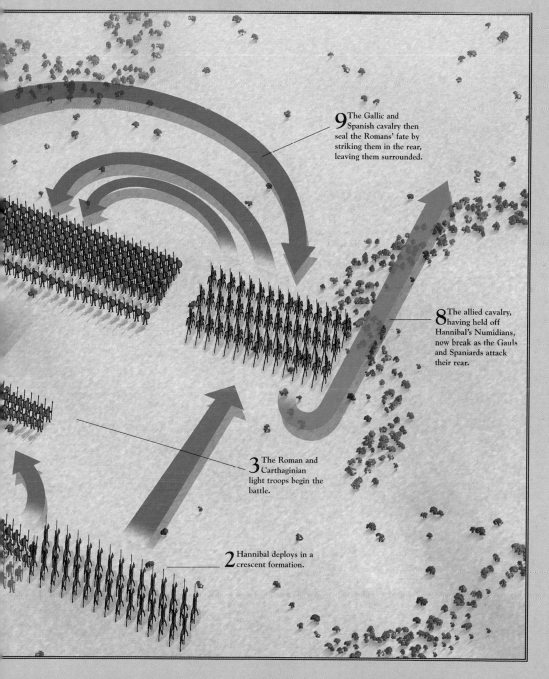

9 The Gallic and Spanish cavalry then seal the Romans' fate by striking them in the rear, leaving them surrounded.

8 The allied cavalry, having held off Hannibal's Numidians, now break as the Gauls and Spaniards attack their rear.

3 The Roman and Carthaginian light troops begin the battle.

2 Hannibal deploys in a crescent formation.

ALESIA

52 B.C.E.

Caesar's victory at Alesia, where Roman skill at military engineering enabled him to defeat a vast Gallic army coming to relieve their chieftain Vercingetorix, besieged in the town, secured Roman rule in Gaul. But for all his fortifications, Caesar had a hard fight of it.

In 59 B.C.E., Gaius Julius Caesar was elected consul in Rome. He used his position and political connections to secure his appointment as the governor of Cisalpine and Transalpine Gaul and Illyricum at the conclusion of his consulship. He took up the governorship the following year and used the migration of the Helvetii, and the trepidation this caused among Rome's Gallic allies, as a pretext to intervene militarily in Gaul. While it does not seem that Caesar initially intended to conquer Gaul, his victory over the Helvetii may have provided him with the opportunity to contemplate doing so. Over the next five years Caesar waged a number of successful, if sometimes close-run, campaigns in Gaul, forcing many tribes to submit to him, at least temporarily. Moreover, Caesar also launched campaigns across the Rhine and twice invaded Britain.

ALESIA FACTS

Who: Gaius Julius Caesar (100–44 B.C.E.), with an army of 45,000 men, besieged an army of around 70,000 Gauls under Vercingetorix of the Arverni (d. 46 B.C.E.) and faced a relief force reputed to number 250,000 warriors.

What: Caesar made use of the Roman skill at siege warfare by constructing lines of siege works facing both inward and outward and Roman discipline to defeat threats from both the besieged and relieving forces.

Where: Alesia, some 30 miles (48km) northwest of modern Dijon in France.

When: Late September/early October 52 B.C.E.

Why: Caesar sought to defeat Vercingetorix's threat to Roman rule once and for all.

Outcome: The battle was the last major effort by the Gauls against Caesar. The defeat of the charismatic Vercingetorix and the sizeable forces mustered for the battle ended the Gauls' ability to resist the Romans.

LEGIONARIES CONSTRUCT DEFENSIVE WORKS. The Roman army were unparalleled in the ancient world as builders of small fortresses. They were also highly skilled at building defensive walls.

Despite his success, there was definite unrest in Gaul which began to manifest itself in late 54 B.C.E. Due to a bad harvest, Caesar was forced to disperse his troops in winter quarters throughout much of northeast Gaul, requiring the various tribes to provide his troops with provisions. This led to serious resentment that burst into open rebellion. Two legionary encampments were attacked during the winter of 54/53 B.C.E. A legion of 10 cohorts with five additional cohorts, perhaps the cadre of a new legion, under the command of Quintus Titurius Sabinus and Lucius Aurunculeius Cotta, was destroyed when the Romans were lured from their fortified camp, ambushed, and annihilated. This was followed by an attack on a legion in winter camp under the command of Quintus Tullius Cicero (the brother of the famous orator Marcus Tullius Cicero). Cicero wisely remained within his fortifications and, although his force was hard-pressed and suffered extraordinarily heavy losses, was able to hold out until he was relieved. Caesar spent the remainder of 53 B.C.E. raising additional forces, intimidating Gallic tribes, and dealing with the Germans, both campaigning across the Rhine and fighting off a major raid.

THE CAMPAIGN AND THE ARMIES

At the beginning of 52 B.C.E., the Gauls planned a coordinated effort that would become a general rebellion aimed at expelling the Romans. The revolt began early in the year with the massacre of Roman citizens living at

A RECONSTRUCTED FORT at modern-day Alesia. The double ditch and abatis (sharp sticks projecting from the wall) were not intended to stop attackers so much as to slow them down so that missile fire from within the fort could kill more of them.

Cenabum, city-state of the Carnuntes tribe. This signal inspired the Gauls, and a young, charismatic noble of the Arverni, Vercingetorix, to put together a coalition of tribes and put a significant army in the field. The Gauls began by attacking the capital of the Boii, a tribe still allied with Rome, but Caesar, who had been away in Italy, returned and forced the Gauls to withdraw. Meanwhile, Caesar attacked several Gallic towns, no doubt in order to procure supplies at this difficult time of year. Vercingetorix realized that logistics were Caesar's weak point and so the Gauls adopted a Fabian strategy where they would avoid open battle with the Romans and fall back on and defend their fortified towns in an attempt to deny the Romans much-needed supplies.

Meanwhile, Caesar continued to attack Gallic towns and attempted to force a confrontation. He moved into the territory of the Bituriges and attacked their major stronghold, Avaricium. Vercingetorix had tried to convince the Bituriges to abandon the town, but they were confident in its defenses. Though he camped outside the town, he was unable to prevent the Romans from investing the town. Caesar attacked the town in a rainstorm when it was least expected and was able to take it, forcing Vercingetorix to retire. Caesar took six legions and marched on the capital of the Arverni at Gergovia. This town was clearly important to Vercingetorix and he intended to defend it. When Caesar reached the town, which was located in very hilly terrain, he seized a hill and established a fortified camp there. He quickly took another hill, established a small camp there, and connected the two with a pair of parallel ditches. Caesar noticed a small hill, which provided access to the town and was virtually undefended. He ordered some of his troops to

provide a distraction and the launched an attack on the hill, which he took with relative ease. The troops, however, continued on to the town walls, whether at Caesar's direction or, as he would have it, having simply been carried away by their success, where they met stiff resistance and were driven off with heavy losses, particularly among the centurions. At that point, Caesar was forced to raise the siege and withdraw from Gergovia.

The defeat at Gergovia was a serious blow to Caesar and a benefit to Vercingetorix. The defeat caused some of Caesar's oldest Gallic allies to defect to the enemy. Vercingetorix set about recruiting additional troops for the rebellion and, using a large cavalry force, began interdicting Roman efforts to gather supplies. Caesar was not idle. To make up the losses caused by the defections, especially in his cavalry, he recruited German cavalry and light infantry to support them. It became clear to Vercingetorix that his forces could not stand up to Caesar's in open battle, particularly with the addition of the German cavalry, and decided to fall back on the fortified town of Alesia, hoping to repeat the defeat of the Romans at Gergovia. Caesar followed him and prepared to invest the town.

DISPOSITIONS

Vercingetorix and his army built a fortified camp adjacent to Alesia defended by a ditch and rampart, 6ft (1.8m) high. Caesar concluded that Alesia and the Gallic camp were far too strong to be assaulted and so decided instead to surround and blockade the town. He started by constructing seven fortified camps supported by 23 redoubts to defend key positions. While these fortifications were being constructed, Vercingetorix sent out his cavalry to interfere with the Romans. A cavalry battle ensued in which the Gauls were badly mauled by Caesar's cavalry, especially the Germans. Vercingetorix then decided to have his cavalry attempt a breakout during the night. The Gallic horsemen slipped out through gaps in the Roman lines and went back to their communities to raise a new army to relieve the siege.

With the escape of the Gallic cavalry and the likely appearance of a relief army, Caesar decided to augment his siege works. First, he constructed a 20ft (6m) ditch with perpendicular sides to prevent the Gauls in Alesia from interfering with his construction of more complete fortifications. Behind this ditch, two additional ditches were dug, and the inner one filled with water to become a

BALLISTA

In the third century B.C.E., the Romans began adopting Greek siege warfare technology. The ballista was a new version of the stone-throwing lithobolos. The frame and base were now sturdier, the holes through which the rope was inserted and the washers by which it was secured went from being square in earlier models, to an oval shape. This allowed more rope to be used in the springs and these were also twisted tighter. The springs were now exclusively made of sinew, much stronger than the old horse-hair versions. All of this gave the machine much greater range and accuracy.

moat. Behind these a rampart 12ft (3.6m) high was erected from dirt excavated from the ditches. This was surmounted with a palisade and protected by sharpened stakes. To further reinforce the rampart, towers were placed along its length at regular intervals. The length of these works was nearly 10 miles (16km).

THE PRIMARY WEAPON of the legionary was his deadly sword, used from behind the protection of his shield. Enemies were softened up before a charge, or their charges were broken up, by massed volleys of pilae, or javelins. The pilum was a "fire" weapon used to weaken the enemy so that the "shock" effect of the legionary assault could more easily shatter his formations and drive him from the field.

During the construction of the fortifications, Vercingetorix made a number of substantial and coordinated sorties from the town, which interfered with construction and made it difficult for Caesar to send out foragers. He therefore added three lines of traps to make enemy attack more difficult. The first consisted of five rows of sharpened tree trunks and stout branches set in trenches, in front of them were pits 3ft (90cm) deep arranged in the fashion of a chessboard, with sharpened stakes set inside, and in front, iron hooks set in wooden blocks were scattered around.

In order to defend against the relief army a similar set of fortifications 17 miles (28km) in length were built facing outward with plenty of room in between for Caesar to move his troops. Caesar also had his men collect a one-month reserve of food and fodder. The Gauls within Alesia recognized that supplies would become short so they sent out of the town all of those who were not able to fight. The non-combatants went to the Roman lines but were turned away by Caesar and so were left to starve in a no-man's land.

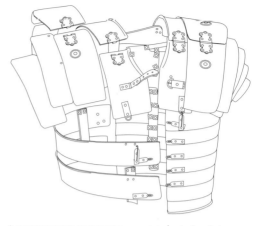

A RECONSTRUCTION OF THE LORICA *segmentata showing how the iron segments are held together with hooks and riveted leather straps to produce a flexible yet effective armor.*

THE BATTLE

The battle began as the relief force arrived and, after having camped within a mile of the Roman lines, sent out their cavalry into a plain 3 miles (4.8km) wide. The Gallic horse

"VERCINGETORIX THROWING HIS WEAPONS AT THE FEET OF CÉSAR," Lionel-Noël Royer's (1852–1926) depiction of Vercingetorix offers a romanticized view of the Gallic leader's surrender. Caesar is depicted dressed as a political figure rather than a soldier.

had archers and light infantry interspersed, while the main body of infantry formed up to watch their cavalry who were the elite of the army. When the Gauls within Alesia saw the cavalry formed for battle, they came out of the town and started to fill in the Roman trenches with fascines in preparation for a sortie. Caesar responded by manning the ramparts with all of his infantry, making sure each man knew

his post, and sending out his Gallic allied and German horse to meet the enemy cavalry. The cavalry action was fiercely contested, the Gallic horse benefiting from the support of the infantry in their midst, something the Romans had not expected. The fighting lasted from noon until sunset, but eventually the Romans had the better of it when Caesar massed his German cavalry at a single point and they broke the Gallic cavalry. The latter fled leaving their infantry supports to be slaughtered and were pursued back to their camp. The Gauls within the siegeworks despaired and retired back to Alesia.

The Gauls of the relief force spent the following day preparing the materials needed for a major assault, including ladders, grappling hooks, and fascines. At midnight, they quietly advanced and, once near the Roman siegeworks, gave a shout to let the besieged know they were beginning the assault. As a result Vercingetorix led out his forces to attack the Romans at the same time so the Romans would be engaged to front and rear. Although the Gauls were able to cause a number of casualties by hurling javelins, slinging stones, and others missiles, the obstacles set up by the Romans before their ramparts made it extremely difficult and caused heavy losses. The Gauls were unable to penetrate the Roman lines and, fearing a counterattack, therefore retreated.

The Gauls held a council of war and decided to use the main army to threaten the siegeworks while a force of 60,000 picked men attacked a Roman camp on the north side of the town. This fort was defended by two legions, but due to the nature of the terrain, it lay outside of the lines of circumvallation. Meanwhile Vercingetorix would again lead an attack so the Romans would be forced to defend both the inner and outer defenses against simultaneous assaults. The Gallic force of warriors marched through the night and rested until noon at which point they attacked. At the same time Vercingetorix attacked the inward-facing fortifications so the Romans were hard-pressed at several places. Caesar noticed that the 60,000 Gauls were having some success against the isolated fort and so he sent his most trusted lieutenant, Titus Atius Labienus, to its relief with six cohorts. He ordered Labienus to defend the fort but if it appeared he could no longer defend it, he should instead counterattack. In the meantime, Vercingetorix's troops had breached a steep section of the inner wall where the fortifications were not as complete.

Caesar sent reinforcements to this position, eventually repulsing the Gauls when he personally led some troops to the breach. By this point the situation had become desperate and Labienus was preparing for a last-ditch counterattack. Caesar rushed to aid the counterattack leading a mere four cohorts, but he also ordered his cavalry to sally out and assault the Gallic warriors from behind. Although the Gauls

GALLIC WARRIOR

The archetypal barbarian warrior with bare chest, fierce mustache, and patterned pants. The Gallic tribesman was a dangerous foe. Roman writers such as Tacitus praised their courage and stoicism. Gauls had defeated Roman armies on previous occasions, but their main weakness was a lack of good organization. Where the Roman army was a well-drilled and obedient body of professional troops, the Gallic force facing it was a loose collection of proud and aggressive men bound together by ties of personal, tribal, and family loyalties. In a short campaign or while they were winning this was not a problem, but once supplies became an issue and victory was doubtful there was a tendency for Gallic armies to break up and groups to begin to drift away.

put up a fight, the appearance of cavalry behind them was too much and they were routed. The Roman cavalry were able to cause tremendous casualties among the routing Gauls. The besieged Gauls were dismayed by this turn of events and retired into Alesia.

AFTERMATH

With the rout of the relief army, the Gauls within Alesia were forced to surrender. Vercingetorix was handed over to Caesar. Some of the Gauls were used to help gain the loyalty of their tribes but many were distributed to the troops as booty and ended up as slaves. The victory at Alesia effectively broke Gallic resistance, although Caesar would spend the next two years consolidating his position. Vercingetorix would remain a prisoner for some six years until, after having been paraded in Rome during Caesar's great triumph, he was publicly strangled.

ALESIA

5 A large relief army of about 250,000 men arrives, and makes three serious attempts to lift the siege of the town.

KEY

← ROMAN ARMY

← GALLIC FORCES

6 The men inside Alesia coordinate their attacks with the relief army, but are defeated by Caesar's Germanic cavalry.

1 Vercingetorix and approximately 70,000 soldiers take refuge in the fortified hilltop town of Alesia.

4 The women and children are forced out of Alesia to save food, and have to camp between the two forces.

2 After the Gallic cavalry escapes, Caesar builds inner and outer walls of approximately 17.4 miles (28km) in length.

3 Forts are constructed along the walls with plenty of space between them to move troops to trouble spots.

ADRIANOPLE 378 C.E.

Described by the soldier and historian Amminaus Marcellinus as the worst Roman military disaster since Cannae, the Battle of Adrianople saw the field army of the Eastern Roman Empire virtually destroyed and the Emperor killed. But the Goths were unable to fully exploit this success thanks to the fortifications of Constantinople.

In 376 C.E., two Visigothic chieftains, Fritigern and Alavivus, made a request to the Eastern Roman Emperor Valens to cross the Danube and settle on the Roman side of that great river. The reason behind the request lay to the east. The Goths were being pressured by a migration of steppe nomads, the Huns, who were on the move westward, driving the Goths and other Germanic groups before them. Valens agreed to the Goths' request with the stipulation that the Visigoths surrender their arms and convert to Christianity, both of which were acceptable to the Gothic leaders. Valens' reasons for allowing the Visigoths within the empire were that they would provide the imperial army with a valuable source of recruits and that he could then transmute the

ADRIANOPLE FACTS

Who: The Eastern Roman Emperor Valens (d. 378 C.E.) with an army of 20,000 men faced a slightly smaller army of Goths under Fritigern.

What: The Goths took advantage of the impetuous advance by the Romans and the serendipitous arrival of the Gothic cavalry (who had been away foraging) to catch the Romans between the Gothic fortified wagon laager and their returning Gothic horsemen.

Where: Near Adrianople in Thrace.

When: August 9, 378 C.E.

Why: The Goths, driven west by the Huns, invaded Thrace to take by force supplies the Romans had promised them but withheld.

Outcome: The battle was a devastating tactical defeat for the Romans who lost two-thirds of the eastern field army.

THIS DRAMATIC DETAIL *from the Ludovisi Sarcophagus (c. 250–260 C.E.), shows Roman troops in a life-or-death struggle with barbarian invaders.*

ROMAN AUXILLIARY

By the time of the battle of Milvian Bridge in 350 C.E. the appearance of the Roman soldier had changed dramatically from when the empire was at its peak. This figure is armed with a long spear and carries a long sword more suitable to the cutting strokes favored by the Germanic auxiliaries in Rome's service than the gladius. His shield is oval, made of wood with a leather or linen covering and a metal rim and boss. He wears a simple iron helmet made in two halves and joined in a central ridge, with flexible cheek pieces. He wears no armor, relying on his shield for protection. Instead of the Roman sandal, he wears a hobnailed boot.

local provincial manpower levies into much needed financial contributions. By the end of the year the Goths, perhaps numbering 75,000 men, women, and children, had crossed over the Danube into Roman territory.

THE GOTHS BETRAYED

Valens ordered that the Goths be given land to farm and that they be supplied by local officials until they could be settled. Unfortunately, the local Roman administrators did not provide the promised supplies. They are often portrayed as being exceedingly avaricious, extorting almost everything the Goths possessed, including their children, in exchange for substandard provisions including dog meat. As might be expected, this caused a great deal of resentment among the tribesmen. The Goths continued their migration deeper into Roman Thrace. Along the way, they made contact with some Ostrogothic warriors who had crossed the Danube without Roman permission while the latter were

preoccupied with the Visigoths. At Marcianopolis, a local Roman commander invited Fritigern and Alavivus to a banquet, apparently planning on either capturing or murdering the Gothic chieftain. Fritigern seems to have secured his own safe return, perhaps in exchange for promises of good behavior by his men, but Alavivus is not heard of afterward and was, presumably, killed.

Upon the safe return of Fritigern, the Goths decided to take what they needed from the Romans by force and open warfare broke out, the Goths defeating the local troops in and around Marcianopolis. Fritigern's forces were then reinforced by other Gothic tribes that had earlier been allowed across the frontier, and the Gothic army moved to Adrianople and attacked the town. Their assault was bloodily repulsed and Fritigern famously noted afterward that he "kept peace with walls." It was clear to the Romans, however, that this was a serious situation that called for additional troops. Consequently, Valens, who was with the elite eastern field army in Antioch dealing with the Persians, dispatched reinforcements to Thrace.

There were soon joined by troops from the western Emperor Gratian, who was also the nephew of Valens. Throughout much of 378 C.E., there was some indecisive fighting but for the most part the Romans were content to keep the Goths contained in some of the more inhospitable parts of the country and to employ a Fabian strategy, avoiding major combat and attacking Gothic foraging parties while awaiting reinforcements from both the western and eastern field armies.

At the end of the year, the Goths, aided by newly acquired Alanic and Hunnic allies, managed to break out of containment and were poised to ravage the more populated and fertile regions of Thrace. To complicate matters, Gratian was faced with an incursion by some of the Alamanni and was delayed while his army dealt with the raiders. The raid turned into a full-scale invasion, which postponed his advance in support of Valens further, even though the invasion was crushed.

THE CAMPAIGN AND THE ARMIES

In the meantime, Valens had left Antioch and in May 378 C.E., he reached the imperial capital of Constantinople. Valens encamped his army on the European side of the Hellespont and sent cavalry out to determine the position of the enemy and scout ahead of the main force. He began a slow advance toward the town of Nike, only a short distance from Adrianople. With the Eastern Emperor and his army advancing against them, the Gothic forces retreated, shadowed by a large force of Roman horsemen. During the advance the Romans managed to defeat some Gothic foragers. In the meantime, Gratian had expeditiously advanced toward Thrace, moving part of his army by ship

EMPEROR VALENS makes a treaty with with the leader of the Visigoths, just two years before the massacre at Adrianople.

along the Danube. Valens decided to advance on Adrianople and make a new camp where he would await the arrival of his nephew and the western field army. At this point, the Goths managed to slip past Valens' troops and took up a position to his southeast, at Nike.

While encamped at Adrianople, Valens received word that Gratian and his army were about to enter Thrace and would soon be able to rendezvous with him. He was also informed by his scouts that they had spotted the Gothic army, who they estimated to be approximately 10,000 strong. At this point, Valens was faced with the decision to remain where he was for the arrival of Gratian and his troops or advance and attack the Goths since he now knew their exact position. He convened a council of war with his high-ranking officers and the issue was debated. Some of the more cautious argued for waiting: the arrival of Gratian's troops would give him an overwhelming numerical advantage. But the majority argued that they should attack immediately, flattering the Emperor by noting that if he defeated the Goths by himself, the glory for the victory would be his alone. They no doubt also considered that the Goths had evaded them once and it would be wise to attack before they slipped away again. Valens decided to attack immediately

and gave orders for his army to prepare to march against the enemy. Fritigern seems to have learned of these preparations and sent an envoy, who was also a Christian cleric, to negotiate a settlement, but Valens dismissed him and continued preparing for battle.

The eastern army that Valens was preparing to march with him probably numbered some 20,000 men. There were more troops in the theater of operations, but Valens had to leave a garrison consisting of a few legions at Adrianople to guard the important base and his baggage train that was to remain there. Moreover, given the fact that the Gothic army was quite close to the imperial capital at Constantinople, other troops had been detailed there to defend the city. Valens' force was composed of many veteran troops, some of whom had been recalled for the current campaign and, as an imperial field army, consisted of troops of good quality. The army was also a well balanced force, consisting of legions and auxiliaries, including bowmen, and apparently was well provided with cavalry.

The Gothic army had been reported at 10,000 men, but this seems to have been an underestimate. The Goths numbered something more like 15,000 warriors, all infantry, encamped in a wagon laager. The Gothic infantry were a mix of warriors armed with spear and shield, and archers. But the Roman scouts were unaware that the entire force of perhaps 4,000 Gothic cavalry, mostly Ostrogoths with some Alan allies under the chieftains Alatheus and Saphrax, were out foraging and had not been spotted by the Romans.

EMPEROR THEODOSIUS I (ruled 379–395). A successful general before being named emperor, Theodosius was the last emperor to rule a united Roman Empire.

DISPOSITIONS

At first light on August 9, Valens led his army out, marching in columns. It appears that both the vanguard and rearguard of the Roman army were composed of cavalry while the main body was formed by infantry; no doubt there were outriders along the flanks as well. It seems clear that Valens and his commanders were still concerned about their intelligence regarding the Gothic army's location and were using cavalry to protect the army from surprise while on the march. After several hours of marching in very hot conditions, the Romans sighted the Gothic camp, a large laager formed from wagons, and began deploying for battle. The Romans moved the cavalry of the vanguard forward to form the right flank of their battle array while the infantry were formed up to support them. The cavalry of the rearguard moved to take up their position as the army's left flank, but because they had to wait for those troops in front of them to deploy and had to travel a considerable distance to take up their positions, were unable to form up properly before the battle commenced.

For their part the Goths, who were probably outnumbered by the Romans and who were, at least temporarily, without any cavalry support of their own, decided to defend their wagon laager. Fritigern did, however, quickly send word to Alatheus and Saphrax requesting their immediate return to join the battle. In an effort to gain time for the return of the Gothic horsemen and their Alanic allies, Fritigern sent an embassy to Valens in order to parlay, but the Emperor refused to meet with them on account of their low birth, requesting that suitable chieftains be sent instead. Fritigern responded by sending one of his warriors as a herald, requesting that Valens send a man of suitable rank as a hostage, apparently as part of an exchange. Valens agreed, no doubt hoping that the delay would give him time to properly deploy his army, especially his left wing. Eventually, one of the Roman commanders, Richomeres, agreed to go to Fritigern's camp. Meanwhile, the Roman cavalry of the right wing and the infantry of the center, waited in formation in the scorching heat. Their discomfort was exacerbated by brush fires that had been started by the Goths. Moreover, the Romans had marched and were now deployed, but did not have an opportunity to eat and so hunger, thirst, and heat were taking their toll on the army.

THE BATTLE

Before Richomeres reached the Gothic camp to meet with Fritigern, the battle was unexpectedly joined. Two units of Roman cavalry, including one of archers, had been skirmishing with the Goths, got carried away and launched an unexpected and ill-considered attack against the wagon laager. These skirmishers, who may have been formed on the army's right, were probably neither in the proper formation for such an attack nor would they have had the necessary supporting troops. As a result, they were forced to retreat. At that very moment, the Gothic cavalry made their return to the battlefield and charged impetuously into the Roman army. It appears that the Gothic horsemen attacked the units of the cavalry on the left flank who were still strung out while they moved into position. The Roman cavalry were hard-pressed by the Goths, and those who had made their way as far as the Gothic laager found themselves without support from the other Roman troopers who had not yet reached their assigned positions. As a result, the Roman cavalry were quickly and decisively defeated. No doubt this played havoc with the Roman infantry who were still attempting to form themselves into a line of battle.

VISIGOTH CAVALRY

Visigothic cavalry charging. Unlike the nomadic peoples of the steppe, who relied on mounted archers, Gothic cavalry fought in Greco–Roman style, with short thrusting spears and swords. They were the most feared cavalry in eastern Roman empire.

The defeat of the cavalry on their left created a large gap in the Roman line, a gap which the Gothic cavalry were quick to exploit. At this point in the battle, front-line units of the Roman infantry found themselves engaged with the Gothic infantry. The Goths had begun to sally forth from the wagon laager and were now pressing the Roman infantry. With the defeat of the skirmishers and the left wing cavalry, the Roman infantry found themselves attacked not only from the front but also in the flank by the Gothic horsemen. The fighting was incredibly fierce, but the excellent Roman infantry fought on, even as those in the front found themselves pressed together so tightly it became difficult to make proper use of their weapons.

The battle went back and forth and for a considerable amount of time and the combat was a close-run affair. But after repeated attacks, and exhausted not only by fighting but by the heat, hunger, and the weight of their armor, the Roman lines began to give way. Some units, however, held on. Valens took up position with two legions, the Lanciarii and Mattiarii, who were still holding out, but then even the Roman reserves began to flee, including the elite Batavian auxiliaries. All resistance broke and a general rout ensued. The Goths pursued, which led to the destruction of two-thirds of the Roman army.

As the army began to disintegrate, Valens was wounded by an arrow. His body was never found and he is assumed to have died on the battlefield. One tradition had him and a small group of bodyguards falling back to a farmhouse with a well fortified second story. Valens' Roman guardsmen fiercely defended their wounded emperor and the Goths eventually burned the place to the ground with the Romans inside. In addition to the Emperor a number of high-ranking officers and 35 unit commanders were slain.

CATAPHRACT CAVALRY

It is likely that the Roman and Visigothic forces at Adrianople both contained at least some heavily armored cavalry, sometimes known as cataphracts. Mounted on horses that could bear the weight of their own body armor, as well as the weight of their armored riders, such horsemen could break up an enemy line by their sheer weight on impact. Since their armored horses were less susceptible to crippling injuries, such troops were also more willing to close with the enemy, where their weapon of choice, the thrusting spear, could be devastatingly effective.

A GOLD COIN of Roman emperor Valens (364–378 C.E.), later converted into a necklace. Valens was one of the last Roman emperors to appear on coins in civilian garb.

AFTERMATH

The virtual destruction of the eastern field army allowed the Goths to march on Adrianople where Valens had left his baggage train, including his treasury and the imperial regalia. The Goths tried to take the city but, once again, the walls held by the legions left by Valens were simply too strong to be stormed. They then moved to Constantinople where the city's defenses and the troops left to defend it thwarted the Goths. Gratian and his western army returned to Gaul to deal with an invasion by the Vandals, but Gratian handed over command of the eastern armies to his general Theodosius whom he named Eastern Emperor on January 19, 379 C.E. Theodosius fought several inconclusive campaigns against the Goths and eventually made peace with them in 382 C.E. Under the terms of the treaty the Goths were granted land in Thrace in exchange for serving as allies.

ADRIANOPLE

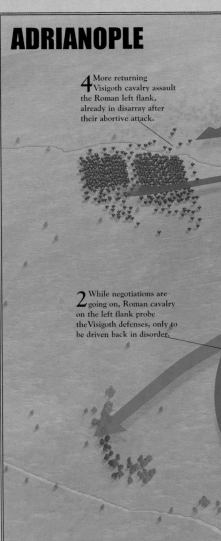

4 More returning Visigoth cavalry assault the Roman left flank, already in disarray after their abortive attack.

2 While negotiations are going on, Roman cavalry on the left flank probe the Visigoth defenses, only to be driven back in disorder.

6 Visigoth cavalry strike the Roman infantry on both flanks, rapidly surrounding and annihilating the Roman center.

KEY

⬅ VISIGOTHS

⬅ ROMANS

1 As the Romans approach, the Visigoths adopt a defensive position, circling their wagons into laagers to protect women and children and manning the makeshift defense with infantry.

3 The Visigoth cavalry return from a foraging expedition and fall on the Roman right flank.

5 The Roman cavalry are driven from the field in disorder.

TOURS/POITIERS

732 C.E.

The battle of Tours/Poitiers was a turning point in world history that decided the fate of Western Europe. It was here that the tide of Muslim conquest was turned back, with enormous implications for the future of the entire world.

After the fall of the Western Roman Empire, Europe fragmented into many small kingdoms and tribal groupings. This era has been called the "Dark Ages" but in fact culture and civilization flourished in most areas. However, it was a turbulent time in which many successors to Roman power fought one another and battled barbarians along their frontiers. By 700 C.E., several large kingdoms had arisen. Spain was more or less dominated by the Visigoths, who had migrated there from the east. The Duchy of Aquitaine ruled southwestern France. But by far the largest of the western European states was the kingdom of the Franks, which stretched from the

TOURS/POITIERS FACTS

Who: A force of Franks under Charles Martel (688–741 C.E.), versus a superior army of Muslim Moorish cavalry under Emir Abd-ar-Rahman (d. 732 C.E.).

What: The Frankish infantry established itself in a defensive position and awaited attack by the Moorish cavalry. After a hard-fought battle the Franks emerged victorious.

Where: Between modern Tours and Poitiers in France.

When: October 10, 732 C.E.

Why: Muslim forces had taken Iberia and were spilling over the Pyrenees to conquer

more of Europe. They were opposed by the Christian Franks.

Outcome: A decisive victory for the Franks. Charles Martel made his reputation in this battle. The Moorish commander was killed and his army retired to Spain.

FRANKISH KINGDOMS

✝ TOURS

UMAYYAD CALIPHATE

THIS DRAMATIC NINETEENTH CENTURY painting by Carl von Steuben (1788-1856) depicts Charles Martel's stand at Tours/Poitiers. Though somewhat romanticized, the painting conveys the desperate nature of close-quarters fighting.

English Channel and North Sea coasts to the Mediterranean, and from a narrow holding on the Atlantic coast north of Aquitaine to Bavaria and Saxony.

The Frankish kingdom was a Christian state, like most of Europe, and could field a powerful army based around a core of elite armored infantry and bound to their leader by oaths and family bonds. The remainder of the force was made up of lighter-armed foot soldiers; armored cavalry were not yet the dominant force in European warfare, though their day was coming soon.

The Franks were powerful and warlike. No less martial, but far less potent, was the Visigothic kingdom of Iberia, which by 700 C.E. was in dire straits. With famine in some areas and the nobility fighting among themselves, central authority had broken down and rivals of the king, Roderick, decided that the time was ripe for a takeover. Roderick's

THE FRANKS ENTERED *the Arab camp late in the battle. The infiltration and looting of their camp was a major factor in weakening the Muslim's assault on the Frankish positions.*

rivals turned for aid to what was probably the greatest power of the era, the Umayyad (or Omayyad) Caliphate, the vast Muslim empire that stretched all along the north coast of Africa through Egypt, Arabia, and on to Mesopotamia. In 711 C.E., assistance was granted by Tariq ibd Ziyad, governor of Tangiers, in the form of 10,000 troops. With their Visigothic allies, this force landed at Gibraltar and so began the Muslim conquest of Iberia. Defeating Roderick in battle, the Muslim forces rapidly conquered much of the country. Whether or not they had initially intended to help Roderick's opponents, they now set out to make themselves masters of Iberia.

EXPEDITIONS INTO EUROPE

After the initial invasion, Tariq ibd Ziyad was superseded in command by his superior, a member of the Umayyad dynasty, named Musa ibn Unsay. Ever-larger forces entered Iberia and turned it into a province of the Caliphate. Some areas were overrun but retained a degree of autonomy, retaining their religious freedom, such as the principality of Murcia, while other regions, notably Asturias, held out as best they could or revolted against Umayyad rule.

Some of those holding out were in the Pyrenees, between what is now France and Spain. Expeditions were sent against them, and ultimately through the mountains against the kingdoms there, which were thought to be supporting the rebels. As the Muslims crossed the mountains and began making forays into Europe, alarm grew. By 720 C.E. Moorish forces had a toe-hold in southern France and were expanding their control. They launched raids as far as the Rhône valley.

A series of internal problems and revolts slowed Muslim expansion into Europe for several years, but in 730 C.E. the then leader, Abd-ar-Rahman, launched an expedition into Aquitaine to remove the threat to his northern border. Defeating the Aquitainians at Bordeaux, Rahman's army rampaged through the Duchy of Aquitaine, breaking its power and reducing its strongholds.

The neighboring Frankish kingdom had several princes with various titles, but the greatest of them, ruler of the Franks in all but name, was Charles. It was in the coming campaign that the Frankish prince earned his title Martel, which means "The Hammer." Born in what is now Belgium, Charles Martel had been previously imprisoned to prevent succession complications. This was not entirely successful. He escaped and during the ensuing civil war he learned the value of, what today would be called, logistics. After a shaky start he emerged as a wily and surprisingly modern commander. Coming to the field with forces capable of winning the battle was part of his pattern of strategy. He also learned the value of striking unexpectedly and of defying convention when it was advantageous to do so. The great

Chinese military thinker Sun Tzu, of whom Charles of course had never heard, would recognize many of his tactics. His military brilliance allowed Charles Martel to create a unified kingdom under his rule, though he did not take the title of king. By 732 C.E. Charles was an enormously powerful figure in Europe. He was also popular with the Church as a champion of Christianity.

Who better, then, to lead the Christian Franks in repelling the invaders and their foreign religion? In fact Charles had been preparing to do just that for some years. Although he did engage in various campaigns between 720 and 732 C.E., he was well aware of the threat from the southeast and had begun to create an army to defeat it. This is typical of the man—he did not rush in to fight his foes but instead worked out how they could be beaten before offering battle. The core of Charles' strategy against the invaders was the creation of a force of elite heavy infantry who were professionals capable of training all year round. This was not the practice of the time; other than small bodyguards, fighting men were normally raised for a campaign then went home to their farms afterward.

Charles equipped his professionals lavishly and protected them with good armor. He trained them well and allowed them to gain experience in combat, increasing their confidence and steadiness. He did have some mounted troops but cavalry was not much in use in Europe at that time and they lacked stirrups. These mounted soldiers, who were not true cavalry and could not stand against the excellent horsemen of the Moorish Caliphate, were used as a mobile reserve or simply dismounted to fight.

THE CAMPAIGN OPENS

The Moorish forces were overconfident. They had easily beaten everything that Europe could put in their path and did not rate the "barbarians" as fighters or as an army. Although a previous expedition had been defeated before the walls of Toulouse, the Muslims did not believe that Europe could offer any significant opposition.

The victor of Toulouse, Duke Odo of Aquitaine, met the Moors at the Garonne River and attempted to turn back the invasion. This time, however, there was to be no European victory. Large numbers of Berber (North African) and Arab cavalry crashed into Odo's army, which was scattered and ridden down. Suffering massive casualties, Odo's force ceased to be a factor in the campaign and the Muslims pushed on.

However, victories like Garonne contributed to the general overconfidence of the Moorish host. Scouting was neglected and victory became an expectation rather than something won by hard endeavor. This allowed Charles to choose the battleground and achieve a measure of surprise over his opponents, who were unaware of the size or quality of his force. Charles marched his force to intercept the Muslims, who he knew were on their way to attack Tours.

MUSLIM CAVALRY *from the invasion of Spain in the eighth century through to the Battle of Nicopolis in 1396 were generally less heavily armored than their Christian counterparts and relied more on skirmishing than the full frontal charge.*

A FRANKISH SHIELDWALL. This spear-bristling phalanxe-style formation was powerful on the defensive, but only if it could maintain its cohesion. If it was broken, a slaughter often ensued.

He did not use the Roman roads, even though these offered the easiest going, because he expected these to be watched, but placed his force in the path of the opposing army. The exact location is unclear but lay somewhere between Poitiers and Tours, hence the fact that the battle is known to historians by two names.

The advancing Muslims stumbled on Charles' force in its blocking position and were both surprised and non-plussed. Their scouts had brought no word of this force and it had simply appeared in their path. The Moorish leader, Emir Abd-ar-Rahman, hesitated to attack and sought to discover as much as possible about these latest adversaries. The pause, which lasted six days, allowed Rahman to observe the enemy and to pull in his patrols and detached forces, but it also acted in the Franks' favor. The enemy were operating far from home in a colder climate than they were used to while the Franks were on home ground. It was obvious that Rahman was going to have to attack and the Franks were ready for him. They occupied a good defensive position and could remain there indefinitely. Sooner or later, Rahman would have to attack or else turn around and go home.

THE MOORS CHARGE

Rahman had under his command between 40,000 and 60,000 cavalry who had carried before their charge every opponent they had met. Many of their defeated foes had been Frankish infantry like those arrayed before them. Any misgivings Rahman might have felt about charging uphill against a solid defensive formation were outweighed by his confidence in his cavalry. Or perhaps he simply felt that having come this far he could not simply retire. Subsequent events showed the value of discipline and confidence in battle. Conventional wisdom of the time said that infantry could not defeat cavalry, but Charles' troops did just that.

The Franks were drawn up in a large defensive square formation with reserve units inside. The capabilities of the infantry square were well proven at Tours.

The Moorish cavalry made several charges at Charles' square and, despite being tired by their heavy armor and the slope they attacked up, despite their formations being disrupted by the uneven ground and the trees that dotted it, they crashed home again and again.

CRISIS POINT

Several times groups of Moorish horsemen fought their way into the square. If they could establish themselves there it was all over; attack from within and without the square would mean that it would lose its cohesion and its scattered members be ridden down. Reserve forces within the square fell on them—infantry rushed confidently up to attack armored cavalry, something that rarely happened and even less often successful—and killed them or drove them out of the square.

FRANKISH WARRIOR

A Frankish warrior armed with sword and shield. Armor was available to some well off warriors but most had to make do with a helmet and skilled use of their shield.

Matters were in some doubt for a time as the square was heavily beset from all sides, but then the pressure began to ease. Moorish warriors began falling back to their camp, leaving the square battered but intact.

RAHMAN KILLED

Some of Martel's scouts had managed to get into the Moorish camp during the battle, taking advantage of poor scouting and overconfidence on the part of the enemy. There, they freed prisoners and generally caused mayhem. This confusion in their rear, coupled with the worry that their hard-won plunder might be stolen back by the Franks, drew many of Rahman's troops back to the camp and severely disrupted the attack on the Franks' square. Rahman tried to stop the rearward movement but in so doing exposed himself with an inadequate bodyguard. He was killed by Frankish soldiers. The Moors were dismayed and retired in some disorder. The Franks tidied up their formation and remained in their defensive positions.

There was no clear successor to Rahman, and the Moorish force fell into disarray. The force began to retire in the direction of Iberia, though this was not immediately apparent to the Franks who suspected a feigned retreat to draw them off the hill they occupied. The Moors retained the means to defeat the Franks because they were still very powerful. However, its will had been broken and the various sub-commanders, still unable to agree who should take over, decided to continue their journey home. They had gained a considerable amount of plunder and still had much of it; little would be gained by a renewal of hostilities, or so they reasoned.

AFTERMATH

The battle of Tours/Poitiers has at times been lauded as the only reason Europe is not a Muslim state and a part of the Arab Empire. While this is an exaggeration, it is fair to say that Charles deserved the nickname "The Hammer," or Martel, which was conferred on him for handing the Muslim expansion such a dramatic defeat.

Tours/Poitiers represented something of a high-water mark in the Muslim invasion of Europe. Expeditions over the Pyrenees would continue and Charles Martel would oppose them for the rest of his life. He would, in time, create the great Carolingian dynasty that produced Charlemagne, who is considered to be the father of European chivalry.

The Muslim occupation of Iberia continued for many centuries and advantage ebbed and flowed between Muslim and Christian forces in southwestern Europe. Charles Martel's victory did not end the Moorish invasion nor make invasion into further territory impossible. It was, however, the point where the easy Muslim victories ended and the long struggle began.

A WATERCOLOR DEPICTION of Charles Martel's victory at Tours/Poitiers. This was not only the turning point of the Muslim invasion of Western Europe, it also marked the emergence of the great Carolingian dynasty.

ANDALUCIAN HORSE ARCHER

The Muslim forces made great use of horse archers. Combining excellent mobility with good striking power, horse archers could choose when and where to attack and could often evade an enemy counterstroke. By skirmishing, they could erode an opposing force by wearing down and tiring out the troops, and by concentrating at a decisive point they could soften up a formation for assault by other units. Predominantly infantry forces had no effective counter to the hit-and-run tactics of the horse archers.

TOURS/POITIERS

3 Close-quarters fighting ensues. Penetrations of the Frankish formation are sealed and dealt with by reserve forces.

4 As repeated charges fail, word comes that the Franks are attacking the Muslim camp.

6 Demoralized and leaderless, the Muslim forces retreat to Spain leaving the Franks victorious.

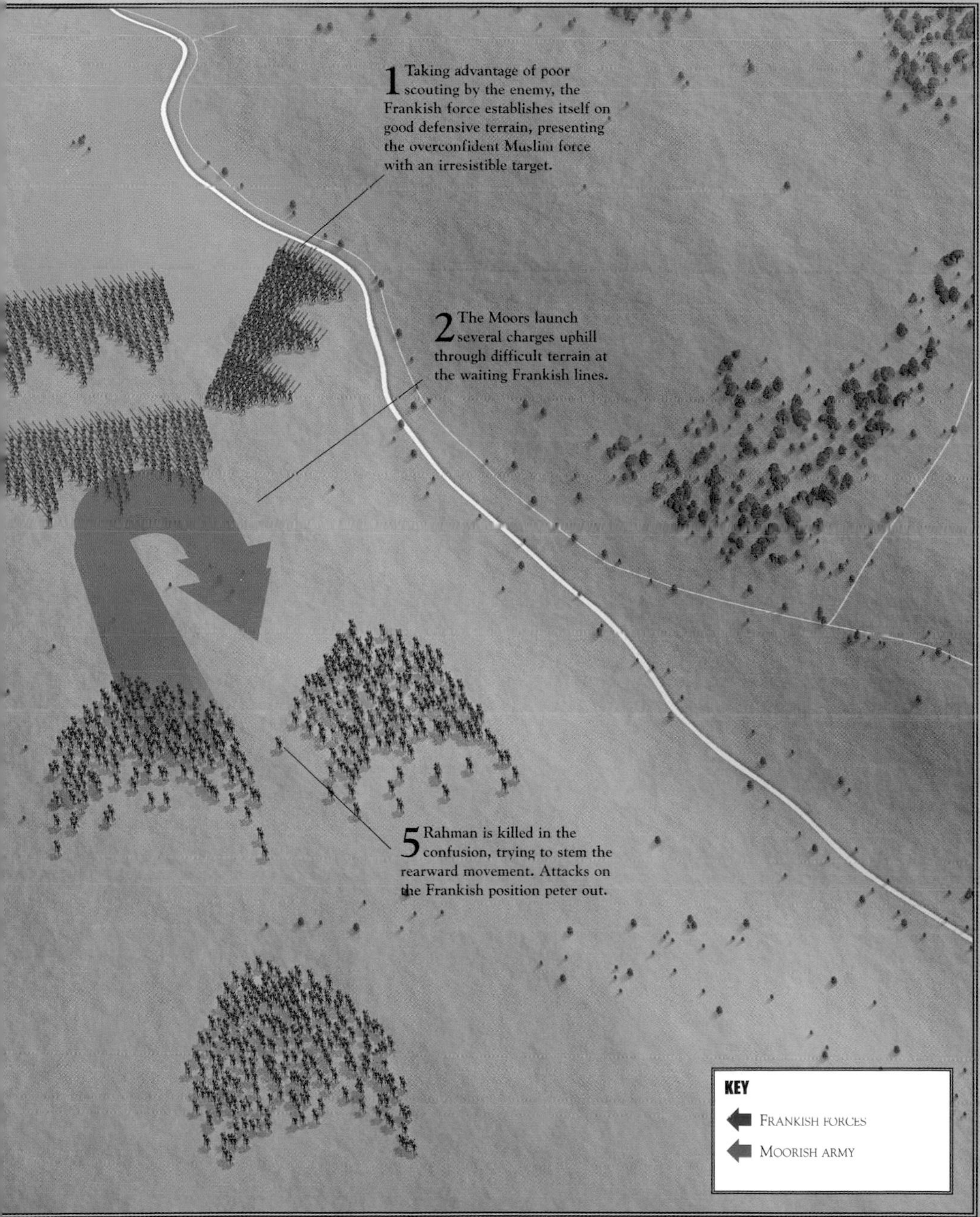

1 Taking advantage of poor scouting by the enemy, the Frankish force establishes itself on good defensive terrain, presenting the overconfident Muslim force with an irresistible target.

2 The Moors launch several charges uphill through difficult terrain at the waiting Frankish lines.

5 Rahman is killed in the confusion, trying to stem the rearward movement. Attacks on the Frankish position peter out.

KEY

← FRANKISH FORCES

← MOORISH ARMY

HASTINGS 1066

Norman mounted men-at-arms met the Anglo-Saxon shield wall in the longest, hardest fought, and most decisive battle in England in the early Middle Ages. William the Conqueror's victory changed English history forever, and ushered in the dominance of the mounted knight in European warfare.

In traditional accounts Harold's reputation was blackened as an oath-breaker, while others viewed William as the villain. It is probably safe to say that both of these remarkably able and ruthless men had their good and bad sides. William was the illegitimate son of the Duke of Normandy and he had to defend his position as Duke, from 1035 onward, against all comers and by the time he wished to invade England had carved out the most powerful duchy in France and northwestern Europe, reducing both Brittany and Maine to vassal states. His influence was also predominant in Paris, where he dominated the young King Philip, and he had created a crucial ally in Flanders by marrying Matilda, the daughter of Duke Baldwin IV.

HASTINGS FACTS

Who: William, Duke of Normandy (1028–87), invaded England with an army of 6,000 men to lay claim to the throne of King Harold II Godwinson (1022–66), who faced him with an army of 6,300.

What: Norman cavalry and archers eventually wore down the Saxon shield wall formation.

Where: Senlac Ridge, 7 miles (11.2km) north of the town of Hastings, England.

When: October 14, 1066.

Why: William wanted to conquer England.

Outcome: Harold and most of the Anglo-Saxon nobility were killed, and William secured the throne of England.

THIS DRAMATIC DEPICTION of the battle of Hastings by R. Caton Woodville shows King Harold Godwinson making his final stand against the Normans on Senlac Hill.

THE NORMAN ARMY AS DISPLAYED IN THE BAYEUX TAPESTRY *consists of cavalry and archers. Other contemporary sources indicate that the cavalry greatly outnumbered the archers, but the latter's role in the death of King Harold Godwinson no doubt accounts for their exaggerated presence.*

William's claim to the English throne was very tenuous and lacked solid legal foundations. William had forced his rival, Harold Godwinson, in 1064 to swear an oath to leave Edward the Confessor's throne to him. But Harold had no intention of honoring an oath forced upon him through blackmail and threats. As the Earl of Wessex, vice-regent under Edward since 1064, the elderly King's brother-in-law, and with undoubted ability and good character, no man had a stronger or more legitimate claim to the throne of England. As a consequence when Edward died, on January 5, 1066, Harold was crowned in Westminster Abbey.

STAMFORD BRIDGE

Harold was no fool and he knew that the ruthlessly ambitious William would use his "breaking" of the "oath" as a spurious excuse to invade. Until May there was no threat of invasion but during the early summer William unleashed an ambitious naval building program to create an armada of 500 ships to carry his 6,000-strong army (of Normans, Bretons, French, and Flemings) across the Channel.

In response Harold mobilized his 4,000-strong Royal Guard, known by their Scandinavian name of huscarls, and the territorial Saxon militia, the fyrd. The fyrd could, in theory and given time, resources, and money, mobilize 15,000–20,000 men but during the summer of 1066 it probably numbered no more than 4,000. Harold strung out his army of 8,000 men along the south coast waiting for the Normans. Harold ordered the fyrd to be disbanded on September 8 so these men could return to their farms and gather in the all-important harvest. Unfortunately Harold had acted precipitously because news arrived that his brother, Earl Tostig, had joined forces with King Harald Hardrada of Norway and had invaded northern England. As

Harold gathered his men and rushed north, the Saxon army of the north, led by the Earl of Northumbria, were defeated on September 20 at Fulford Gate. Five days later Harold surprised and annihilated the Norwegian invaders, slaying Tostig and Harald in the process, at Stamford Bridge.

WILLIAM'S INVASION

Back in France, William had been kept in Normandy by contrary winds. It was only on September 12 that his armada could sail to St. Valéry on the Somme River from where he intended to invade England. It was only a short day's sailing across the Channel to England from this small port. The winds proved fickle and it was not until September 27 that a southerly wind allowed William's fleet to set sail northward. He made landfall at Pevensey Bay the following morning and immediately started gathering supplies, erecting his wooden forts (portable ones brought from Normandy in sections), and plundering the surrounding countryside for intelligence, food, and fodder for his horses.

News that William had finally landed reached Harold at York on October 1 amid celebrations following Stamford Bridge. Harold rushed south picking up the fyrd and other troops along the way back to London. He left the capital on October 11 heading south with an army of 6,000–7,000 troops. Many of his men rode to the battle on horses but would fight on foot. It was late in the afternoon on October 13 that Harold reached Senlac Ridge, a location that he had, during the summer's idleness, chosen as a possible battleground. His choice was based on his experience fighting the Welsh (1064) and his familiarity with the Hastings region.

Senlac was a gently sloped ridge with a marsh area to the south around the Asten brook with its western and eastern flanks protected by deep ravines covered by thick brushwood. An even steeper ridge protected the northern side and would thus prevent the Normans from attacking Harold's army in the rear. William was rapidly informed about Harold's movement and the arrival of his army. Because the Saxons had arrived late in the day they would opt to rest and then make a lightning attack in the morning. But William would himself make the first move. His men were roused little after five in the morning and by 6 A.M. the Normans were marching northward to face Harold's host. Before they set off William spoke to them telling them, "You fight not merely for victory but also for survival."

William's claim may seem melodramatic but it was the naked truth: if they failed to defeat the Saxons on hostile English soil then they would probably not escape home to Normandy alive. William divided his army into three divisions that marched off with the Bretons as the vanguard, followed by the Franco-Flemish troops and then finally William leading his own Normans. William had chosen as the assembly point the Blackhorse Hill, on the Hastings to London road, where the Bretons arrived by 7:30 A.M. Here, out of sight of the Saxons, William left his baggage train and ordered his men to put on their chain-mail hauberk armor which they had slung across the back of their horses. Unfortunately William put his hauberk on back-to-front, viewed by his superstitious men as a bad omen, but one that the cynical William simply laughed off. The Norman army marched north to take up position opposite the Saxons.

DISPOSITIONS

William remained on a small knoll out of the way under the Papal banner and his own Norman leopard standards. From this position he could give orders and had a good view of the battlefield. He could observe how the Bretons under Count Alan of Brittany followed the Asten brook to take up position opposite Harold's right flank. On William's left, Count Eustace of Boulogne led his French and Flemish mercenaries to the bottom of Senlac Ridge facing the Saxon left. In the middle now stood the largest and most formidable of the divisions: William's own Normans with auxiliaries from Anjou and Main. The archers and crossbowmen were

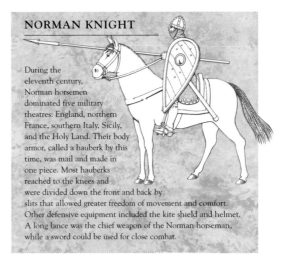

NORMAN KNIGHT

During the eleventh century, Norman horsemen dominated five military theatres: England, northern France, southern Italy, Sicily, and the Holy Land. Their body armor, called a hauberk by this time, was mail and made in one piece. Most hauberks reached to the knees and were divided down the front and back by slits that allowed greater freedom of movement and comfort. Other defensive equipment included the kite shield and helmet. A long lance was the chief weapon of the Norman horseman, while a sword could be used for close combat.

at the front, then came the more heavily armed infantry and finally William's mounted men-at-arms.

For his part, Harold had been aware that the invaders were on the move since 8 A.M. when his scouts reported that the Normans had left Blackhorse Hill. If the weather had been wetter, forcing William to postpone his attack for a few crucial hours, Harold might have had time to erect proper defenses atop Senlac Ridge but there was no rain and the ground was firm. Harold's army was roused and began to deploy along the ridge in a shield wall that stretched for 600 yards (549m) from the Asten brook to the junction of the roads to Hastings and Seddlescombe. The Saxon phalanx was 10 ranks deep with 2ft (0.6m) of frontage for each of his warriors meaning that he had about 6,300 men under his command. William had placed his strongest division in the center so Harold followed suit, placing his more experienced

ENGLISH SHIELD WALL, mid-eleventh century. The troops are mainly spearmen, though some hold axes and swords. The formation depended on the mutual support of the men within it for its strength.

A ROMANTIC PORTRAYAL of William the Conqueror from a nineteenth-century illustration. Born an illegitimate son of the Duke Robert of Normandy, he became one of the greatest military leaders in history, fighting off rebels in his own duchy and conquering Maine, parts of Brittany, and England.

huscarls in the center. He placed his lighter armed and armored men of the fyrd on the flanks, reinforced by a line of sharpened wooden stakes in front.

THE BATTLE BEGINS

The October 14, the Feast of St. Calixtus, dawned with brightening skies, a thin cloud cover and no indication of rain. Aged 44, Harold faced the 38-year-old William. They were both gifted and experienced commanders in their prime leading two of the best armies in western Europe, whose morale was superb: the Normans because of the prospect of conquest and loot; the Saxons because of the need to defend their homeland and their recent spectacular victory at Stamford Bridge. The Normans, who would have to make the first move, were 150 yards (137m) from, and 50ft (15.24m) below, the Saxon shield wall. The Bretons were the least experienced of William's troops and the weak link in his army. Harold's equivalent were the fyrd and he trusted his shield wall to hold back the onrush of Norman cavalry—it was the first time a predominantly cavalry army was fighting infantry in this fashion. The outcome would decide the nature of medieval warfare thereafter.

Sharp trumpet blasts at 9 A.M. announced the beginning of the battle as William's three divisions advanced up the slope of Senlac Ridge. The archers at the front showered the Saxons with arrows but to little effect—these either overshot their intended target or got lodged in the shield wall. The Saxon response with javelins, spears, and axes proved far more effective against the onrushing Normans. Because they had the gentler slope, the jittery Bretons were the first to smash into the shield wall and be repelled by the fierce resistance of the Saxons. Unnerved by this and the failure of the archers' fire to make any impact on the shield wall, the Bretons

retreated by 10–10:30 A.M. The retreat turned into a rout when the undisciplined fyrd militia left the safety of the shield wall to purse the fleeing Bretons.

WILLIAM'S ATTACK

From his vantage point, William saw what was happening and with a curse he gathered part of the advancing Norman cavalry to assist the hard-pressed Bretons. Riding into the fyrd with a charge of armored knights, the Saxons were taken by surprise and, as lightly armored infantry on open ground, they were cut down to the last man. William's timely and ferocious cavalry charge had saved his army from disaster. Undoubtedly morale, especially among the defeated Bretons, was low. William recalled his other two divisions, halted for half an hour to regroup for another attack. This time the advance would be slower and more deliberate with the cavalry at the

THE MOST FEARSOME military tactic of the Middle Ages was the cavalry charge, as demonstrated here by Norman horse. At a time when success in battle often depended more on forcing one's enemies to flee the battlefield than on actually killing them, resisting such a charge depended on the discipline of lower-class infantry troops.

helm supported by archers and infantry following behind. William, taking personal charge, began the second attack at 11:00 A.M. The ground was slippery from the previous attack and littered with dead men and horses, so progress was slow and hesitant.

Waves of attacks were launched against the shield wall for two hours. The Normans managed to make a few, small holes in the line but Harold and his commanders, including his brothers Gyrth (Earl of East Anglia) and Leofwine (Earl of Kent), steadied their men, plugged the gaps, and showered the enemy with missiles. Harold's Fighting Man standard and the Dragon Pennant of Wessex had been placed at the center of the Saxon lines to encourage the defenders.

NEAR ROUT

Finally, by 1 P.M., even the tough Flemish and French troops had had enough, they broke and began to flee from the ridge. Their commander Eustace grabbed the Papal standard, rallied his fleeing men, and admonished them to return to the fight. William had already lost his Spanish charger and was fighting on foot when a rumor reached him that he was dead. Eustace gave the Duke a horse to mount and show himself to his men. William tore off his helmet so that his troops could recognize him and shouted: "Look at me well. I am still alive and by the grace of God shall yet prove victor!" In reality William was losing the battle and he stared defeat in the face. Should the Saxons hold their line indefinitely then he would have been forced to retreat back to Hastings and return across the Channel.

At 2 P.M. William called his men and returned them to his own lines below the ridge to regroup, rest, and feed his hungry men. Harold used this respite to shorten his thinning line since Saxon losses, whatever the Normans may have thought, had been considerable and Harold was worried that he would run out of men to plug the ever-rising number of holes in the line. But at least his men were more rested than the Normans who faced an ever more debris-ridden and cluttered slope as they prepared for a renewed attack.

Having lost one-quarter of his army, or around 1,800–1,900 men, in five hours of almost continuous fighting, as well as a horrendous number of horses, cut down by the axe-wielding Saxons, William saw that many of his men-at-arms were now fighting on foot. He decided that the whole army would attack in a single formation of all arms combined.

The third and final attack saw the entire army advance with archers at the back, from around 3 P.M., at a slow pace. It took the Normans an agonizing half-hour to reach the Saxon line. William had ordered the archers to shoot as high as possible while the infantry, dismounted knights, and still-mounted cavalry gave their utmost in attacking the shield wall. Finally the shield wall began to waver, break in places and then come apart under the Norman onslaught. Once a

hole had been created in wall the Norman cavalry poured through and, with their lances, sword, and spears, tore at the soft underbelly of the Saxon army. After 4 P.M. the breach became unstoppable and the fighting degenerated into group actions and hand-to-hand combat. This fighting went on until 5:30 P.M. with undiminished ferocity as men fought for their lives. Then the fyrd began to retreat, fleeing into the woods while the huscarls fought on until they were overwhelmed and killed. A large group rallied around Harold's standard as William joined his men on the ridge and had his third and final horse killed under him. Harold led his men with customary tenacity and courage, setting a personal example for his huscarls. But there were not enough of them to fight back the Normans. Gyrth and Leofwin, leading their own huscarls, were killed.

The final straw was the death of Harold himself. He was cut down by the Normans leading his few remaining huscarls. As darkness closed in on the battlefield, small groups of Saxons continued fighting until they could slip away into the surrounding countryside. They rallied and ambushed the pursuing Normans at Oakwood Gill, a small stream north of Senlac Ridge, and managed to cut down Eustace of Boulogne. That was small consolation for the death of Harold.

AFTERMATH

Both sides had lost more than 2,000 men, the Normans well over one-third of their army. For William, it was a triumph against the odds that led to him being crowned as king of England on December 25, 1066. The Saxons would continue to resist their Norman invader for decades after their defeat at Hastings, but were eventually defeated.

SAXON HUSCARL

The Huscarls were an oath-sworn bodyguard of the Anglo-Danish aristocracy, which ruled England prior to the Norman Conquest of 1066. This man wields a long-handled axe, which could decapitate a horse. He has slung his kite-shaped shield on his back to allow him a double-handed grip for extra weight in the blow.

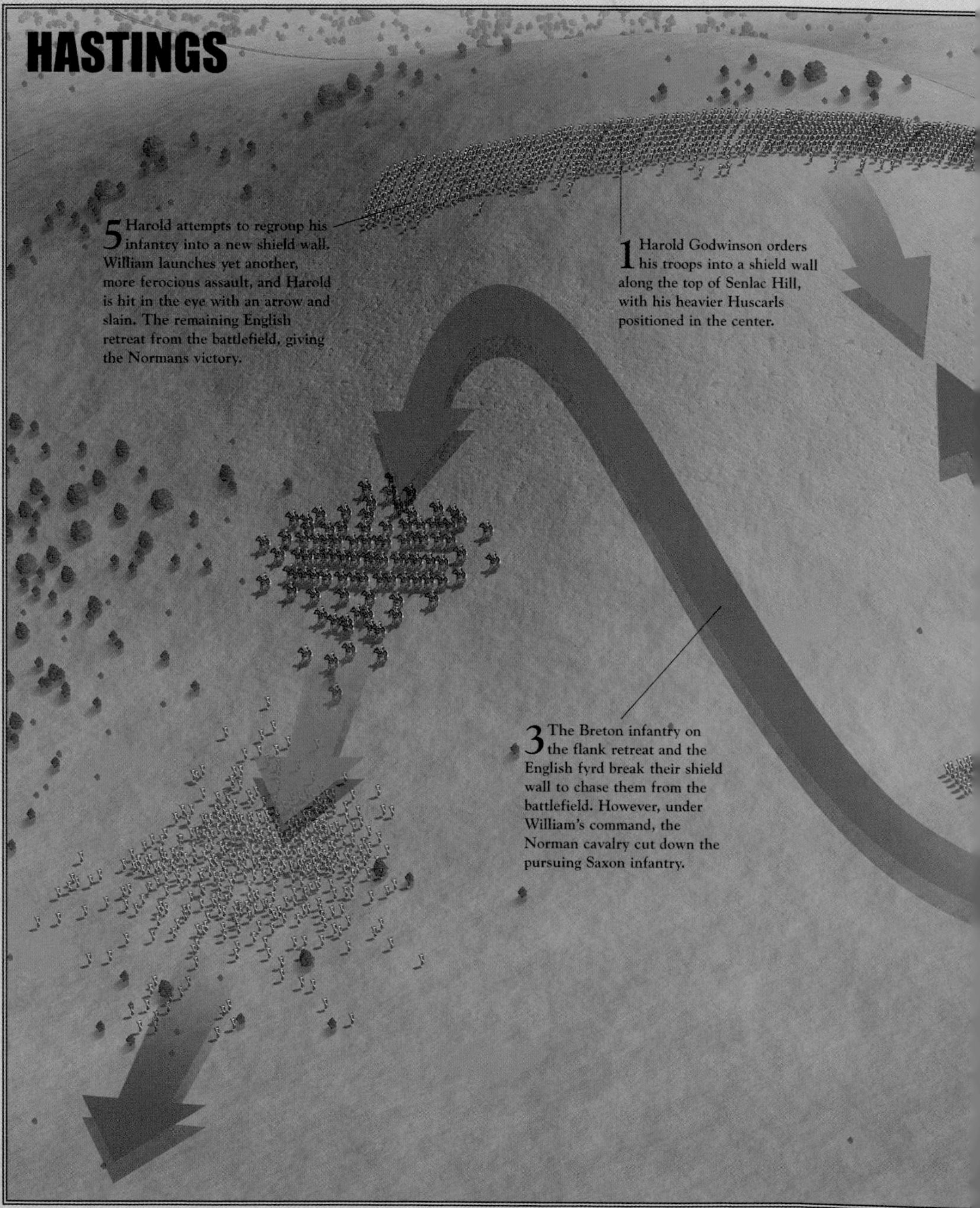

HASTINGS

5 Harold attempts to regroup his
infantry into a new shield wall.
William launches yet another,
more ferocious assault, and Harold
is hit in the eye with an arrow and
slain. The remaining English
retreat from the battlefield, giving
the Normans victory.

1 Harold Godwinson orders
his troops into a shield wall
along the top of Senlac Hill,
with his heavier Huscarls
positioned in the center.

3 The Breton infantry on
the flank retreat and the
English fyrd break their shield
wall to chase them from the
battlefield. However, under
William's command, the
Norman cavalry cut down the
pursuing Saxon infantry.

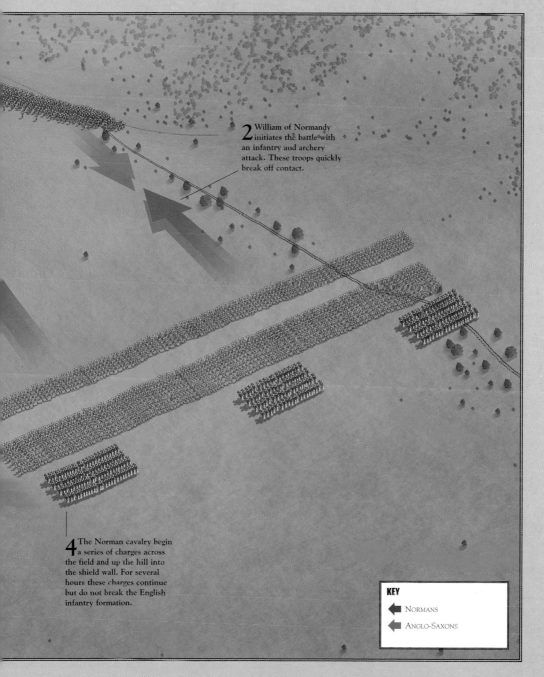

2 William of Normandy initiates the battle with an infantry and archery attack. These troops quickly break off contact.

4 The Norman cavalry begin a series of charges across the field and up the hill into the shield wall. For several hours these charges continue but do not break the English infantry formation.

KEY

Normans

Anglo-Saxons

HATTIN
1187

Hattin was a great victory for Saladin, who used his faster, lighter forces to great effect. He was assisted to a great extent by his enemy King Guy, who chose to march heavily armored troops through a waterless region at the hottest time of the year.

The Crusades pitted two very different military systems against each other. On the Christian side, the arm of decision was the heavily armored cavalry, which could smash an enemy formation and ride down the broken remains —assuming it made contact. This knightly host was supported by infantry— spearmen and crossbowmen—who were not greatly valued by their social betters among the cavalry. The fighting style of the Christians tended to be undisciplined and badly coordinated, though aggressive and courageous.

Against this powerful but clumsy blunt instrument was ranged the lighter, more mobile and (usually) highly trained Muslim militia, which contained lighter troops for the most part but was better disciplined and organized than its enemy. Its cavalry component was largely made up of mail-armored askari from Egypt and Syria, armed

HATTIN FACTS

Who: Crusader forces numbering around 32,000 under King Guy of Jerusalem (reigned 1186–92), versus a Seljuk Turkish army of 50,000 under Saladin (1138–93).

What: Harried to exhaustion by the more maneuverable Turks, the Crusaders were surrounded and eventually overwhelmed.

Where: The Horns of Hattin, Galilee.

When: June 1187.

Why: The Crusader force was marching to relieve a fortress and was intercepted by Saladin's army.

Outcome: The Crusader force was virtually annihilated.

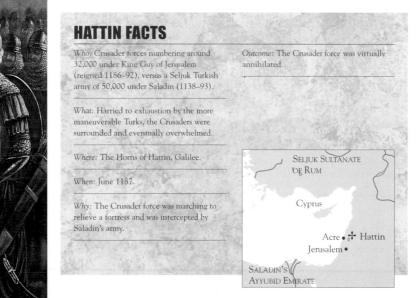

A ROMANTICIZED VERSION *of the remaining Crusader leaders surrendering to Saladin after the battle (painting by S. Tahssin). Shortly after this the man who broke the truce, Reynald de Chatillon, and all the surviving Knights Templar and Hospitaller, were executed by Saladin.*

with bows, lances, and shields. They were skilled skirmishers as well as hand-to-hand fighters, and well versed in hit-and-run tactics. The askari cavalry were paid regulars, and they were backed up by irregular cavalry drawn from local Bedouin, Kurdish, and Turkish groups. The Saracen force also included a large infantry component. These were mostly bowmen or spearmen, who also carried shields. The Muslim forces also had the advantage of a unified command whereas the Crusaders came from all over Europe and answered to many rival leaders. Many Crusaders spoke different languages and could not effectively communicate with one another.

THE CRUSADES

The Crusades came about as a result of the defeat of the Byzantine Empire by the Seljuk Turks, otherwise known as Saracens. This meant that Christian holy places were now in the hands of Muslims (to whom many of the same areas were holy). This offended Christian leaders in the West, and Pope Urban II called for a Crusade to take control of these important places. Several Crusades then ensued, interspersed with smaller expeditions. Some were truly inspired by religious fervor and others were little more than smash-and-grab raids. Most fell somewhere in between—however holy their motives, few Crusaders were above enriching themselves if an opportunity presented itself.

Naturally, these armed expeditions to capture areas of the Holy Land brought the Crusaders into conflict with the current overlords of the region, and a series of sporadic wars then ensued. At times the Crusaders were strong enough to hold kingdoms in the Holy Land, and at other times their presence was all but removed. Treaties and agreements were made at various times, but here the disorganized nature of the Crusaders made it unlikely that any agreement would last. No sooner had one group negotiated a deal than

someone else would arrive and stir things up again. Conflict was inevitable even if those involved tried to honor their agreements. Quite often, they did not. The Battle of Hattin stemmed from such a disregarded treaty. In 1186, the Crusader leader, Reynald de Chatillon (d. 1187), raided a caravan and captured a substantial amount of booty and prisoners. The Crusader leader of the time, King Guy of Jerusalem, was not impressed and ordered the return of both loot and prisoners. Saladin, leader of the Turks in the region, made a similar demand. Reynald declined. So Saladin declared war on the Crusaders and began gathering his forces.

A COINCIDENTAL DEFEAT

A Saracen reconnaissance force numbering about 6,500 was sent out to discover as much as possible about the Crusaders' forces, dispositions, and intentions. It achieved rather more than this, though mainly through a combination of good luck and Crusader stupidity.

The Orders of the Temple and the Hospital (the Knights Templar and the Knights Hospitaller) were important and

SALADIN IS DEPICTED here as the wise and kindly father figure who cared for the poor and sick. He was also shrewd and ruthless—an admirable and necessary combination in a leader of his time.

powerful among the Crusaders, and at that time the Grand Masters of both orders were in the field with just 140 knights and 350 infantry between them. They were there to resolve a dispute between King Guy and Count Raymond of Tripoli, but quickly decided to go looking for the Saracen force.

The Saracens were located at Kishon, and the Grand Masters decided to attack them. Vastly outnumbered, they left their infantry behind and plunged into the attack—140 men against 6,500. The result was predictable enough. Only three men, including the Grand Master of the Knights Templar, survived. The Saracen reconnaissance force went on with its mission, gaining information. The Christian garrison at Nazareth was overwhelmed and destroyed.

Meanwhile, the Crusaders were trying to organize themselves. Even though Reynald had betrayed the truce and unilaterally committed the Crusaders to war, his fellows stood with him. They probably decided that they had no choice—Saladin had declared war on all the Crusaders and not just Reynald's people, and so they would have to stand together or be defeated individually.

Whatever their motivation, the Crusaders decided to rally at Acre, and some 2,200 knights made their way there. What was left of the Hospitallers and Templars joined the host, some 40 and 80 men respectively, along with 650–750 knights from the various Crusader kingdoms. The remainder of the Crusader strength was made up of mercenary knights or opportunists seeking their fortune in the Holy Land. They were professional fighting men of course, but less reliable than those who owed allegiance to the Crusader commanders. They were backed up by about 4,000 Turcopole light cavalry—local warriors who had converted to Christianity—and around 32,000 infantry.

With the Crusader army was the True Cross, supposedly the very cross upon which Christ had been crucified. Its presence inspired more devout men among the Christian force. An army marching behind the Cross was—it was claimed—invincible. Perhaps too much reliance on relics and divine power was one reason for the unwise strategy employed by the Crusaders.

CRUSADER IMPATIENCE

The Saracens were threatening the fortress of Tiberias, which was held by the wife of Count Raymond. The castle was well defended, and though the nearby town was pillaged Raymond knew that his castle and his wife were safe for the time being. The Christians could afford to take their time,

and indeed might be able to force the enemy to come to them, tiring themselves out in the process.

Unfortunately, Raymond's wise counsel was ignored. King Guy was determined to bring the Saracens to battle and defeat them as soon as possible. The Christian army had camped at Saffuriya, about 6.2 miles (10km) short of Tiberias. The most direct route toward the enemy was across the waterless plain of Toran. Attempting to march an army with thousands of horses and tens of thousands of men in heavy armor across such an arid region was folly. To do it in the face of a waiting enemy was suicidally stupid, but nevertheless Guy decided to press ahead.

King Guy was heavily influenced in his decision by Reynald de Chatillon and Gerard de Ridefort, who urged him to throw caution to the winds and attack like a proper Christian knight. Guy's only concession to survival was to advance using the Wadi Hamman, which might have water available but was not the most direct route. Nevertheless, Saladin's scouts reported the move to him in time to counter it, and from then on the Crusaders' fate was sealed.

As the Crusaders pushed up the wadi, the advance guard under Raymond, and the rearguard, both came under attack from fast-moving Muslim skirmishers. The only troops capable of countering these attacks were the Turcopoles, whose equipment was light enough to allow fast countermoves. The Saracens therefore concentrated on destroying the Turcopoles, which would then expose the rest of the Crusader force to destruction at their leisure.

THE CORE OF THE REGULAR TROOPS in the Fatimid Egyptian army were made up of Turkish slaves, known as Mamluks (from the Turkish word meaning "owned"). The Mamluk warrior (left) carries the short cavalry bow favored in Saladin's armies, which was ideal for skirmishing and harassing Crusader forces. Askari warriors (right) were members of the emir's personal bodyguard. This Askari is armed with a heavy javelin.

The Horns of Hattin in Galilee today. This photograph shows a rough, rocky terrain. It would have proved hard going for the Crusader heavy cavalry, but would not have hindered the lighter Muslim horse archers.

As the Turcopoles were driven off or destroyed, the Crusader column had no counter to the attacks of the Saracen skirmishers, except to keep the valuable knights and their horses inside a protective screen of infantry. While still about 1.25 miles (2km) short of the intended battle area, the column was halted and preparations made to camp. There was no water available but the troops were too tired to go on. Between the heat and the constant attacks of the skirmishers the powerful column had been nibbled to death. The rearguard in particular was in a terrible state.

Having camped overnight without water, the Crusader army was in a desperate plight the following day. There was no possibility of going back, not through that wasteland with mounted skirmishers dogging every step. The objective lay only a couple of miles ahead, and obtaining water was now a critical requirement. The only option was to go on.

The Crusader force gathered its resolve and set off early in the morning, driving onward to try to reach the nearest source of water, which lay in the village of Marescallia. The exhausted troops were halted well short of their objective by Muslim forces, who had been resupplied by camel trains during the night and were in good shape to fight.

THE BATTLE OPENS

In accordance with the ancient principle of not giving battle until you have already won, Saladin had allowed his enemy to exhaust himself, cut off his own retreat, and then stumble to a disorganized halt in the face of relatively light opposition. And still Saladin did not commit to a decisive charge. He was a clever and patient man, who did not need dramatic results to know he had won. He would settle for quietly getting what he wanted at a lower price and always had an eye to the long-term strategic situation.

Saladin's forces advanced in a crescent formation, but stopped short of contact. Instead they poured arrows into the exhausted and disordered Crusader force. This placed the Crusaders in a terrible dilemma. The Crusaders could unleash their famous cavalry charge which, weakened as it was, still represented a tremendous amount of striking power. However, it was likely that the charge would hit only empty air as the Saracens faded away, shooting all the time. Alternatively the Crusaders could do nothing, and be steadily shot down. All the while their strength was being depleted by heat and thirst, and by arrows shot deliberately at the knights' horses to rob the Crusaders of their main striking power.

It was all too much for the hard-pressed infantry. Desperately thirsty, with the wasteland to their backs, and thoroughly sick of being little more than walking archery butts, they tried to push on to the Sea of Galilee, which was visible not far away. The disorganized mob that had been the Crusader infantry was unable to break through to the shores of the sea, and was deflected by elements of the Muslim force. The infantry took refuge on the slopes of the easternmost of two hills nearby, known as the Horns of Hattin. There they stayed, refusing or ignoring orders, pleas and demands to rejoin the battle. Most were massacred after the battle proper. The rest were sold as slaves by their captors.

THE KNIGHTS ATTACK

There was no option now but to attack and try to break through the Muslim force. Raymond, with about 200 knights of the vanguard, was ordered forward and made his gallant, if ultimately doomed, run at the enemy.

As had happened many times before, the Saracens declined to receive the Crusader charge, but melted out of the way, shooting at the knights from flanks and rear as they passed. Raymond was wounded in three places and had been unable to make contact with the enemy. His weakened horses were blown and there was no prospect of achieving anything but a fairly inglorious death, so Raymond led what was left of his force out of the deathtrap and headed for Tyre. Saladin seemed content to let him go.

The remainder of the Crusader knights also launched charges at the Saracen force. The result was much the same; the highly mobile Muslim force evaded the clumsy charges and shot down the knights and their horses, closing in to cut off small contingents that could then be overwhelmed.

Some of the knights, perhaps 300 in all, were able to

break free and reach Acre. The remainder were gradually driven onto the western Horn of Hattin where they were no better off than the infantry on the eastern one. King Guy had his tent pitched on the hill, marking the center of the defensive position.

Saladin had already won, but the cornered Crusaders might still inflict heavy casualties on his force if he decided to charge in and seek a dramatic ending. Instead he was content to bottle the Crusaders up on their waterless refuge and slowly destroy them with archery.

The Crusaders defended the area around the king's tent for as long as they were able, launching weak and abortive counterattacks that had no chance of success. Even when the Saracens set fire to the brush, tormenting the thirsty Crusaders with smoke on top of all their other miseries, the knights held out as best they could.

Finally, though their strength gave out and the king's tent was overrun. The survivors surrendered, among them King Guy, Reynald, and Gerard as well as about 150 knights. The Saracens took so many prisoners they could not find enough rope to secure them all.

MUSLIM SOLDIERS *set upon a fallen Crusader cavalryman. Once a horseman had been brought down from his mount, his opponents generally had the advantage.*

VICTORY FOR SALADIN

Saladin had his most implacable enemies executed: Reynald and every Knights Templar or Hospitaller he could find. He also massacred the surviving Turcopoles, who were seen as traitors by their countrymen. Thousands of Crusader soldiers were sold into slavery, causing such a glut in the market that the price dropped considerably. Saladin did show mercy, however. King Guy was spared, as was Raymond's wife. She had to surrender the castle, but was allowed to depart unharmed. Guy was freed upon payment of what was literally a king's ransom. Saladin's victory at Hattin was partly due to failures of logistics, planning, and common sense among the Crusaders, though it also owed a lot to the patience and cunning of Saladin himself. One of the great military axioms says "do not interrupt the enemy while he is making a mistake" and Saladin was clever enough to let his foes hang themselves before he even considered joining battle. When he did fight it was with good tactics and sound logistics—a potent combination on any battlefield.

AFTERMATH

Hattin was the beginning of the end for the Crusaders. More Crusades would be launched and some successes would be scored, but the days of the great Crusader kingdoms were more or less over. Some 30 Crusader castles fell within the year, and Jerusalem surrendered to Saladin. This was in addition to the 11 cities handed over to Saladin's control as the ransom for King Guy.

The struggles for the Holy Land would go on, of course, but it was at Hattin that the Crusaders threw away all their advantages, and perhaps their chances of winning in the long term.

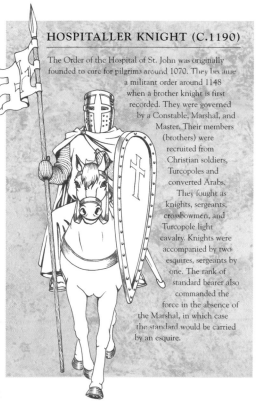

HOSPITALLER KNIGHT (C.1190)

The Order of the Hospital of St. John was originally founded to care for pilgrims around 1070. They became a militant order around 1148 when a brother knight is first recorded. They were governed by a Constable, Marshal, and Master. Their members (brothers) were recruited from Christian soldiers, Turcopoles and converted Arabs. They fought as knights, sergeants, crossbowmen, and Turcopole light cavalry. Knights were accompanied by two esquires, sergeants by one. The rank of standard bearer also commanded the force in the absence of the Marshal, in which case the standard would be carried by an esquire.

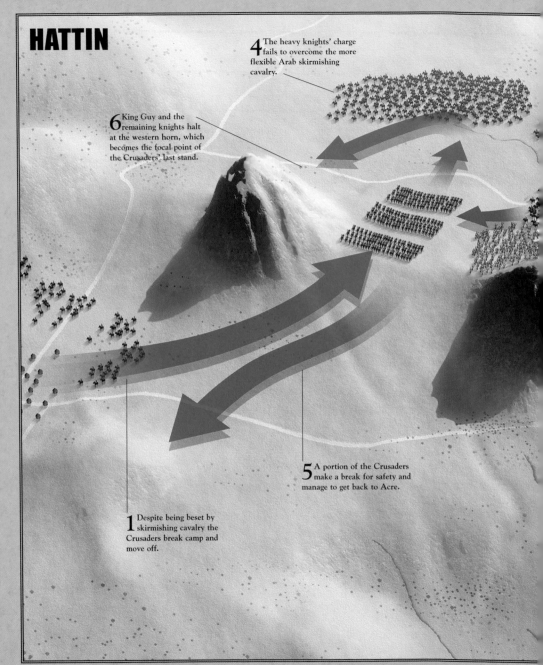

HATTIN

4 The heavy knights' charge fails to overcome the more flexible Arab skirmishing cavalry.

6 King Guy and the remaining knights halt at the western horn, which becomes the focal point of the Crusaders' last stand.

5 A portion of the Crusaders make a break for safety and manage to get back to Acre.

1 Despite being beset by skirmishing cavalry the Crusaders break camp and move off.

2 Desperately thirsty, the infantry break off from the line of march toward the Sea of Galilee. Arab cavalry quickly move to exploit the division of forces.

3 Like so many sheep, the Crusader infantry are herded onto the eastern horn. Those that are not cut down are rounded up to be sold into slavery.

KEY

SARACENS

CRUSADERS

TANNENBERG · 1410

The decisive battle of Tannenberg, between the army of the Teutonic Knights and the Royal Army of Poland-Lithuania, brought to a halt the eastward expansion of the hitherto invincible military order and secured the independence of Poland-Lithuania.

Founded in Acre in 1190 to defend the Holy Land, the Teutonic Order was a military order of warrior-monks whose military and religious reputation could be equated with the Knights of St. John or the Templars. But unlike their rivals the Teutonic Order moved the seat of their activities and crusades to the southern and eastern coasts of the Baltic. The neighboring Poles, whose once united kingdom by this time had become divided into independent duchies, were under constant attack from these hostile pagans, although the Lithuanians, who had carved out a huge realm by conquering Mongol-occupied western Russia, had eventually become Christian and allies of the Poles.

But that still left the marauding and savage Pruzy to be dealt with. Lacking resources or the willpower to deal with them, Prince Conrad of Mazovia, whose duchy

TANNENBERG FACTS

Who: The army of the Teutonic Order under their Grand Master Ulrich von Jungingen (d. 1410) fought the Royal Army of Poland-Lithuania under King Wladislaw II Jagiello (1350–1434).

What: The Royal Army of Poland-Lithuania, with Tartar (Mongol) and Russian auxiliaries, annihilated the more experienced and heavily armed Teutonic army.

Where: On a shallow grass plain between the East Prussian (Mazurian) villages of Tannenberg and Grünwald.

When: July 15, 1410.

Why: The Royal Army were caught by surprise when the whole Teutonic army bore down on them before they were prepared but the Teutons squandered a great opportunity to secure a victory by not attacking first.

Outcome: The Polish-Lithuanian victory halted the Teutonic Order's eastward expansion and effectively broke its power.

THIS PAINTING BY POLISH MILITARY ARTIST *Wojciech von Kossak (1824–99) gives a taste of the bloody battle, with the Royal army in close combat with the Teutons—the screams of wounded men, the neighing of horses, the clank of armor; dust, heat, and sudden death.*

was most exposed to Prusy attacks, in 1230 invited the Teutonic Order to crush the Prusy. The Order was only too glad to oblige and a decade later the Prusy threat had been eliminated leaving only pockets of resistance. Conrad quickly regretted ever having invited these rapacious and acquisitive Germans into territories that Poland viewed as vassal states.

EASTWARD EXPANSION

By 1283 the Order controlled both western and eastern Pruthenia or Prussia including the vitally important seaport city of Danzig (now Gdansk)—Poland's only port and point of contact with the West. As if this was not bad enough the Teutonic Order merged with the Order of the Sword Brethren—it too composed of German warrior-monks—that had conquered the Baltic states including the great seaport of Riga. The Order was now the dominant military and political power in the region and a growing threat to its neighbors especially because its huge state was backed by the region's best army and cavalry force. The Poles, Lithuanians, and the Novgorod Russians were equally threatened by the Order. Through a victory over the Sword Brethren in 1242 at Lake Peipus, Novgorod had been saved. It was Poland's turn next. The Order, meanwhile, had not only conquered Prussia but during the period 1310–50 encouraged German colonists to establish 1,400 villages in the territory. Clearly the Order intended not only to conquer but colonize Poland and Lithuania as well, despite both nations being loyal Christians.

In the face of an overwhelming threat Poland was finally, in 1320, reunited under King Wladislaw I (1320–33). Civil

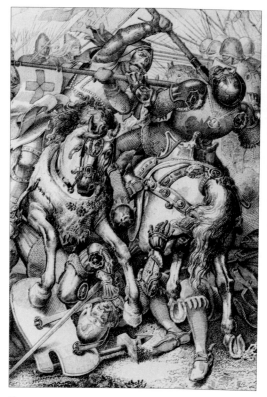

THIS DRAMATIC BATTLE SCENE shows Grand Duke Jagiello supposedly tearing the standard from a Teutonic Knight, signaling the order's defeat.

LITHUANIAN INFANTRYMAN of the fifteenth century were armed in a variety of ways, including long-handled axes (as here), conical, Norse-style helmets, and chainmail. This was a consequence of Lithuania's geographical location, which reflected a mixture of Nordic and Russian military and cultural influences.

war and chaos threatened when he left no male heirs, Poland being ruled by his daughter Queen Jadwiga. She, however, proved a shrewd and able ruler in her own right and she offered her hand in marriage—in order to unite Poland and Lithuania—to the much older Lithuanian Grand Duke Jagiello (1350–1434) who had only recently been christened, appropriately enough, Wladislaw.

Poland had acquired a powerful ally in their quest to crush the Order and regain control over Danzig and Prussia. Lithuania had a formidable army in its own right, which had defeated the Mongols and emulated their superlative tactics, equipment and horsemanship of the steppes' lightning war. In 1386 Jadwiga married Jagiello and the Royal Commonwealth of Poland-Lithuania was founded. When the Order sought to wrest the Lithuanian province of Samogitia from the Grand Duke, Poland was ruled by Jagiello. War was now inevitable but shrewdly Jagiello wanted his enemy to make the first move.

THE OPPOSING ARMIES

Fighting, let alone defeating the Order, was no easy proposition for Jagiello since the Order's army had been victorious ever since its appearance in the region in 1230. Its heavy cavalry of men-at-arms clad in white surcoats with black crosses, numbering some 2,000–3,000 men, were probably the best in Europe and formed the superlative core of an outstanding military machine. Superbly disciplined, mounted, equipped, trained, and experienced, the Teutonic Knights had no equals in Europe let alone the east Baltic region. But with the technological progress of the fourteenth century, the Order had to supplement its knights with mercenaries and specialists such as English longbowmen, Genoese crossbowmen, German and Swiss infantry, and French artillery. All in all the army of the Order was a dangerous and formidable foe.

By contrast the Poles and Lithuanians were far weaker and with less reason to be confident of a victory if faced with the grim-faced German warrior-monks. The Poles had a conventional European-style medieval army of no particular distinction or reputation as yet. As in France the Polish infantry was made up of reluctant, poorly disciplined and motivated peasant conscripts who would rather be working on their farms than fighting their proud and uncaring Lord's wars. In the face of the superior Teutonic infantry they would either fight with customary Polish bravery or, if the mood took them, simply run away at the first enemy charge. The cavalry, mainly composed of Poland's proud and insanely brave nobility, were well mounted, equipped, and motivated. While they were more than a match, man-for-man, to the Teutons, they lacked the warrior-monks experience and discipline.

MEDIEVAL ARMOR SUITS were most often made of chain links or metal scales. Chain armor (favored in Western Europe) consisted of thousands of round metal rings, the ring ends welded or riveted together. Scale armor (favored in Eastern Europe and Byzantium) was made of a large number of metallic scales attached to each other by wire or leather laces.

By contrast the Lithuanian host was more Asiatic than European in appearance, equipment, and tactics because they had fought for centuries against the Mongol occupiers of Russia. As a consequence they placed great reliance upon skirmishing, maneuvering, and mobility with light and medium cavalry forces rather than a head-on collision with heavy cavalry and massed infantry. If these warriors faced the

IN THIS PAINTING by Jan Matejko (1838–93), the Polish-Lithuanian army is at the point of crushing the reeling and bleeding troops of the order, with a triumphant Jagiello in the center of the action.

TEUTONIC KNIGHT

The roots of the Teutonic Order were military-monastic in the simple white garb with its equally simple cross as the only decoration on shield, uniform, and horse. The main strength of the order's military might was its mounted knights, who acted as the foremost offensive arm. They wore scale armor, instead of plated armor, to improve mobility, speed, and striking power in the face of ever better-equipped, better-disciplined, and better-led infantry armies. Tannenberg was a cavalry battle, but one in which infantry and support forces played a vital role in the defeat of the hitherto invincible Teutonic Knights.

Teutons in open pitched battle in a confined space—as they were to do at Tannenberg—it was dubious whether they would be able to make a stand.

THE CAMPAIGN

In December 1409 during a meeting at Brest-Litovsk Jagiello, the Polish commanders and his cousin, Duke Witold, the Viceroy of Lithuania, agreed to combine their armies at a rendezvous on the Vistula, called Czerwinsk, where it was safe to cross the river barrier. It was safe from there to invade Prussia and hopefully defeat the Order on home ground. Meanwhile Jagiello secured the neutrality of the Order's Livonian knights while the friendly king of Hungary, who had signed an alliance with the Order, assured the Poles that he would not support his newfound allies. Thus the Commonwealth had no reason to fear a diversionary attack on their extensive southern and northeastern frontiers leaving them free to concentrate their considerable military strength against the Teutons.

To keep the Order's army (dispersed along the frontier) on its toes, Jagiello ordered diversionary offensives against Pomerania and Memel. In the meantime, using a 550-yard (600m) long pontoon bridge across the Vistula, the Poles and

Lithuanians had combined at the Czerwinsk bridgehead by June 30. They marched northward on July 2. Ulrich von Jungingen, Grand Master of the Teutonic Order, had failed to concentrate his army because he underestimated his enemy in general and his technical expertise—he could not believe the "primitive" Poles and Lithuanians capable of building pontoon bridges! His racial arrogance was to cost him his life and the existence and reputation of his army as well. In a mere eight days the Royal Army had covered 82 miles (90km)—a phenomenal rate of advance for a medieval army —crossing the Prussian frontier already on July 2, 1410. Ulrich was caught by surprise again and was forced to concentrate his scattered army at Kurzetnik where, on July 3, Jagiello's army joined him. The two armies were now poised for battle.

DISPOSITIONS

Ulrich built a series of bridges across the Drweça River in order for his army to cross over to its eastern bank where the battlefield formed a rough triangle between three small Prussian villages—Tannenberg, Grünwald, and Ludwigsdorf. In this partly wooded and rough terrain visibility could have been better. The battlefield was shaped like a shallow soup dish measuring 1.9 miles (3km) in diameter.

Jagiello's combined army numbered 10,000–20,000 infantry and as many as 40,000 cavalry (including Tartar auxiliaries) while the Grand Master had 21,000 cavalry and a mere 6,000 infantry. The Royal Army's camp was situated 4.5 miles (7.2km) east of Grünwald at Lake Lubien while the Order's army had moved across the river into the field. At dawn on July 15 a Polish knight and scout, Hanko, entered the camp and informed Jagiello that the enemy was already drawn up for battle. Ulrich had caught the enemy—only forming up slowly—by surprise and should have, in hindsight, attacked immediately with all force and determination. Instead Ulrich ordered his men to dig ditches and form the army in two lines. His decision was the more faulty since here was open ground with good visibility well suited for a massed cavalry attack up to the slopes of the ridge that led to Lake Lubien and the Royal army's camp.

THE BATTLE

But nothing happened because Ulrich wanted the enemy to make the first move and they—primarily the cautious and shrewd Jagiello—were reluctant to act. As the morning hours wore on and his men grew impatient, Ulrich decided to goad the "cowardly" Poles and Lithuanians into action. He sent Duke Kazimir of Stettin (Szczecin) whose shield bore the Black Eagle on a gold background (symbol of the Holy Roman Emperor) and the Imperial Herald to rebuke Jagiello for not fighting like a man. Jagiello, hoping to negotiate a peaceful settlement, received the two knights politely but was rudely told that his army should come out to fight like men on the

field of battle. Jagiello gave as good as he got, telling the two arrogant knights that they would regret their insults in a few hours and they, like the Grand Master, would get more than they had bargained for. He gave a signal for Witold to commence the battle.

The Poles advanced in good order on the left while the Lithuanians, Russians, and Tartars could not control themselves and threw themselves at the Germans who buckled under the onslaught. The Teutonic knights counterattacked, slaying the enemy, and the Lithuanian army began to falter and retreat as the Tartars (either fleeing or executing a feigned retreat) moved out of range. Only Witold's central regiments held the line and Witold was forced, in person, to beg his cousin to save his flank.

Jagiello sent his last remaining reserves that managed to stem the Teutonic advance but as the dust settled Ulrich noticed how exposed the Polish king was on a small knoll on the battlefield, and sent a small force to either kill or capture Jagiello. The assassination attempt failed since some alert Polish knights saw what was happening and moved to intercept the Teutons. Witold used this time to rally his men who turned around and rode back to the center of the battlefield. It was the Teutons' turn to be caught unawares as Tartar arrows, Russian battleaxes, and Lithuanian swords cut

In this romanticized nineteenth-century oil painting by the Polish artist Maksymiljan Piotrowski (1813–75), the Polish-Lithuanians, led by their venerable-looking king, Wladislaw II, prepare for battle on July 15, 1410.

at them. The Poles, having held their line, forced the Order's knights back and surrounded them. Ulrich, stubborn, proud yet brave, chose like his men to stand and fight where they stood and as consequence they were cut down. Few remained alive when the battle finally ended, at 7 P.M., at the village of Grünwald. Some 14,000 of the Order's knights and soldiers had been taken prisoner while the rest (18,000) lay strewn dead or dying on the dusty battlefield.

AFTERMATH

Instead of marching on the Teutonic Order's capital of Marienburg to the west, the utterly exhausted Polish-Lithuanian army remained on the battlefield to divide the loot, rest, and recuperate. When it was ready to march on Marienburg, held by Count Heinrich von Plauen and 3,000 troops, it was too late. This immense fortress complex with stone walls 27ft (8.2m) high and 7ft (2.1m) thick and ample supplies of food and water proved impregnable. Jagiello's victorious army arrived on July 25 but failed to make any headway during the two-month siege. The war would continue for years and the Order would eventually recover.

TANNENBERG

3 The Grand Master believes, with the enemy's right in disarray, that the time has come for a final push and sends a group of his toughest men to capture Jagiello. This lunge fails and with it any hope of a Teutonic victory.

6 The Order's army is completely wiped out with 18,000 dead littering the battlefield and the remaining 14,000 captured.

5 The battlefield is by afternoon a confusing tangle of struggling, dying, and wounded men fighting each other in close combat where no mercy is given or expected. One by one the Teutonic Knights are overwhelmed.

1 After the Teutonic emissaries' taunts at first light, the Polish-Lithuanian army advance across the open fields toward the Teutonic lines. Their left flank attack with abandon but are stemmed by heavy Teutonic Knights.

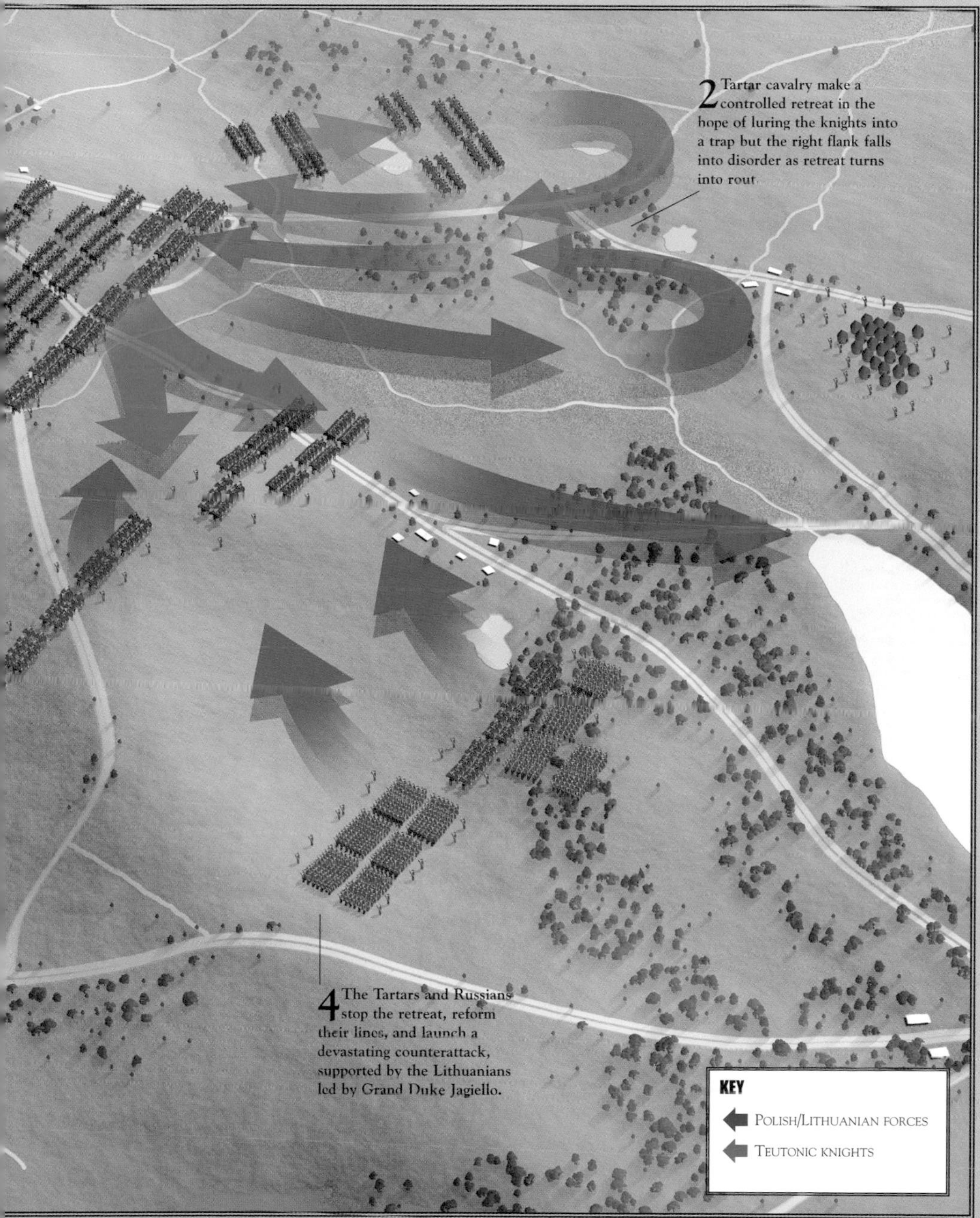

2 Tartar cavalry make a controlled retreat in the hope of luring the knights into a trap but the right flank falls into disorder as retreat turns into rout

4 The Tartars and Russians stop the retreat, reform their lines, and launch a devastating counterattack, supported by the Lithuanians led by Grand Duke Jagiello.

KEY

← POLISH/LITHUANIAN FORCES

← TEUTONIC KNIGHTS

AGINCOURT 1415

The victory of Henry V's small, exhausted, and starving army against a vast French host was the greatest triumph of the English longbow in the Hundred Years War between England and France. But despite the arrow-storm, the battle came to hand-to-hand combat, and was not the walkover for the English that it has often been portrayed as.

In 1413 Henry V, aged only 27, mounted the English throne with the ambition to wrest control of northern France. By early July 1415 Henry V had gathered in utmost secrecy a 12,000-strong army around Winchester while he collected suitable tonnage to ship his troops to France. On August 11 his army set sail from the south coast in 1,500 ships, reaching the tip of the peninsula north of the Seine two days later. Early the next morning, August 14, the English began to disembark. Fortunately for the English, the French Constable Charles d'Albret had expected Henry to land his army on the south side of the Seine as a prelude to a march on Paris. Paris was not Henry's objective. Instead he had his eyes on the great fortified port city of Harfleur (Le Havre) located 1 mile (1.6km) up the Lézarde River, a tributary of the Seine,

AGINCOURT FACTS

Who: An English army of 6,000 under King Henry V (1388–1422) defeated a French army of 36,000 under the command of Charles d'Albret, Constable of France (1369–1415).

What: Agincourt saw a small, well disciplined and entrenched English army defeat a far larger French army through massed archery.

Where: The battle took place near the Castle of Azincourt approximately half way between Calais and Abbeville in northern France.

When: Friday October 25, 1415.

Why: Henry sought to revive the English claim to the throne of France.

Outcome: Agincourt (Azincourt) was the greatest English victory of the Hundred Years War against France.

KING HENRY V MAKES *a rallying speech to his troops on St. Crispin's Day, inspiring his men for the desperate battle ahead. By nightfall the English had won one of the greatest victories of all time.*

AT AGINCOURT, KING HENRY V ordered that every archer should cut himself a stake to provide portable protection against cavalry charges. This worked to great effect in defeating the French.

undermine the walls and English artillery fired into the city both day and night. A month later and both sides were suffering from the effects of dysentery, the "bloody flux" as it was called, and an acute shortage of food. Henry met Gaucourt on September 17 but the stubborn French nobleman, impervious to Henry's threats and flattery alike, refused to accept terms for surrender despite having lost one-third of his garrison during the five-week siege.

Gaucourt's only hope was that the Dauphin, Prince Louis de Guienne, would come to his relief. Guienne—a fat, indolent, foppish 18-year-old—was hardly the man to risk leading a relief force to aid the hard-pressed garrison of Harfleur. Fearing an English assault and subsequent massacre, the populace beseeched Gaucourt to capitulate, which he did on September 22. It was sweet revenge for Henry who had been left fuming five days earlier.

THE MARCH TO CALAIS

Henry's counselors, including Clarence, urged the king to return in triumph to England and leave France to its civil wars and strife. Henry refused, so Clarence took his own advice and returned home in a huff, leaving the king to plan

protected by tidal salt marshes and a lake. Harfleur was held by 400 knights under the command of the experienced and courageous Raoul de Gaucourt.

By August 19 the English had invested Harfleur from all sides, with the Duke of Clarence in the east blocking access and relief (if it ever came) from Rouen while Henry was camped on the port's western side. Henry ordered siege lines to be erected while Clarence's Welsh miners dug tunnels to

AN ENGLISH FOOT SOLDIER takes a French nobleman captive at the Battle of Agincourt in 1415. This image symbolizes the superiority that infantrymen could exercise over their social betters.

the next stage of his campaign. Harfleur was a small prize for such a huge effort and Henry was hardly a man to rest on his laurels. He wanted to lure the French into fighting a pitched battle and defeat them decisively—anything less would be a failure.

Trusting in God and his men—5,000 archers and 900 men-at-arms—Henry left Harfleur on October 6 expecting to cover the 150 miles (241km) to Calais in a mere eight days. It would take a lot longer and prove a trying ordeal for his army—halved through the grueling siege of Harfleur. The French, ably led by d'Albret, shadowed the movements of the English along the Somme and at the fording point of Blanche Taque 6,000 French blocked their advance across the river, forcing Henry to continue along the southern bank of the river. On October 15, when they should have reached Calais according to Henry's wildly optimistic calculations, the English slipped past Amiens. Both the troops and Henry's advisers began to wonder if they would ever get across the Somme.

Finally, four days later, having evaded the French army at Péronne by cutting across country and avoiding a bend in the Somme, the English reached Nesle where they found two undefended crossing points. They were safely across in a single day and could advance northward on October 21 in good order, although in daily expectation of a French attack.

Wisely the French bided their time and d'Albret argued, like the Duke de Berry, that the French should avoid a pitched battle. Henry would have little to show for his efforts if he returned to Calais without having fought and won a battle. Harfleur could then be retaken. But the Royal Dukes (Orléans, Bourbon, and Alençon) swept aside d'Albret's objections. They wanted to crush the English in the field and earn some much needed martial glory for themselves and France.

AGINCOURT

On October 24 came the news the English had dreaded but also looked forward to: the French army were drawn up in a flat plain between the villages of Azincourt, Tramecourt, and Maisoncelle. Henry turned to his Welsh retainer, Dafyd Gam, asking him to estimate the vast French horde and Gam replied cooly: "Sire. There are enough to kill, enough to capture, and enough to run away." In fact the French outnumbered the English six-to-one with 36,000 troops in all as they drew up a strong defensive position along the Calais road that cut across the Azincourt plain. Their flanks were protected by woodlands, their backs by open fields, and only a small, shallow valley separated them from the puny English army.

During the night, Henry enforced total silence upon his men who were reduced to whispering. This eerie silence unnerved the French who expected it was an English ruse to escape their inevitable doom the following morning. They set up a picket line with fires at regular intervals along the road to prevent such an escape. Henry expected a night attack so he kept his men in battle order during much of the night. Henry did not sleep either as he made preparations for the coming battle and sent out scouts that returned with news that the ground resembled a muddy soup.

DISPOSITIONS

Henry decided to extend the English line between the woods and hedges surrounding the villages of Maisoncelle and Tramecourt. As the ground in front of the English line, fronted by a line of sharp stakes, had turned into a quagmire the French attack would be slowed down and prove a most welcoming target for his archers. Conditions were ideal and Henry placed the dismounted men-at-arms in the middle of his battle line and the archers on the flanks. The center would be under Henry's personal command while the right was commanded by the Duke of York and the left by Thomas, Lord Camoys.

But Henry knew that his was a desperate and dangerous gamble. He had no reserves, there was no fall-back and he had nowhere close to escape to should he be defeated.

FRENCH KNIGHT

The large amount of warfare taking place in the fifteenth century led to some dramatic military technological changes. By 1400 cavalry began wearing a more solid breastplate made from a single piece of metal fashioned to cover the chest and sides. By the end of the century this had been joined to metallic plates covering the back, neck, legs, arms, and feet, and was topped by a helmet with visor that fitted tightly around the head. Over this, the knight usually wore a heraldic surcoat. The knight would be armed with a lance and sword.

In this nineteenth-century illustration of Agincourt, it is the mounted knight that takes centerstage. Even today, it is widely (and erroneously) believed that medieval warfare was the exclusive province of the armored nobleman.

Henry's single line could be outflanked should the French use part of their army to go around the woodlands and attack him in the rear. Even if the French made a frontal assault the English might be crushed by the sheer weight of the attack.

The French did, in fact, have a battle plan drawn up a few days before the battle. Boucicaut, Marshal of France, and Constable d'Albret would command the first French battle composed of 8,000 dismounted men-at-arms, 4,000 archers, and 1,500 crossbowmen. The main (center) battle or division would be under Prince Charles d'Artois and Alençon with a similar number of troops, and flanked on the right and left by two wings of mounted men-at-arms under the respective command of Richemont and Bourbon.

There was a small rearguard of 1,000 knights and a small force of 200 knights that would be sent around the woods to attack the English baggage train. In fact, the plan broke down even before it was implemented and instead of being preceded by a shower of arrows from their archers and crossbowmen, the French men-at-arms pushed them to the back of the formation. Instead, it was the flower of French chivalry that was to be sent forward to crush the small English army into the ground.

THE ENGLISH MEN-AT-ARMS *were always prepared to dismount to fight alongside the archers, who were their social inferiors. These longbowmen usually deployed on the flanks or in broken ground to give them protection against more heavily armed opponents should it come to hand-to-hand fighting.*

ST. CRISPIN'S DAY

After a long, cold night of torrential rain the fields were even muddier as the sun rose on St. Crispin's Day—Friday October 25, 1415. The English had spent the night in the open while the French had slept in tents and gorged themselves on wine and plentiful provisions. The French were sure they would win an easy victory.

Hours passed as each side waited for the other to make the first move. The French had every reason to wait. With every passing hour their strength would increase and the English grow weaker. It was this realization that prompted a frustrated Henry to make the first move. It was a calculated gamble as he ordered his men to pull up their stakes, move forward in full view of the enemy, and erect a new line of stakes further in the gap between the woods, closer to the French, hoping to goad them into attacking. This narrowed the front considerably—a change that favored the English and tore up the French plan. The French had originally thought of sending their cavalry to attack the flanks of the English line but now they were forced to make a frontal assault—exactly what they had hoped to avoid. The French realized that the ground sloped downward toward the English line and the field tapered off into a funnel shape the closer they got to the stakes. Furthermore it was only now, quite belatedly, that the French—who had failed to send out scouts—realized the ground was dangerously muddy and soft.

Yet they were committed to a plan and stuck to it with disastrous results. The French chose to open the battle with

KING HENRY V, a portrait by Benjamin Burnell (1790 1828). One of England's great captains, Henry's real-life deeds at Agincourt and Harfleur would grant him a place in heroic legend, even if he had never been immortalized in Shakespeare's plays.

a cavalry charge that proved too puny—of 1,200 knights on horse and only one-third (420 men) actually attacked. Their noble colleagues on foot were quickly in trouble as their heavy armor pulled them into the mud below. As they floundered and sunk into the mud up to their knees Sir Thomas Erpingham (in command of the archers) gave the signal and then shouted the dreaded order—"Now strike!"

Strong arms nocked arrows, pulled the bowstrings to their maximum extent, and sought the greatest elevation before loosing off the first volley. Thousands of arrows whined through the air like a cloud before hitting the target or plopping into the muddy ground. Enough steel-tipped, armor-piercing bodkin arrows struck home to break up the French advance. Their effect upon the less protected horses was terrifying and masterless horses, bleeding and neighing wildly, ran back into the French lines trampling the dismounted knights into the mud.

Now an additional hindrance of dead and dying horses and men had been created for the dismounted knights to advance over. Despite the massed volleys, huge casualties, and confusion, the dismounted knights pressed on with determination and heroism. They could see little because the arrows made it dangerous to put one's head up, even with an armored helmet, as the English archers aimed straight at their visors. The knights were trapped inside their armor and their mobility, vision, and breathing was dangerously restricted. Yet they continued advancing in their thousands.

HAND-TO-HAND COMBAT

The greatest honor of saving the English army from destruction at the hands of the French dismounted men-at-arms must go to the small number of English men-at-arms who halted and bloodied the French advance that reached right up to their lines. They were joined by squires, camp followers, and an increasing number of archers who had run out of arrows, using any weapon at hand—axes, daggers, and the mallets they had used to drive in their stakes—to cut, thrust, gouge, and stab at the faltering French. Sheer numbers had crowded the French line preventing their knights from using their weapons effectively. The French were now so close the archers could fire at them at point-blank range with devastating effect.

In this confused and grim hand-to-hand combat no quarter was given. As commoners, the English archers knew they would be slaughtered out of hand by the French since they had no value in terms of ransom. As a consequence the English were, quite literally, fighting for their lives and fought with even more ferocity than usual against the French

knights who might be captured alive and ransomed at a later date. This simple difference in psychology might explain the outcome of the battle.

For three gruesome, bloody hours the slaughter went on as the French dead piled up in heaps in front of the English lines. The English were growing weary with their deadly task. There was a last minute flurry among the French as the Duke of Brabant arrived in the afternoon. It came to nothing as Brabant was killed with his men. Alarmed by this, and fearing that the scores of French prisoners might take up arms again if there was another attack, Henry took no chances and broke all rules of chivalry by putting his prisoners to death where they stood.

AFTERMATH

There was no French rally or second attack as feared. Instead what remained of the French army fled the field of battle leaving thousand of dead, wounded, and captured to the less-than-tender mercies of the English. The English had lost a mere 112 men, two-thirds archers, and had won the most miraculous of victories against all the odds and expectations. A month later Henry was back in England, his men were amply paid and England celebrated that wonderful Day of St. Crispin while the traumatized French simply referred to Agincourt as "that unfortunate day" (la malheureuse journée) for generations to come. The Hundred Years War was set to continue for another four decades.

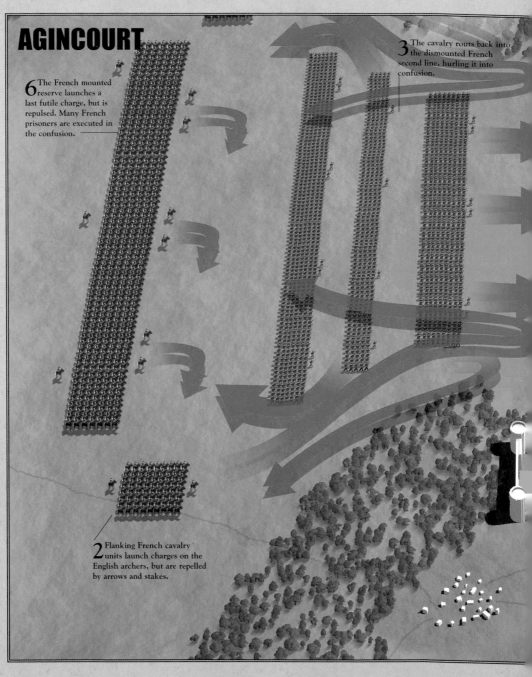

AGINCOURT

6 The French mounted reserve launches a last futile charge, but is repulsed. Many French prisoners are executed in the confusion.

3 The cavalry routs back into the dismounted French second line, hurling it into confusion.

2 Flanking French cavalry units launch charges on the English archers, but are repelled by arrows and stakes.

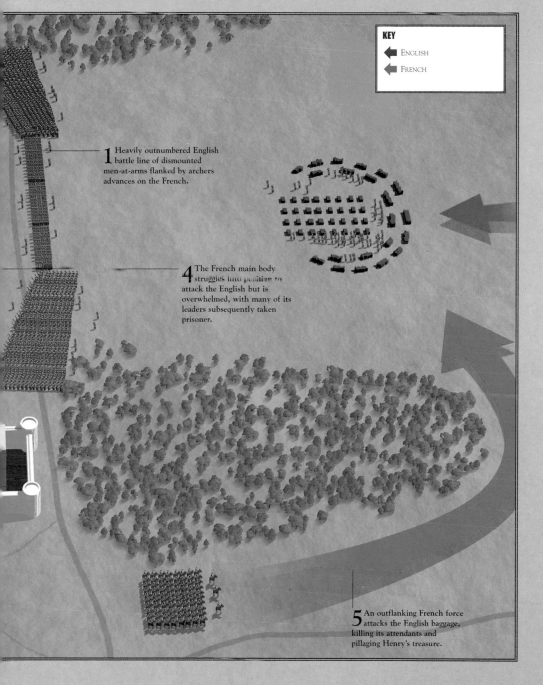

KEY

ENGLISH

FRENCH

1 Heavily outnumbered English battle line of dismounted men-at-arms flanked by archers advances on the French.

4 The French main body struggles into position to attack the English but is overwhelmed, with many of its leaders subsequently taken prisoner.

5 An outflanking French force attacks the English baggage, killing its attendants and pillaging Henry's treasure.

THE AGE OF GUNPOWDER

Gunpowder and artillery revolutionized European warfare after its introduction during the fourteenth and fifteenth centuries and forced military commanders to develop fortresses and military tactics and strategies to deal with this new, devastatingly effective technology.

Having played a secondary role during the Middle Ages, the infantry regained its primary role on the battlefield with the rise of the musket. The musket was a great leveler, in that large numbers of men could be trained quickly to use it, putting an end to the dominance of the expensively armed and armored knight of the Middle Ages.

During the seventeenth and eighteenth centuries, muskets became less unwieldy, lighter, and more accurate. By that time massed infantry armies made up of professional, regular troops fought each other in huge, packed series of lines, firing at each other with musket and canon shot at close range. In these deadly, close-range firefights just a handful of musket volleys could decide the outcome of a battle.

AS PART OF A REENACTMENT to commemorate the battle of Austerlitz, military-history enthusiasts dressed as French soldiers shoot at the enemy, November 2003. This photograph suggests the deadly effectiveness of massed musket volleys, which could decimate an enemy column in a matter of minutes.

CONSTANTINOPLE
1453

The fall of Constantinople in 1453, its once-impregnable walls breached by Ottoman siege guns, brought to an end the Byzantine Empire and established the Ottoman Empire as the major threat to Christendom in the Mediterranean and Eastern Europe for the next two centuries.

The Byzantine Empire, once the bulwark of the Christian West against the Arabs and Turks, had been defeated by the Seljuk Turks at Manzikert in 1071 and in 1389 their descendants, the Ottoman Turks, defeated a Serb army at Kosovo Polje. By 1400 most of Asia Minor was in the hands of the Ottomans and it seemed only a matter of time before this once flourishing Imperial capital of a million inhabitants would fall to them. The irruption of Tamerlane (Timur Lenk) (1336–1405) into Asia Minor and his defeat of the Turks at Ankara in 1402 gave the hard-pressed Byzantines a short breathing space. In 1422 Sultan Murad II (ruled

CONSTANTINOPLE FACTS

Who: Sultan Mehmed II Fatih (1451–83) laid siege to Constantinople with an army of 120,000 men, opposed by a mere 10,000, Christian Greek and Italian defenders led by Emperor Constantine XI (1449–53).

What: Turks used, for the first time, massive siege artillery to blow a hole in the Theodosian Wall protecting the city.

Where: The city of Constantinople was the Imperial Byzantine capital (303–1453) located on a peninsula by the Bosporus, the Sea of Marmara, and facing the Golden Horn in what is now Turkey.

When: April 5–May 29, 1453.

Why: The Ottoman Turks had expanded their empire in every direction and wished to

make Constantinople their capital and eliminate this Christian stronghold behind their lines.

Outcome: The city was taken with great bloodshed, and became the capital of the Ottoman Empire.

CONSTANTINOPLE ✚

OTTOMAN EMPIRE

THE TURKS ENTERED CONSTANTINOPLE *on May 29, 1453. The Byzantine Emperor, Constantine XI, was killed. The sultan, Mehmed II, gave the city up to his troops to destroy and loot for three days.*

1421–51) laid siege to the city but Constantinople's defenses repelled him and this gentlemanly scholar of a ruler left the Byzantines alone.

THE CANNON OF MEHMED II was cast in 1464 and used by the Turks to protect the Bosporus strait. The gun was divided into two parts for ease of transportation. It weighed 18 tons and was 17ft (5.25m) long.

MEHMED THE CONQUEROR

Unfortunately Murad died in 1451 leaving the throne to his arrogant and aggressive 19-year-old son, Mehmed (Muhammed) II, who for the next 30 years was to be a scourge upon his Muslim and Christian neighbors alike. Mehmed set out to prove himself an ardent Ghazi (holy warrior) by conquering Constantinople and all of Asia Minor and the Balkans.

The key to a successful siege of Constantinople was the ability to breach the massive 3.5 mile (5.7km) long

THIS DETAIL of a sixteenth-century fresco depicts Ottoman horse cavalry during the Siege of Constantinople.

Theodosian land wall with its moats, towers and triple layered lines of walls, walls that no army had been able to overcome in over a millennium! But Mehmed II had found a renegade Christian, Urban of Transylvania, willing to build a monster of a gun measuring 26ft 8in (8.1m) in length, with a calibre of 8in (20.3cm) that could lob a solid stone cannon ball weighing a ton more than 1 mile (1.6km). Urban's monster gun was completed and ready for inspection by a most satisfied Mehmed in January 1453. It would take a crew of 700 to transport, load, and handle the monster gun but it would prove most effective against the Theodosian Wall.

Unlike his father, Mehmed never honored treaties made with the Christians. He occupied Byzantine lands across the

Bosporus and cut the city's supplies of grain from Romania and southern Russia vital for its population. In five short months (April–August 1452) Mehmed had built a fort named Boghaz-Kesen (appropriately enough called the Throat Cutter) on the Bosporus whose sole purpose was to prevent shipping supplies from reaching Constantinople. In November a Genoese vessel that ignored Mehmed's blockade was sunk with a single shot from one of the massive guns inside Boghaz-Kesen and its captain, Antonio Rizzo, was impaled while his men were put to death. Mehmed had warned the infidels not to try his severely limited patience and that the Byzantines were now at his mercy.

THE OPPOSED FORCES

The final nails in Constantinople's coffin came during the winter of 1452–3. Firstly, the Catholic West failed, as ever, to assist the Orthodox Christians against the common foe. Admittedly the Pope made frantic but ineffectual efforts to drum up support for a crusade against the deadly Turkish threat, but Genoa, which held the fortified suburb of Pera across the Golden Horn, refused to abandon her lucrative yet dubious "neutrality." Only Venice, Genoa's sworn enemy, with extensive and vulnerable Balkan colonies, proved willing and able to assist Constantinople.

No such mercenary spirits prevailed in the doomed city itself as Christians of Slav, Greek, or Italian origin buried the hatchet in the face of the approaching, ruthless foe. Constantine XI who had only ascended the throne four years earlier proved not only a great orator but an inspired leader: he pointed out that they were all in the same boat, that they could not expect any mercy from Mehmed given the Genoese crew's gruesome fate, and that the West might aid them after all.

These were no more than words of truth but of scant comfort to the outnumbered and now surrounded defenders with no more than 10,000 armed men. Mehmed's elite guard, the Janissaries, alone numbered 12,000 men and his whole army would be ten times that size (figures vary from 100,000 to 150,000 troops). What was far worse was that Mehmed had managed, through a massive effort, to create a real galley fleet—the first in Ottoman history—built and manned by renegade Balkan Christians. Its commander, the Grand Admiral of the Fleet (Kapudan Pasha), Suleyman Balthoghlu was a converted Bulgarian. To the consternation of the defenders this fleet entered the southern (Marmara) Sea in early March 1453. Now the Marmara Sea Wall was threatened as well, requiring a garrison from Constantine's tiny army.

THE SIEGE BEGINS

The first Ottoman troops, the vanguard, appeared beneath the Land Wall on April 1 and at a signal from Constantine

himself the gates were shut, the wooden bridges across the moat burnt and the walls manned. Constantinople was now clearly under siege and cut off from the rest of the world. Five days later Mehmed arrived with the main army and set up camp beneath the walls. The Byzantines were master fortifiers who had reinforced the massive Land Wall where it was weak, such as at Blachernae. They had left the Sea Walls along the Marmara and Golden Horn relatively weakly held, since intelligence reports told them Mehmed would concentrate upon the Land Wall.

On April 9 the Ottoman Fleet made a failed attempt to break through the boom that stretched across the Golden Horn from the Sea Wall to Pera while the army dealt with two outlying forts, Therapia and Studius. Both held out for two days. On Mehmed's express orders the defenders were impaled as a warning to Constantinople's defenders that the same gruesome fate awaited them. Mehmed's barbarity only made the besieged Christians more determined to fight to the death rather than capitulating to such a capricious and bloodthirsty tyrant. A third fort, on the island of Prikipo, saw the garrison burn themselves alive rather than surrender.

Three days later the Ottoman artillery began an unrelenting bombardment of the Land Wall that went on for six weeks. Urban's gun fired seven times a day but the damage wrought was easily repaired by the diligent defenders. By April 18 the wall across the Lycus valley—the weakest spot in the defenses of the Land Wall—had

TURKISH JANISSARY (C.1450)

Founded in 1330, these Turkish slave-soldiers, drawn from converted Christian tribute-children and prisoners of war, were essential to the military success of the Ottoman state and went on to become the model for discipline in the Western armies of the sixteenth century. This infantryman is armed with the standard curved scimitar of the period and a short bow. Janissary bowmen first proved their worth at the battle of Nicopolis (1396), where they were deployed against cavalry to great effect behind stakes in a skirmishing formation. By the time of the siege of Constantinople, they were an essential part of the Ottoman Turkish army.

SULTAN MEHMET II FAHTI, known as the "The Conqueror." Italian court painter Giovanni Bellini (1430–1516) was called to Constantinople in 1479 and painted the portrait in the year before Sultan Mehmet II's death.

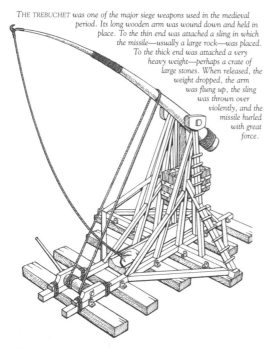

THE TREBUCHET was one of the major siege weapons used in the medieval period. Its long wooden arm was wound down and held in place. To the thin end was attached a sling in which the missile—usually a large rock—was placed. To the thick end was attached a very heavy weight—perhaps a crate of large stones. When released, the weight dropped, the arm was flung up, the sling was thrown over violently, and the missile hurled with great force.

crumbled but the Byzantines, led by the Italian general Giustiani Longo, repaired it in time. Having ordered the moat filled Mehmed unleashed his men in the first assault, costing him 400 men. The Christians, heavily armed knights on foot led by Longo, suffered no casualties. Obviously taking Constantinople was not going to be a walkover and the defenders' morale soared.

ITALIAN REINFORCEMENTS

Two days later a small fleet of heavy and well armed Italian merchant vessels broke through the Ottoman Fleet's blockade with little trouble using artillery and Greek Fire. Their arrival with news and much-needed grain boosted morale further. Mehmed, who had witnessed the defeat in person, was so enraged he fired Balthoghlu on the spot and reduced him to a common sailor.

The defenders' luck now ran out as Mehmed managed to move his galleys on rolling logs across the land side of Pera to the Golden Horn. Constantinople was now threatened from the north as well. A bravely led, but ineptly executed, night attack with fire ships failed leaving the Genoese and Venetians accusing each other of treason. Constantine XI was appalled with the Italians' behavior telling them "The war outside our gates is enough for us. For the pity of God do not start a war between yourselves."

On May 7 and 12 the Turks made two failed night-time assaults against the Lycus section. Mehmed was now losing heart and his Grand Vizier, Halil Pasha, urged him to abandon the siege. Mehmed gave the old man a violent dressing down telling him that he would have the "Apple of Rum" (i.e. Constantinople) whatever the cost and time it would take. A major threat to a city or castle under siege during this period was tunneling. Here the Turks, thanks to Serbian expertise, had an advantage and they had begun digging a series of tunnels to undermine and blow up the Land Wall. As luck would have it the Byzantines were ably led in countermining by a Scottish crusader knight, Sir John Grant, whose efforts in flooding the Turkish mines neutralized these efforts.

As if this was not bad enough the defenders made a surprise night attack on May 18 and left the Turkish siege towers in flames. Five days later the defenders captured the Serbian mining master who revealed the whereabouts and depths of the remaining Turkish tunnels. This good news was tempered by the arrival of a lone Venetian galleon with the news that the Pope had not been able to collect a relief army.

BAD OMENS

On the days of May 23 and 24, natural phenomena served to undermine the city's morale with devastating results. There was always the lingering fear that the city was doomed once the West would not succor the defenders. There was also the ancient prophecy that Constantinople would fall when the ruler was named Constantine and the present Emperor was named Constantine XI. During the procession to take out the Holy Icon of the Mother of God, the icon was carelessly dropped to the ground amid gasps of disbelief and horror. Once the icon had been picked up and the procession continued its progress through the capital it was interrupted by a sudden flash flood. During the following day, May 24, Constantinople was enveloped in a thick blanket of fog quite unheard of for this balmy month and which, the Byzantines whispered in shock to each other, hid the departure of God's protection from the city. It was God's punishment for the Orthodox allying themselves with the schematic Catholics from the West.

Morale among the besiegers was no better and again Halil Pasha forced Mehmed to agree to one final, massive assault during the night of May 28/29. If that failed then the previously so boastful Sultan agreed he would lift the siege once and for all. By the late evening of May 28 Mehmed and his generals had completed all preparations while the defenders braced themselves for what would prove the final battle. That same evening an ecumenical Mass was held in Hagia Sophia with Constantine in attendance where Catholic and Orthodox rubbed shoulders.

THE FINAL ASSAULT

At 1:30 A.M. some 20,000 irregulars (bashi-bazouks), screaming and running at top speed, rushed the Land Wall but after two hours of bloody and merciless fighting the heavily armored defenders had left only heaps of Turkish dead on the ground. The Anatolian army regulars failed equally miserably and assaults against the Sea Wall were also fiascos. Then, through treason or carelessness on the part of the defenders, some irregulars found that the small Kerkaporta gate between the Blachernae Palace section of the wall and the main Theodosian Wall had been left slightly ajar. Wasting no time the Turks, hundreds strong, rushed the gate and were through between the first and second walls where the few defenders were simply unable to stem the tide.

During the fighting on the main outer wall Longo was mortally wounded and instead of remaining to fight by the side of the Venetians and Byzantines he chose, with disastrous results, to be evacuated down to

the port. The Genoese, who had fought until that moment with outstanding determination and bravery, saw their commander leave on a stretcher and they panicked fleeing down to the port as well. Constantine's desperate pleas for Longo to stay went unheeded and the Venetians howled that those dogs from Genoa had betrayed them.

The Turks had by this time been able to open the main gate and poured through, where small groups of defenders, including the armor-clad Constantine, were cut down where they stood. The Catalans fought with grim Hispanic fatalism secure in the knowledge that fighting the Infidel assured them a speedy passage to Heaven.

AFTERMATH

Some 4,000 defenders lay dead, and it was claimed most of the population was enslaved while churches, monasteries, and houses were burnt to the ground or defiled. Mehmed immediately converted Hagia Sophia into a grand mosque. The fall of Constantinople was the end of the Byzantine Empire, and established the Ottoman Turks as a threat to Europe that lasted until their failed siege of Vienna in 1683.

CROSSBOWMAN WERE MORE effective in a siege situation, and some Aragonese and Genoese crossbowmen mercenaries were employed to defend Constantinople. By this time Western plate armor had become so heavy that knights ceased using a shield, freeing them to use heavy two-handed weapons.

CONSTANTINOPLE

1 Mehmed II establishes his camp outside the Land Wall in early April 1453. The city is cut off and the walls receive a constant battering.

4 On the night of May 28/29 the Turks break in over the wall and through a small postern gate.

5 Constantine XI is killed. For three days the city is sacked and looted.

KEY

← OTTOMAN TURKS

← CHRISTIANS

3 Mehmed sends Turkish ships overland around Pera on rollers and into the Golden Horn. Constantinople is now fully blockaded.

2 A small Italian fleet breaks through and is let into the Golden Horn, giving temporary relief.

LEPANTO 1571

In the last great Mediterranean galley battle, the combined fleet of the Western Christian powers decisively defeated the Turkish fleet thanks to superior gunnery and better-armed fighting men. The Turks' losses were so great that their naval power never really recovered.

The last Venetian stronghold, Famagusta, fell on August 1, 1571 the Turks massacring the population and brutally murdering the Venetian commander Marcantonio Bragadino—he was flayed alive and stuffed with straw. In response to the Turkish threat, Spain, the Papacy, Venice, Genoa, and Malta had formed the Holy League on May 25, 1571 and mobilized their combined naval power for war. Only the acute threat from the east would have compelled Venice to make allies of her sworn enemies Genoa and Spain, while accepting a "Spaniard" Don Juan of Austria as Grand Admiral of the Combined Fleet. Juan was the 26-year-old illegitimate half-brother of King Philip II of Spain.

As if to heighten such fears, the Sultan, Selim II, ordered his Grand Admiral (Kapudan Pasha) Ali Pasha—as young and tempestuously proud as Don Juan—to

LEPANTO FACTS

Who: Philip II of Spain and Pope Pius V founded the Holy League to fight the Ottoman Turks under Sultan Selim II. The League's Fleet was commanded by Don Juan of Austria (1545–76) while the Turks were led by Ali Pasha (d. 1571).

What: Lepanto was the greatest Christian naval victory against the Muslims and the last sea battle fought exclusively with oared galleys.

Where: In the Gulf of Patras on the western coast of Greece, taking its name from the port of Lepanto (Naupáktos).

When: October 7, 1571.

Why: The Ottoman Turkish Empire posed a deadly threat to Italy and the rest of Europe.

Outcome: Christian gunfire smashed the Ottoman fleet, breaking Turkish naval power in the Mediterranean.

THE BATTLE OF LEPANTO, *as depicted by the Venetian school of painting, the home city of some of the victors. The painting accurately portrays the crowded nature of the battle, where ships came alongside each other to exchange close fire and occasionally board to engage in hand-to-hand fighting.*

ITSELF A GUIDED PROJECTILE, galley engages galley with the ram striking into the hull as the attacker's heaviest cannon fire. Grappling and boarding follow as the marines of the attacking vessel attempt to swarm on board the target.

move his fleet of 274 ships (220–230 galleys) to the sheltered and fortified port of Lepanto. Ali Pasha sent his most feared commander, the Dey of Algiers Uluch Ali, to raid the Italian coast and Venice's outposts in the Adriatic. Uluch Ali was a renegade Italian from Calabria who hated Christians with a venom even unknown to a genuine Turk like Ali Pasha. It was therefore decided that the League, or Combined Fleet, would rendezvous at Messina in August 1571. The first to arrive were the Maltese (with three galleys) whose Knights were sworn enemies of the Turks having defeated the "Infidels" at their home island back in 1556. They were commanded by the Papal admiral Marcantonio Colonna who had a particular grudge against the Turks ever since they had sacked his family estate years earlier.

THE FLEETS

Since Antiquity, naval battles in the calm, blue waters of the Mediterranean had been fought between oared warships called galleys. These were long, sleek vessels with a shallow draft, with sails but propelled in battle by rows of oars manned by slaves or prisoners of wars. These unhappy men were manacled to their oars and went down with their galley should it sink in battle.

The Combined Fleet was the largest and most sophisticated galley fleet ever to fight in the Mediterranean and its commanders had introduced a series of innovations that

was to secure a devastating victory at Lepanto. One was to rely on gunnery and as consequence the Christian ships had removed the reinforced prow (used as a boarding ramp, not a ram) from the bow of their vessels. Another was to introduce boarding nets to make it harder for the Turks to board them. Furthermore the fleet had six heavy Venetian galleasses, each carrying 50 heavy guns and some 500 arquebusiers. These floating artillery platforms would meet the first onslaught of the Turks and blunt their attack.

Don Juan, who had left Barcelona on July 20 with 47 Spanish galleys, arrived to pick up Doria's squadron at Genoa six days later. This combined Spanish-Genoese contingent finally reached Messina on August 23 where the Venetians, under Sebastian Veniero, had arrived already on July 23 with about 100 vessels. Unfortunately these galleys were poorly manned and maintained and Veniero—who hated the Spanish as arrogant, brash upstarts—gritted his teeth and accepted, with bad grace, 4,000 Spanish soldiers aboard his galleys. These would be desperately needed to protect his vessels or board the enemy's galleys. The Combined Fleet was an impressive sight with well over 200 galleys and 22 large sailing ships manned by 43,000 oarsmen and almost 13,000 sailors.

Most importantly, the Christians had plenty of troops onboard—a total of 28,000. Of these 7,000 were German and 6,000 Italian mercenaries but the best equipped, heavily armored, experienced and disciplined troops were 10,000 Spaniards. It was these troops that would tip the balance in the Christians' favor during the forthcoming battle against the Turks. The Ottoman Fleet at Lepanto was nothing to sneeze at either. It consisted of almost 300 vessels (two-thirds galleys)

THE EARLIEST BREECH-LOADING naval cannon spat fire around the breech, which was potentially disastrous for the gunner. The gunner would place gunpowder in the hollow breech and the ball in the barrel, then use wedges, weights, and prayers to hold the weapon together as it fired.

but was short of troops (only 25,000) and these were poorly equipped and armored compared to the fearsome Spanish. This deficiency, coupled with a lack of artillery, would prove fatal for the Turks.

COUNCILS OF WAR

The Combined Fleet under Don Juan's command sailed into Corfu harbor on September 27. The island had only recently been raided and sacked by the Turks and its condition showed what might happen to Italy should the Turks ever reach its exposed coastlines. The following day came news that the enemy's fleet lay at anchor in Lepanto harbor.

Both sides held councils of war. The Genoese admiral, Gian Andrea Doria, had been defeated by the fearsome Uluch Ali in person off Tripoli years earlier and his self-confidence had taken a permanent knock. He urged a hostile Don Juan not to risk an open battle. Doria's colleagues did not share his defeatism—Colonna and the Spanish admiral, Don Álvaro de Bazán, Marquis of Santa Cruz, urged Juan to attack. At Lepanto most of Ali Pasha's commanders likewise counseled caution because they believed the Combined Fleet was strong and their crews and soldiers thirsted for revenge after Cyprus. Only Hassan Pasha of Algiers believed the Turks were stronger and would easily defeat the despised and cowardly "Infidels."

DISPOSITIONS

On October 5 the League's Fleet sailed out of Viscando harbor in fog and strong winds that bode ill for the future campaigning season. Obviously if the season advanced the weather would deteriorate so badly there would be no hope of fighting a galley battle in calm seas.

Juan divided his fleet into three divisions and decided to fight the forthcoming battle in a line. The Venetian fleet with 64 galleys were on the left and with Antonio and Ambrosio Bragadino in command of the two galleasses. The galleasses would break the Turkish attack with a hail of fire. On the right were the Genoese under Doria, flying the green pennant (the Venetians flew the white one). Doria had a

series of most distinguished subordinates. Commanding three galleys was an Englishman, Sir Thomas Stukeley, Alexander Farnese (the Duke of Parma) commanded his own 200-strong contingent of troops, while onboard the Spanish galley *Marquesa* was a young, bookish volunteer by the name of Miguel Cervantes. No one knew it at the time but he would be the author of *Don Quixote*. The Reserve Division (30 galleys) was commanded by the Marquis of Santa Cruz who would intervene to shore up the Christian lines wherever the greatest threat of a Turkish breakthrough appeared. That left Don Juan with 64 vessels in the center headed by his own flagship the *Real*, a three-year-old galley built of Catalan pine, ornately gilded and carved with murals. The Center Division was divided between the left commanded by the cantankerous Venetian septuagenarian Sebastian Veniero while the right was under Colonna with his Papal and Maltese vessels.

During the night of October 5/6 Ali Pasha moved his fleet from Lepanto into the Gulf of Patras while Don Juan told those, like Doria, who still wished to avoid a battle that the time for fighting had finally arrived. There was to be no more talk or second thoughts.

THE DAY OF BATTLE

That Sunday morning of October 7 Mass was held with special solemnity aboard the Christian vessels because battle was upon them. The League fleet edged around the northern shore of the Gulf of Patras as an observant boatswain with a lash gave any galley slave not pulling his weight a stroke or two. Coming from the east Ali Pasha's fleet amounted to 274 ships of which little over 200 were galleys. Uluch Ali, mirroring the self-serving caution of Doria on the other side, urged Ali Pasha to

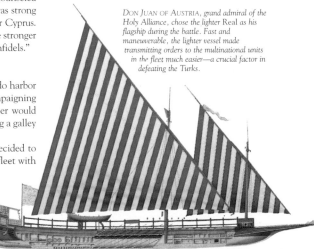

DON JUAN OF AUSTRIA, grand admiral of the Holy Alliance, chose the lighter Real as his flagship during the battle. Fast and maneuverable, the lighter vessel made transmitting orders to the multinational units in the fleet much easier—a crucial factor in defeating the Turks.

avoid a battle but was brushed aside by the young, brash Kapudan who said that the Sultan's orders were clear: to find and destroy the enemy where he stood. Fluttering from Ali's flagship was the Prophet's Green Flag that would ensure a victory against the "Infidels." The Turkish vessels were alive with the sounds of fiery martial music and the din of pipes, cymbals, drums, and flutes.

By contrast total and solemn silence reigned on the Christian vessels where Juan had ordered that there was to be no swearing or blaspheming since this was tantamount to treason when fighting the Muslims. Swords were sharpened, the decks were greased to make boarding more difficult and the armorers knocked the fetters off the feet of the galley slaves—they were freed and handed arms. Not a shot was fired as the galleasses were towed into line, half a mile ahead of the main fleet line. Don Juan, in a frigata, rowed along the fleet line and admonished his men to fight to the death.

The Turks were formed in the shape of a massive crescent that extended from one shore to the other—thus 1,093 yards (1km) longer than the Christian battle line. Ali would use this to try to outflank and roll up the Christian line. Aboard his imposing flagship *Sultana*, Ali was in command of the Turkish center with 92 galleys, while Mehmed Scirocco with his 56 Egyptian galleys sought to outflank the Venetians by moving his vessels as close to shore as possible. Uluch Ali, on the left, with 63 Algerian and Turkish galleys, faced his old adversary Doria whom he was sure he would defeat this time too.

THE CENTER DIVISION

When the wind turned the Christians took this as a sign that God was truly on their side this day and the *Real* fired a shot straight at the *Sultana*—a signal that the battle could begin. In fact it had already begun as the Turkish vessels passing the galleasses were shot to pieces—some even sank or were so damaged by the deadly arquebus and cannon fire they could not advance. Juan had given orders there was to be no firing until the Turks were at point-blank range and the Christian crews fired three rounds to every Turkish one. Their shots hit the waterline with devastating results while the Turkish shot high, either only hitting rigging or missing completely.

The *Sultana*'s prow smashed into the *Real*'s forecastle as grappling hooks were flung from either side. The Janissaries were frustrated by the boarding nets allowing the *Real*'s Spanish and Sardinian troops to invade the *Sultana*'s deck. The vicious hand-to-hand battle on her deck flowed back and forth.

Don Juan was wounded in the leg while Ali was struck in the head by an arquebus bullet. Before he could get up a Spanish trooper cut his head off and put his head on a pike. Turkish morale collapsed at the sight of their dead Grand Admiral's head and by 2 P.M. the *Sultana* had surrendered. The Turkish center was broken.

ENTITLED "THE NAVAL BATTLE OF LEPANTO," *this huge canvas was painted by Andrea Micheli (1539–1614) to celebrate the victory of the Christian fleet over that of the Ottoman Turks. Today, it hangs in the Doge's Palace, Venice.*

THE LEFT

Don Juan's colleagues on either side of him were not having such an easy time of it, however. Scirocco's ships outnumbered the Venetians and their Admiral Agostino Barbarigo's flagship was attacked simultaneously by eight Egyptian galleys. Barbarigo was wounded, handing command to his deputy Federigo Nani who was himself killed. But the individualistic Italians did not care, fighting on regardless. Some six Venetian galleys were sunk and it seemed the Egyptians would win when the Christian galley slaves onboard these vessels revolted. Scirocco was killed in hand-to-hand combat and his head was cut off and displayed. The Egyptians, like the Turks in the center, were utterly demoralized and many fled ashore, where they were pursued by their enemies who cut them down before they escaped inland. The 75-year-old Veniero set an example of bravado for his men, telling them that this was a glorious day to die in battle. He fired off a crossbow with great skill and accuracy while wearing slippers—it gave him, he would tell those who asked, a better grip on the slippery deck.

THE RIGHT

Further south the fighting was not going so well for the Christians and may have even jeopardized their victory thanks to Doria's defeatism and timidity. Doria had a private stake, as had his Genoese colleagues, in not losing their galleys in a battle and the slippery Genoese commander acted accordingly. Doria hoped to outmaneuver Uluch Ali without having to do any serious fighting. But Uluch, himself slippery and treacherous, had read his enemy's mind and extended his line (he had far more ships than Doria) ever closer to the Morean coastline, until Doria had stretched his fleet to the absolute limit. Don Juan had seen what was happening and sent orders for Doria to stop extending his line south or otherwise it would open a gap between his fleet and the main fleet.

Doria (like Uluch) was arrogant and ignored orders from men he considered less intelligent than himself so he ignored Don Juan's warning. Uluch could exploit his corsair galleys' superior speed, turn his ship around and then fill the 1,000-yard (914m) gap that had opened up. Before Santa Cruz or Juan himself could plug the gap Uluch seized the initiative and exploited it for short-term gains. If the bloodthirsty Selim "the Sot" was not to lop his head off when he returned to Constantinople then Uluch needed a token of "victory." He attacked three Maltese galleys with 90 Knights aboard with seven of his own, concentrating on their flagship, the *Capitana* under Captain Pietro Giustiani, while the rest of his squadron (16 vessels) attacked eight galleys commanded by Don Juan de Cardona. Cardona lost 450 out of his 500 Spanish troops on two ships, on *San Giovanni* and *Piamontese* (both lent by the Duke of Savoy to

Spain), there was not a single defender left alive. Uluch finally took the *Capitana* but Captain Ojeda (of the Guzmana)—the spearhead of Santa Cruz's counterattack—recaptured her. Ojeda found that there were only three men, including Giustiani, alive and that 30 Maltese knights had taken 300 Turks and Algerians with them into the afterlife.

AFTERMATH

Uluch escaped with a Maltese flag but his 13 galleys were all that was left of the once proud Ottoman fleet. By 4 P.M. the battle was over. Don Juan never publicly blamed Doria for his conduct and mistakes and Philip II may have been able to excuse his admiral, but the Pope, in a blind fury, made it clear that the Genoese was never to set his foot in Rome again on pain of being hanged like a dog. It was a total Christian victory but one that came a high price. The League lost 7,000 men and 12 galleys but they had freed 12,000 Christian galley slaves. Only 10,000 Turks survived the battle, losing 25,000 men and 180 galleys. It would take the Turks years to recover and Europe was safe—for now.

GALLEASS

Hasty, deadly, and decisive conversions, the six galleasses the Venetian arsenal prepared and sent into the fury of Lepanto began their existences as large merchant galleys on the lucrative spice voyages to East Asia. These monsters freighted castles and cannon after their conversion, rendering them practically, but not completely, immobile. Slow and unwieldy in comparison to ships under sail, the galleass could have a potentially telling advantage in the event of calm or unfavorable winds.

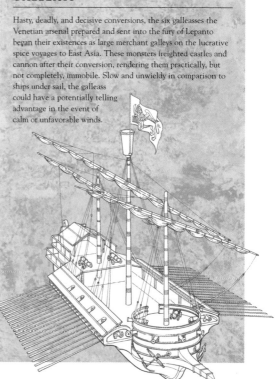

LEPANTO

1 The Christian fleet, having decided upon battle, move into the Gulf of Patras toward where the Turkish fleet are anchored under the protection of coastal artillery.

KEY

◀ CHRISTIAN ALLIANCE

◀ OTTOMAN TURKS

2 Confident in their abilities and past success, the Turks move directly toward the Christian vessels, which form a crescent with the horns toward the enemy.

3 The Turkish fleet flows around the giant galleasses, which inflict heavy damage. Fighting is fiercest in the center, while the struggle on the flanks gradually favors the Christian forces.

4 Some Turks manage to break through the Christian flank, but most are trapped or driven aground as the victorious Holy League presses forward in a battle of annihilation.

THE GREAT ARMADA 1588

The defeat of the Spanish Armada is one of the legendary victories of English history. English gunnery overcame a Spanish fleet equipped for boarding actions, but only after an attack by fireships at Calais scattered the Armada, preventing it from escorting the Spanish army across the Channel.

Until 1585 King Philip II of Spain and Queen Elizabeth I had learned to live with each other. In that year, Francis Drake raided the Spanish coast while the English, now allied to the Dutch rebels, landed 4,000 troops in Holland. It was a declaration of war, if not in name, then in reality against Spain. Parma suggested that he should land 30,000 men from his Army of Flanders directly on the Kent coast while Don Álvaro de Bazán, Marquis of Santa Cruz, suggested sending 510 ships and 95,000 troops against England directly from Spain. Santa Cruz had taken

ARMADA FACTS

Who: Philip II of Spain sent the Duke of Medina Sidonia (1550–1619) with the "invincible Armada" against Queen Elizabeth I of England whose fleet was led by Lord Howard of Effingham (1536–1624) and Sir Francis Drake (1543–96).

What: A landmark naval battle that saw the English system of sea warfare with battle lines firing broadsides introduced, eclipsing the tactics of Spanish "galley style" warfare.

Where: The English Channel from Cornwall to Gravelines on the Belgian coast.

When: July 31 to August 9, 1588.

Why: Philip II was seeking to invade England with the Duke of Parma's

30,000-strong army and end his English problems once and for.

Outcome: A fireship attack at Calais broke up the Armada's formation, the English won the engagement at Gravelines, and the survivors of the Armada were forced to sail around the British Isles to escape.

THIS COLORFUL HAND-TINTED ILLUSTRATION *shows the Spanish and English fleet closing with each other in the English Channel in August 1588. From a painting in the National Maritime Museum.*

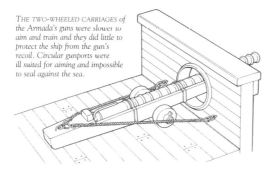

THE TWO-WHEELED CARRIAGES of the Armada's guns were slower to aim and train and they did little to protect the ship from the gun's recoil. Circular gunports were ill suited for aiming and impossible to seal against the sea.

the Portuguese islands of the Azores (1582–3) and had fought at Lepanto in 1571 when the Holy League crushed the Turkish fleet. Hesitant and cautious by nature, Philip II chose a compromise between the two. He would send the Armada into the Channel to then escort Parma across from the Netherlands. This strategic compromise would prove the undoing of the Armada before it even left port.

To gain time for English anti-invasion preparations the famous English buccaneer (or pirate as the Spanish referred to him) Sir Francis Drake set sail with 22 ships and on April 19, 1587 attacked Cadiz where he burnt or captured 36

Spanish vessels at anchor, and in May raided the Azores. Drake's dangerous presence forced Philip to delay the sailing of the Armada until the following spring.

Philip II had appointed Santa Cruz to command the Armada but the Marquis died in February 1588 in the middle of the preparations. Santa Cruz's place as Captain-General of the Ocean Sea was taken by the 38-year-old Don Alonso Pérez de Guzman, the seventh Duke of Medina Sidonia—an experienced and efficient organizer who soon had the massive Armada project back on track. Whatever the Duke lacked in terms of actual combat experience he made up in cool tactical and strategic skills, common sense, stern discipline, and ruthless determination. He set about with tremendous energy to repair the damage wrought by Drakes' raids and the chaos that Santa Cruz had left behind.

THE ARMADA SAILS

On April 1 the Duke received Philip II's orders: he was to sail to Margate in support of Parma, who was to land at Ramsgate and march along the Thames to take London. Once this had been achieved Philip would force Elizabeth I to make concessions. Philip very perceptively warned Medina Sidonia that the English would seek to avoid close combat and would use their superiority in naval gunnery to sink or damage the Duke's ships.

On May 30, 1588 the Armada, numbering 130 ships with 2,400 guns, 8,000 sailors, and 19,000 troops, set sail from Lisbon. The Armada may have looked formidable at a distance, but it was far weaker than it appeared. The Spanish treated war at sea like an extension of land warfare. Their experience of sea warfare was gained fighting the Turks in the Mediterranean. However, that was with galley fleets where ships were boarded by heavily armed troops, which was why the Spanish carried so many troops aboard their ships. The Spanish hoped to close with the English ships, sink their grappling hooks into them and then carry the enemy ships by boarding.

THE ENGLISH FLEET

The English, however, sought to fight in a completely different way. They had learnt to build fast, sleek galleons with plenty of medium and heavy gun and the English would rely upon firepower and speed to outrun, outgun, and outmaneuver the slower and clumsier Spanish ships. The English had several other advantages compared to their enemy. They were fighting in defense of their country against a ruthless would-be invader who wished to impose his rule and religion upon them. This spurred them on. They

THIS PORTRAIT (c. 1620) shows Lord Howard of Effingham, Earl of Nottingham (1536–1624), the Lord High Admiral who led the British fleet against the Spanish Armada.

were also fighting in home waters, the Channel, which they knew well. The Spanish were not familiar with these cold, gray waters and as attackers were not as motivated.

The English had also something resembling professional and specialized crews and officers. The captains were supreme commanders on their ships while on the Spanish ships command was divided between the military and naval officers where it was often unclear who had precedence. This caused not only confusion but fanned the flames of discord between the officers and troops/crew. The English had a well trained corps of gunners on board used to loading, firing, and reloading their guns swiftly and efficiently despite the rolling decks, while the Spanish used their army artillerists to do this. The English rate of fire was, therefore, three to four times faster than that of their enemy's.

Finally the ships themselves were quite different. Not even Philip II could afford a standing fleet on the scale of the Armada so most of the vessels had been hired or lent by individuals or friendly powers. Most of the Spanish tonnage was neither suited nor fitted out for a proper sea battle and the largest vessels (in the supply fleet) were not properly armed. By contrast the English vessels were specifically designed as warships, built for fighting in home waters, and for fast and intense fighting at short range. In 1588 the English had 24 newly constructed or fitted-out vessels in the Royal Navy and to this number could be added privateers and merchant ships. In total the English navy, under Charles Lord Howard of Effingham, numbered 105 vessels and the main fleet under Howard was anchored at Plymouth. Aged 52, Howard had in fact little experience of sea warfare or high command but his subordinates, such as Drake and Frobisher, had plenty from their numerous privateering raids against the enemy. Drake had divined, from whatever source, that the Armada would sail up the Channel and try to neutralize its English foe before Parma landed in England.

So far so good, from an English point of view, but they had no idea where Parma would land. Elizabeth had convinced herself they would land in Essex placing her favorite Robert Dudley, Earl of Leicester, with the bulk of the English army (14,000–20,000 men) there. That left only 4,000 poorly equipped levies to guard the Kent coast where in fact Parma's veterans were going to land.

THE FIRST DAY

Having been delayed at Corunna by a storm that temporarily scattered the huge fleet on July 19–21, the Armada sailed slowly across the Bay of Biscay and on July 30 entered the

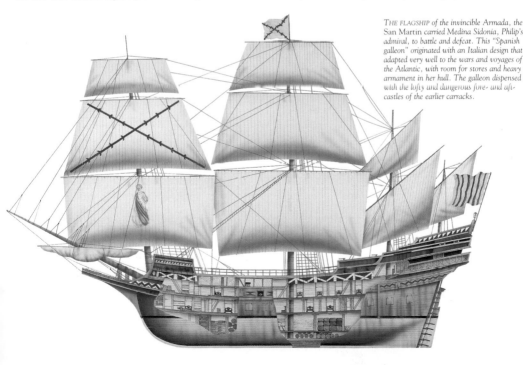

THE FLAGSHIP of the invincible Armada, the San Martin carried Medina Sidonia, Philip's admiral, to battle and defeat. This "Spanish galleon" originated with an Italian design that adapted very well to the wars and voyages of the Atlantic, with room for stores and heavy armament in her hull. The galleon dispensed with the lofty and dangerous fore- and aft-castles of the earlier carracks.

Channel. During the night of July 30/31 Howard's fleet of 64 ships sailed across the path of the advancing Armada while Drake's squadron was left inshore. Medina Sidonia formed his vast Armada into a huge crescent where he commanded the center (90 ships). The left flank (20 ships) was under the command of Don Alonso Martinez de Leiva and the right flank (also 20 ships) under Don Juan Martinez de Recalde. The whole battle formation spread out some 2 miles (3.2km) from the tip of the left horn to the tip of right. It was an impressive and terrifying sight.

As no formal declaration of war had been made between England and Spain, Howard sent out the appropriately named *Defiance* to fire a token shot at the approaching Armada. This was the signal for battle to commence. As Howard's fleet prepared for battle it was the turn of the Spanish to be perturbed as the English ships turned in a formation *en ala*, a line. This was the new flexible system of giving battle at sea attacking the enemy using a broadside. The English were sensible and cautious avoiding all close contact with the Spanish ships. They had good reason to be careful as the Spanish ships were packed with men armed with grappling hooks, ropes, and hand grenades at the ready. In close hand-to-hand combat the lightly armed English sailors and crews stood little chance.

FURTHER ENGAGEMENTS

The following day (August 1) Don Pedro de Valdés in the crippled *Nuestra Senora del Rosario*—having been abandoned by the rest of the Armada—was forced to strike to Drake aboard the *Revenge*. Drake's many English detractors believed he had veered off during the night in order to seize the *Nuestra Senora* as a prize.

During the previous day's fighting some of the Spanish captains had wavered in holding their positions in the rigid battle formation and in the light of this Medina Sidonia gave orders that any commander who broke ranks would be hanged without mercy for cowardice. Then he divided the command: he would lead the vanguard in person while Leiva brought up the rear, and to steady the nerves of his crews and officers he created two heavy battle groups with the largest and gunned vessels in his Fleet.

On August 2, as the Armada was west of Portland, Bill Howard attacked again and the English found however that their fire had little effect. They fired 500 rounds at the *San Martin* without causing any serious damage. Howard broke off

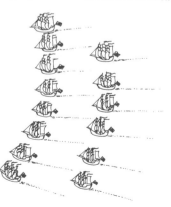

LINE OF SIGHT limited the formations of the era into two basic shapes: line of battle (ships side to side with their bows to the enemy) or column (ships proceeding bow to stern toward the foe). The ships in line of battle have the options, wind or sea permitting, to present their broadsides to the advancing foe. The ships in column can close the range and attempt to sail through the enemy's formation or they may turn suddenly to form a line of battle of their own.

the battle because his ships were running out of ammunition, noting that the Armada seemed, after all, invincible. By the evening Medina Sidonia contemplated sailing into the Solent to capture Portsmouth and use it as a base. Howard was determined to prevent this and divided his fleet into four squadrons, each commanded by himself, Drake, Hawkins, and Frobisher. While the other three squadrons detained the Armada, Drake went out in to the Channel, turned and attacked unexpectedly. The English forced the Armada to abandon its attack on the Solent and it drifted into the Channel again. A Spanish victory turned into a crucial English success. Nevertheless, the Armada was left unmolested for two days and reached Calais by the afternoon on August 6.

FIRESHIPS

Calais was a dubious sanctuary for the hard-pressed Spanish since the harbor was shallow and open with hardly any natural defenses against an English attack. However, in the ongoing religious civil war in France between Catholics and Protestants, the port of Calais was in the hands of the former and the French governor was an ardent Catholic who welcomed the Armada with open arms. That same evening Parma's courier arrived by pinnace from his headquarters with the grim news that he would not be ready for another six days. Medina Sidonia realized the English and their Dutch allies—with 140 vessels hovering off the coast—would be most unlikely to give them that long.

His hunch was right as Howard had called a Council of War aboard his flagship the *Ark Royal* during the morning of August 7 where it was decided to send some eight fireships against the anchored Armada. Howard hoped to spread confusion and disorder thus enabling the English to move to point-blank range and blast the Spanish vessels. His scheme went according to plan. Medina Sidonia had suspected the English would launch an attack with fireships and posted lookouts so when the attack was launched during the night of August 7/8 two of the English craft were intercepted and ran aground. That left six that got through. The English had loaded the vessels' gun barrels with double shot, so the explosion, the smoke, and fire were tremendous, spreading panic and fear. Most captains of the Armada cut their cables in a wild and thoughtless scramble to get away and save their skins despite the Duke's orders to save the anchors and return to their previous positions once the attack was over.

By dawn on August 8 the Duke was left with his flagship and only four escorts to protect him. Little by little the vessels returned with the heavily armed galleons protecting the scattered Armada's rear as the Spanish vessels reformed. The stark truth, however, was that the English had them where they wanted them—strung out along the shallow coastal waters of Flanders. At last the English could use their superior firepower at point-blank range with devastating effect. The battle of Gravelines (August 8) was fought in the shoal waters between Gravelines and Ostend, lasting nine hours. The *San Martin* received 200 shot, was badly damaged and began to take on water while her Portuguese sister-ship, the *San Mateo*, was riddled with English shot. Both vessels ran aground between Nieuwpoort and Ostend where they and their crews were captured by the Dutch. Two more vessels, including the *El Gran Grifon* ran aground while one, the *Maria Juan*, was actually sunk—the only one to be so.

AFTERMATH

The Spanish had 1,000 dead and 800 wounded and morale collapsed. Medina Sidonia made desperate efforts to gather his ships by signaling and then he called his remaining captains together. They failed to convince the Duke as to why they had failed to return to the Armada and he simply turned to the Provost with an icy order: "Hang the traitors." As it was they were all spared except one, Don Cristobal de Avila, who was hanged from the yard arm and then his corpse was put into a pinnace on display to restore order and discipline.

The Armada had lost the battle against the English and now, with discipline restored, made the arduous and amazing trip around the British Isles back to Spain. It was a measure of Medina Sidonia's leadership and his men's fortitude and toughness that so many ships made it back at all.

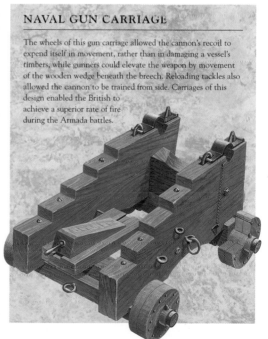

NAVAL GUN CARRIAGE

The wheels of this gun carriage allowed the cannon's recoil to expend itself in movement, rather than in damaging a vessel's timbers, while gunners could elevate the weapon by movement of the wooden wedge beneath the breech. Reloading tackles also allowed the cannon to be trained from side. Carriages of this design enabled the British to achieve a superior rate of fire during the Armada battles.

THE GREAT ARMADA (GRAVELINES)

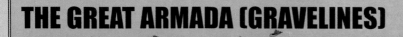

5 Prevailing winds and damage prevent the Spanish from either making a rendezvous with their invasion fleet or descending on the English coast.

4 Medina Sidonia attempts to reform the Armada. The English press their advantage in a furious cannonade in which the Spanish suffer some loss and cannot resume their fleet formation.

3 The prepared Spanish elude the incendiary vessels but are thrown into great confusion.

NORTH SEA

1 After engagements in the Channel, the Armada shelters in the roadstead of Calais while waiting for the Spanish flotilla in the Netherlands to complete preparations for the invasion of England.

2 During the night of August 7, English Admiral Lord Howard unleashes burning fireships among the anchored Spaniards.

KEY

⬅ ENGLISH NAVY

⬅ SPANISH ARMADA

LÜTZEN 1632

In one of the great battles of the Thirty Years War, the "Lion of the North," Gustavus Adolphus of Sweden, faced a revived Imperial army under Wallenstein at Lützen. The Swedish King was killed, but his troops rallied and were victorious after a hard fight against opponents who had learned from their previous defeats.

L ittle did the Bohemian patriots who threw the Imperial delegates out of the windows of the Hradcany Castle in Prague realize that their actions would unleash the longest and bloodiest war in modern European history, lasting a full 30 years. The Holy Roman Emperor Ferdinand II gave command of the Imperial Army to Count Albrecht von Wallenstein, a ruthless, scheming Czech nobleman, who swiftly defeated the Danes at the battle of Lutter in 1626. With an army of 125,000 men Wallenstein had won the war and secured the whole of Germany for Ferdinand II, who repaid his victories with an abrupt dismissal. Ferdinand's timing was disastrous since the triumphant Imperialists were about to meet and be crushed by their most formidable enemy, the Swedes.

LÜTZEN FACTS

Who: King Gustavus II Adolphus of Sweden (1594–1632), commanding the Swedish Army, against Prince Albrecht von Wallenstein, Prince of Friedland (1583–1634), leading the Imperial Army.

What: In a hard-fought battle, the Imperial forces showed they had learned from their previous defeat at Swedish hands, and Gustavus was killed. However, the Swedes rallied and were victorious.

When: November 6, 1631.

Where: The fields outside the small town of Lützen near Leipzig in Saxony (eastern Germany).

Why: Wallenstein threatened Saxony—an ally of Sweden.

Outcome: The battle saved Saxony but the Thirty Years War (1618–48) ground on despite this hard won Protestant victory.

SEEN FROM NEARBY HEIGHTS, *troops maneuver into position as the battle of Lützen develops. The infantry columns favored by Gustavus Adolphus can be seen forming up for the attack.*

THE SWEDISH ARMY

Gustavus II Adolphus had become King of Sweden in 1611, aged only 17, but had gained valuable experience fighting the Russians and Poles between 1611 and 1630. The young King had modernized the Swedish army and created Europe's first truly professional standing army. His artillery was modeled on that of the Dutch but used lighter, more mobile guns of standardized calibers and handled by trained professionals. Artillery was used by Gustavus Adolphus in a new offensive manner in close cooperation with the infantry, where his artillery fired eight rounds to the six fired by the musketeers.

The infantry's pikemen had their armor lightened and their pikes shortened, while the Swedish musketeers used lighter muskets. Both were grouped in mixed, flexible brigades or rectangular columns to increase mobility and speed of deployment. The baggage train was reduced to an absolute minimum to improve marching speed and campaign mobility. His cavalry, unlike the Imperial cuirassiers, were only lightly armored and so attacked the flanks of the enemy under cover of artillery fire, charging at high speed with drawn swords.

BREITENFELD

It was thus a new but inexperienced army that was about to invade the continent of Europe for the first time in 1630. The Swedes feared that Wallenstein's army would take

HAVING PLUNGED into the mêlée to shore up a faltering brigade, the Swedish king's wounded horse carried him into the enemy ranks where, deprived of his escort, he was surrounded by Imperialist troopers and killed.

Stralsund and with the aid of privateers dominate the Baltic and perhaps even threaten Sweden itself.

On July 6, 1630, Gustavus Adolphus landed in northern Germany with 13,000 men. When the new Imperial commander, General Count Tilly (1559–1632), sacked the city of Magdeburg, Gustavus simply marched on Berlin and forced George William the Elector to join him or see his capital—like Magdeburg—burnt to the ground. When Tilly and Imperial army invaded Saxony its Elector, George John, had little choice but to become a Swedish "ally." Consequently, the Saxon-Swedish army of 47,000 men marched on Leipzig on September 16, bumping into the Imperial cavalry commander Count Pappenheim (1594–1632) near a village called Breitenfeld.

Tilly, aged 73, was still a practitioner of "Spanish" style warfare. This meant fighting your enemy in massive squares of 1,500–2,000 men with muskets and pikes, called *tercios* in Spanish, with heavy cavalry on either flank. He lined up his 40,000-strong army in 17 massive *tercios* with 10,000 heavy cavalry in smaller squares on the sides. Gustavus placed his Swedish and elite Finnish troops in the center supported by three brigades of Scottish mercenaries. To the left stood General Count Horn with a mixed force of mainly German and some Swedish troops, while the entire right was made up the Elector's Saxons. The Swedish artillery fired off a massive salvo and their batteries fired three rounds to every one Imperial round.

Tilly's right wing mistook Pappenheim's unauthorized attack as a signal for a general advance against the Saxons who—seeing the invincible tercios advance—broke and

GUSTAVUS ADOLPHUS understood that his horse needed firepower if they were to break their enemies and so copied the Dutch System of deploying bodies of musketeers between those of horse, a practice known as interlarding the horse. These men were thus able to defend the horsemen by outranging the pistols of the enemy horse.

fled, their Elector in the lead. At one stroke one-third of the Allied army was gone. But Gustavus' troops could move and maneuver twice as fast as Tilly's and the Allies quickly took the Saxons' place. The whole Imperial line began to buckle, and finally broke, leaving the field to the Swedes.

Gustavus had reignited the war and during the winter of 1631–2 he occupied much of western and southern Germany even threatening Vienna. On April 16, 1632, he caught and defeated Tilly at Lech—his enemy was dead two weeks later. In sheer desperation Ferdinand II was forced to recall Wallenstein—the only Imperial commander willing and able to put a stop to the rampaging Swedes.

THE LÜTZEN CAMPAIGN

Prospects looked good for the Imperial side, because Wallenstein was a shrewd strategist with a cool and calculating head. He avoided battle at all costs forcing Gustavus to take the initiative and on September 4 the Allied army unsuccessfully attacked Wallenstein's fortified positions at Fürth, losing 3,000 troops. Wallenstein extracted himself from his positions there and invaded Saxony but committed the mistake, on October 22, to go into winter quarters sending his cavalry (5,000 strong) under Pappenheim to Halle.

Gustavus took immediate advantage of Wallenstein's mistake and marched during November 5 as quickly as he could toward Pergau to join up with the Saxons. After 15

years of war the German countryside was ravaged and could not feed the armies and Gustavus needed a battle of annihilation to put an end to this constant movement. The Allied advance was blocked by Croat and Imperial cavalry at the Rippach stream for hours on that day, which left Gustavus no choice but to move his army toward Lützen. Here the Allied (Swedish, Finnish, German, and Scottish) troops spent a cold, miserable and dreary night in the open during the night of November 5/6 with the Imperial army bivouacked only 3 miles (5km) away.

On the other side Wallenstein—so troubled with gout he had to be carried around in a sedan chair—was determined to fight a defensive battle here since he had tried his best to avoid a battle altogether. Lützen was on a flat, featureless north German plain with the main road to Leipzig running

THE DECLINE OF ARMORED cavalry and the return of the infantryman to the centerstage of the battlefield was accompanied by a resurrection of military drill. Here a company of pikemen is shown in three distinct formations, as it would have appeared in a military manual of the seventeenth century.

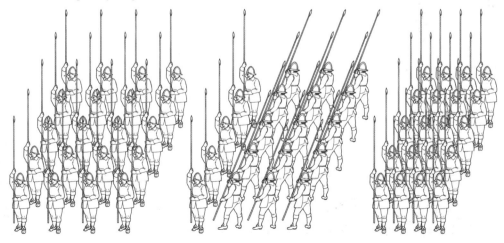

through it from southwest to the northeast atop a raised causeway that formed a natural line of defense for the Imperial side. On either side of that road was a ditch that Wallenstein's men spent November 5 and the following night making into a formidable line of trenches that would be filled with musketeers.

DISPOSITIONS

Wallenstein had 25,000 men—facing 18,000 Allies—with Pappenheim's 8,000 as reinforcements and he would form his order of battle in a single line just north of the Leipzig road. His right flank rested on a knoll just north of Lützen—Windmill Hill—while his left was left hanging in the open. Yet Wallenstein had learned the lessons of the Breitenfeld disaster well. The infantry was now more mobile and grouped in shallower, more maneuverable formations with their own light artillery. The three Imperial batteries, with a total of some 60 guns, were well placed and protected while the cavalry had absorbed some Swedish tactics and equipment. Wallenstein placed himself with the infantry—

WHEN ARTILLERY was first introduced in Europe it was extremely cumbersome, requiring teams of oxen, horses, and men to draw each piece. Monarchs and their generals were constantly seeking better means of producing stronger, lighter cannon that could be moved with less difficulty and employed on a wider scale for both siege and battle.

in four tercios—in the middle while he placed Colloredo's cavalry on the left and Ottavio Piccolomini's cavalry on the right. He then set fire to Lützen to create a smokescreen and prevent the enemy using its houses for cover.

By the early light of a gray dawn the Swedes and their allied troops took up position opposite the Imperials. In the center were Brahe and Kniphausen each with four infantry brigades, the right—mainly Swedes and Finns—were under Gustavus' personal command while the left was under Prince Bernhard of Saxe-Weimar (1604–39). Bernhard was a young but experienced German mercenary commander of dubious credentials as a Protestant "patriot" and he was to show himself a good choice as deputy commander.

THE BATTLE BEGINS

The fog thickened as the morning progressed rather than thinned out as would have been expected. So the planned attack had to be postponed from 8 A.M. to 11 A.M. when the fog lifted temporarily and allowed Gustavus to begin his attack. Due to skilled and coordinated Imperial artillery and musket fire the advance was halted on the left and center. It was only on the right where a breakthrough was achieved but at a high cost. The Swedish and Yellow Brigades managed to clear the trench of musketeers, cross the road, and seize the batteries to the north of the road.

Then the fighting, as the fog descended upon the battlefield yet again, became a murderous stalemate. Just as the Imperial left crumbled, Pappenheim arrived and rescued the Imperial army from being overwhelmed by the Swedish-Finnish onslaught. The Swedish Brigade lost 70 percent of its pikemen and 40 percent of its musketeers in the slaughter that now ensued. The other side was just as badly mauled, as shown by Piccolomini having five horses killed under him and being wounded as many times during the fighting. The Swedish cavalry were reduced to scattered small groups on either side of the raised road and they began to waver. Only the intervention by the army's chief chaplain, Jacob Fabricius, steadied their nerves and brought them back into battle.

ALBRECHT VON WALLENSTEIN, commander of the Imperial army during the 30 Years War, is shown in this oil painting sitting on horseback. He is wearing the layered plate armor still popular with cavalrymen of the time.

THE DEATH OF GUSTAVUS ADOLPHUS

Meanwhile things had gone very wrong for the king. When Colonel Frederick Stenbock of the Småland cavalry was shot in the foot Gustavus took personal command of the unit. He rode north to aid the hard-pressed Swedish and Finnish troops north of the road. Just as they began to advance the fog descended and it was, as one Swedish soldier said, "thick as pea soup." Simultaneously Imperial cuirassiers smashed into the Småland regiment and everything became confused.

Since the Polish war, when a bullet had been lodged in his body, Gustavus had been unable to wear metal body armor and he wore instead thick, hardened leather. But this was hardly any protection against bullets that were flying past thick and fast. His left arm was hit, and he was forced to drop his sword and take the reins of his horse, Steiff, in his right hand, and he got separated from the Smålanders. An Imperial officer, Moritz von Falkenberg, shot Gustavus in the back, but was himself shot from his horse. One of the King's guards tried to prop up the wounded and bleeding King in his saddle but Steiff was now hit in the neck and Gustavus fell off the saddle but he was stuck with one of his feet in the stirrups. He was dragged a few yards but lay on the ground—still alive. When Piccolomini arrived to inspect the rumor that their mortal foe was dying, he gave orders to kill the king and his men did so gleefully—firing a pistol into his temple. They also stole his weapons and clothes.

Meanwhile a bloody and terrified Streiff came galloping out of the fog. The Swedish and allied troops had heard that the king was dead and feared that all was lost. Bernhard, now in command, rallied the wavering men for a counter-attack and as the Swedes advanced they found their hero king's corpse—mutilated and stripped. Bernhard had calculated that they would now thirst for revenge and so they did, more than willing to avenge Gustavus' humiliating death. The general Swedish attack had bent the Imperial line into something resembling a crescent but both sides were now tired and wearying of fighting. They came to a halt as they fired at each other but could not break the deadlock. Bernhard decided that the only way to bring this dismal battle to an end would be to attack Windmill Hill, knock out Wallenstein's remaining 13 guns, and break through between the enemy's center and left.

The Swedish batteries unleashed a storm of shot that silenced the battery atop Windmill Hill and then, at 3 P.M., the Swedes, Finns, and other troops—with drums beating and flags waving—marched swiftly up the slope leading to the hill. They were thrown back by withering fire but regrouped and attacked again until they had seized the hill and the trenches around. These were filled with dead and dying men. Finally, after two hours of intensive fighting, the Swedish colors were raised—at 5 P.M.—atop the hill. The battle was won.

IMPERIAL CUIRASSIER

Cuirassiers of the Thirty Years' War continued to wear plate armor for maximum defense but had discarded the lance in favor of pistols. Their armor was usually of a good quality and could stop both sword cuts and pistol balls. It was also articulated, which means the many layers could slide over each other, allowing a lot of movement. However, it also earned them the nickname of "lobsters."

AFTERMATH

Wallenstein could have fought on but his troops were now utterly exhausted and demoralized. Wallenstein's son, Bertold, was one of the casualties and the whole slaughter had cost 7,000 lives—some 4,000 Imperial and the rest Allied.

Lützen was a Swedish-Allied victory but only just, and it was Bernhard who had led the army to victory. A year later Wallenstein was murdered while Bernhard was defeated by the Spanish and Imperial armies at Nördlingen in 1635. Amazingly the war dragged on until finally, on October 24, 1648, the exhausted combatants finally signed a lasting peace—that of Westphalia.

WITH ITS MORE EFFICIENT MECHANISM, *cavalrymen who were about to ride into combat preferred the wheel-lock pistol. Not only could such pistols be loaded easily but the user could be reasonably sure of being able to fire when they wanted to without the complicated process of using a match for ignition.*

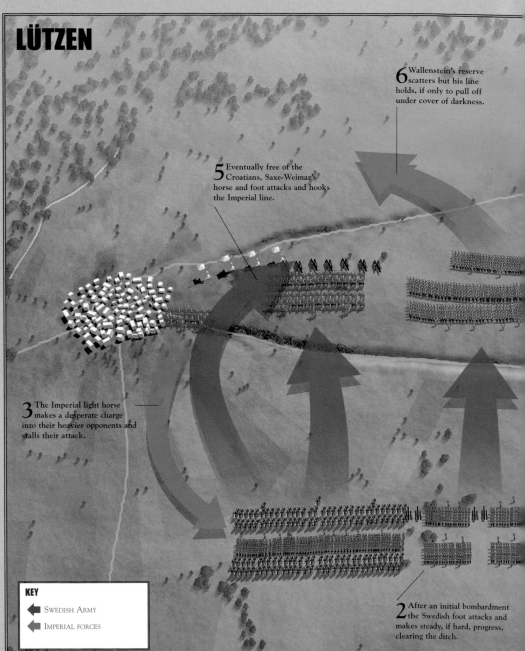

LÜTZEN

6 Wallenstein's reserve scatters but his line holds, if only to pull off under cover of darkness.

5 Eventually free of the Croatians, Saxe-Weimar's horse and foot attacks and hooks the Imperial line.

3 The Imperial light horse makes a desperate charge into their heavier opponents and stalls their attack.

2 After an initial bombardment the Swedish foot attacks and makes steady, if hard, progress, clearing the ditch.

KEY

◄ SWEDISH ARMY

◄ IMPERIAL FORCES

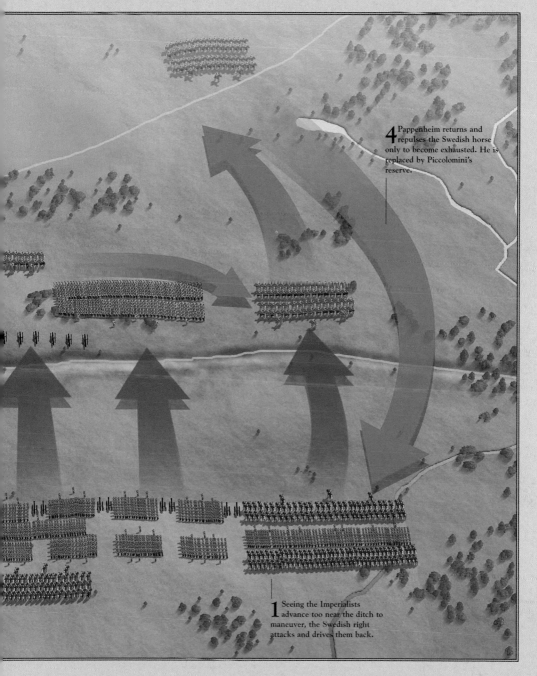

4 Pappenheim returns and repulses the Swedish horse only to become exhausted. He is replaced by Piccolomini's reserve.

1 Seeing the Imperialists advance too near the ditch to maneuver, the Swedish right attacks and drives them back.

BLENHEIM 1704

During the War of the Spanish Succession, the Duke of Marlborough lead a daring march across Europe to defeat a superior Franco-Bavarian force at Blenheim on the Danube. This victory secured not only the safety of the Habsburg capital, but also Marlborough's reputation as one of the great military commanders of history.

On November 1, 1700 King Carlos II of Spain died without a natural heir leaving his vast empire to the grandson of Louis XIV, Philip Duke of Anjou, to be ruled as an undivided realm, something that powers of the anti-French "Grand Alliance" were determined to prevent. Louis XIV had no wish to provoke another war but, at the same time, he could not see an Austrian Habsburg, Archduke Charles, become king of Spain and thus leave France surrounded on all sides by enemy states. If he had wished to maintain peace yet see his grandson Philip on the Spanish throne then Louis went about it totally the wrong way. In February 1701 his armies occupied the Spanish Netherlands including some Dutch-controlled forts, thus violating a series of internationally agreed treaties and provoking his most dangerous enemy King

BLENHEIM FACTS

Who: A Franco-Bavarian army under Marshal Tallard (1652–1728) faced an Allied army under the Duke of Marlborough (1650–1722) and Prince Eugene of Savoy (1663–1736).

What: Marlborough's aggressive and shrewd battlefield tactics coupled with superior infantry firepower, stronger artillery, and cavalry shock tactics marked the end of French military supremacy in the War of the Spanish Succession.

Where: At the village of Blenheim (Blindheim) on the Danube in central Bavaria.

When: August 13, 1704.

Why: The Grand Alliance sought to limit Franco-Bavarian power by decisively defeating their forces in the field.

Outcome: Marlborough and Prince Eugene of Savoy defeated the Franco-Bavarian army and thereby saved Austria from invasion.

LED BY THEIR JUNIOR OFFICERS, *British infantry exchange volleys with their French counterparts before closing for hand-to-hand fighting. It was still common in the early eighteenth century for sergeants and junior officers to be armed with pikes.*

William III of England and the Netherlands into a conflict neither had sought. By September 1701, in response William had revived the Grand Alliance, Austria, the Netherlands and Britain, against Louis XIV.

"CORPORAL JOHN"

Unfortunately William III was thrown from his horse and died of his injuries on March 8, 1702, leaving the throne to his sister-in-law Queen Anne (reigned 1702–14). The Anglo-Dutch alliance was now to be led by the most remarkable military and political leader of his age: Sir John Churchill, the First Duke of Marlborough. As his outstanding abilities as a field commander, politician, and diplomat were to show during the war, the confidence placed in him was more than amply justified.

"Corporal John," as he was affectionately known to his troops, had realized that the development of new flintlock muskets, coupled with the replacement of the pike with the socket bayonet, had restored the offensive to infantry tactics.

THE BATTLE OF BLENHEIM TAPESTRY is displayed in the Green Writing Room at Blenheim Palace. Here, the Duke of Marlborough sits astride a white horse, in commanding posture.

Equally cavalry were to be used in massed formation, using shock tactics and charging with drawn swords. Unlike his peers therefore, Marlborough, following in the footsteps of Gustavus II Adolphus, avoided needless maneuvering and sought a rapid decision through a fiercely fought pitched battle to defeat the enemy with one mighty blow.

THE CAMPAIGN

By early 1704 the war, having proved indecisive for the last three years, had entered a most critical and dangerous state for the Allies. A large Franco-Bavarian army was poised to march on the Imperial capital of Vienna forcing Emperor Leopold I to recall his most brilliant and experienced commander, Prince Eugene of Savoy from Italy with his army. The Austrians also called upon their Anglo-Dutch allies to aid them.

Marlborough knew that the exposed Netherlands and the war would be lost should the enemy defeat the Imperial army and seize control of Vienna. However, the Dutch Estates General asked the English commander to move "their" army away from the Dutch border. Marlborough placated the Dutch by claiming that he would only move

TO PREPARE A CANNON *to fire, the crew would have to go through a number of several first; swab the barrel with a wet sponge; then load powder into the barrel; then ram in the charge with the ramrod; next, direct the gun using a handspike; and finally, apply a lighted match to fire.*

his army to the Moselle River and no further. Leaving 70,000 men to watch the Netherlands, Marlborough—with 70,000 men and 48 guns—marched south along the Rhine. He faced 60,000 French at Strasbourg and the Franco-Bavarian army of 60,000 and it was crucial, should the Allies have any hope of success, to keep these two armies apart. Hence Prince Eugene (with 30,000 men) took up position in Baden to keep Marshal Villeroi at bay while Marlborough—who had reached Donauwörth on July 1—dealt with Marshal Marsin and the Elector of Bavaria, Prince Maximilian II Emmanuel.

Marlborough had to take this strategically placed fortified town without a time-consuming siege if he was to cross the Danube unscathed and be able to defeat the Franco-Bavarians before the campaigning season came to an end. The Bavarian Elector had sent 14,000 troops under Marshal d'Arco's command to build a fortress outside Donauwörth, called the Schellenberg, and to hold this vital river crossing against the advancing Marlborough. The Allied army, now reinforced by Prince Louis, Elector of Baden, had taken up position near the fortress by noon on July 2. Marlborough ordered his quartermaster general to set up tents in order to create the impression that his army would attack the following day. This simple ruse worked.

At 5 P.M. the artillery opened fire on the Schellenberg and at 6:15 P.M. 6,000 British infantry attacked in three columns, supported by cavalry, and made three unsuccessful assaults against the fortified works. D'Arco's garrison was

now pinned down giving Prince Louis the chance to attack with a second force against the northwestern side of the fortress at 7:30 P.M. The affair was now decided in vicious hand-to-hand combat between the Allied and Bavarian troops but in the end the defenders—losing a staggering 10,000 men—were overwhelmed by the force and ferocity of the assault. Marlborough suffered 1,400 killed and 3,800 wounded.

DISPOSITIONS

These casualties were light compared to the gains of the Allies: the road to the Danube via Nördlingen was now open. Marlborough's army crossed the Lech River on July 8 and began to lay waste to the Bavarian countryside in a brutal and systematic fashion that left no villages or farms standing in the path of the inexorably advancing Allies. Marlborough was now nearing the quarry and requested, on August 11, that Eugene join him, especially as the experienced French Marshal Count Camille de Tallard had taken command in Bavaria.

Tallard's Franco-Bavarians had taken up position just west of the village of Blenheim (or Blindheim) on August 12. Their camp was atop a gentle rise 1 mile (1.6km) west of the marshy brook of the Nebel that formed a soggy "moat" facing the north and the approaching enemy. The Elector's Bavarians were stationed around Lutzingen, Marsin at Oberglau and Tallard at Blenheim. The left (west) flank rested on a series of hills and forests while the right (east) flank was anchored on the Danube.

CORNET

Strangely, in the late seventeenth century both the flag and the officer who carried it were called cornets. This one is shown 'dipping' or saluting on a special occasion that merits rosette ribbons being plaited into the horse's mane.

THE TYPICAL THREE-RANK infantry formation in use during the eighteenth century was made possible because of the use of the bayonet. Shown here are infantry prepared to receive cavalry. The front rank kneels to ward off the horsemen with the bayonet while the second and third ranks fire.

Tallard and his colleagues felt quite safe in this "impregnable" position, which resembled a fortress, and they could not believe that Marlborough and Eugene would be bold or rash enough to attack them, especially when they were outnumbered. A fortress mentality is always dangerous and as Napoleon was apt to claim "the side that stayed within their fortifications was already beaten" and this proved no exception. The enemy commanders were ruthless and bold, especially Marlborough and the fall of Donauwörth had clearly shown that not even a real fortress could stand up to "Corporal John" and his ferocious redcoats.

At daybreak on August 12, Marlborough made a personal reconnaissance of the enemy's position in and around Blenheim. At 2 A.M. on the following day the Allied army set out westward in four columns, crossed the Kessel stream at 3 A.M. and three hours later had reached high ground at Wolperstetten. At 7 A.M. the morning mist finally lifted from the field revealing to the Franco-Bavarians the unwelcome presence of the Allied army only a stone's throw from their lines.

Unbelievably enough Tallard, Marsin, and the Elector still believed their enemy would withdraw and it was only with some shock and horror that they realized the Allies meant business. The general alarm was sounded sending troops, horses, and wagons in all directions to take up battle positions.

The Allied commanders could note with satisfaction that they had caught their blithely self-confident enemies completely by surprise and neither the Duke nor the Italian prince were the sort of commanders to squander such a chance. Some 56,000 British, Baden, Imperial, and Dutch troops faced 60,000 French and Bavarians.

THIS EIGHTEENTH-CENTURY ARTILLERY piece has been limbered for movement. Artillery pieces had become lighter and more mobile when compared to cannon of the previous century.

THE BATTLE

The battle could finally begin and it did, with a massive artillery barrage from the French, at 8:30 A.M. answered with an equally ear-shattering blast in reply from the English batteries (some 90-cannon strong). Caught napping, Tallard had no time to devise a sophisticated battle plan. The Franco-Bavarians would remain on the defensive but the two armies would fight separately. Marsin would hold the center, the Elector on the left, and Tallard himself around Blenheim down to the Danube. Marsin and the Elector would hold positions right down to the banks of the Nebel while Tallard's force would hold a position some 1,000 yards (914m) south of the stream. Tallard hoped that Marlborough would advance across the Nebel, get caught in the crossfire from Oberglau and Blenheim—garrisoned with French troops—and thereby allow Tallard to counterattack and drive the British into the marshlands flanking the Nebel.

Marlborough had noticed that the enemy's right was stronger than its left and it was therefore on the stronger flank he would attack. Marlborough had a hunch about Tallard's ruse and sent Eugene to pin down the Elector while he advanced to neutralize the French garrisons at Blenheim and Oberglau. The British and French artillery dueled for four hours while Lord Cutts' column, rushing across five pontoon bridges, crossed the Nebel and created a bridgehead on the southern bank. Marlborough awaited impatiently for news that Eugene—who was finding the country toward Lutzingen rough going—had attacked and pinned down the Elector's Bavarians before he attacked.

At long last the Savoyard's ADC arrived with the welcome news and at 12:30 P.M. Marlborough told his generals, "Gentlemen, to your posts." Fifteen minutes later General Rowe's British brigade attacked Blenheim where—quite uselessly—12,000 French troops were bottled up. Two assaults, in which Rowe and one-third of his men were killed, were beaten back but had served their purpose. In the center Prince Holstein-Beck's Germans attacking Oberglau were in trouble until Marlborough got Austrian cavalry from Eugene to beat back the French cavalry with heavy losses. Holstein-Beck drove the French back to the village and kept them confined there for the rest of the battle.

By 3 P.M. the Elector was kept away from joining the French while the villages had been prevented from supporting Tallard's counterattack. Marlborough finally crossed with the rest of his army an hour later and at 4:30 P.M. came the welcome news that Eugene had driven the Elector from Lutzingen. Tallard finally realized that Marlborough had outmaneuvered him and rushed nine battalions to hold the position near Oberglau. It was "too little, too late." The battalions fought ferociously to hold their positions but were slaughtered to the last man where they stood while the much vaunted French cavalry fled into the waters and marshy banks of the Danube. By 5:30 P.M. the battle was over, with Tallard having fallen into British hands and the whole Franco-Bavarian army having ceased to exist as an organized military force. To their lasting honor the French garrisons of Blenheim and Oberglau held out until 9 P.M. when they too had finally had enough of the slaughter.

AFTERMATH

It had been neither an easy victory nor a bloodless one. One-fifth of the Allied army was gone—4,500 killed and 7,500 wounded—but this was nothing to the destruction wrought on the Franco-Bavarians who had lost 15,000 prisoners and 13,600 dead, wounded, and drowned in the Danube.

Marlborough had marched his army without the French being able to intercept or block his advance 250 miles (400km) into the heart of the enemy's territory, and gained one of the greatest victories in European military history, a victory that could be compared to Agincourt as France's reputation for military excellence and invincibility had been destroyed again. Europe was saved from French hegemony.

BRITISH OFFICERS

In order to defray the cost of maintaining large armies, monarchs often sold commissions. The more prestigious the rank and position, the greater was the purchase price. Although uniforms were standard by the eighteenth century, embellishments were initially permitted to reflect the individual's social and military stature. On the left is a British general, in the center an officer of engineers, and on the right a British Field Marshal. The latter appeared to prefer a less ostentatious display of his rank.

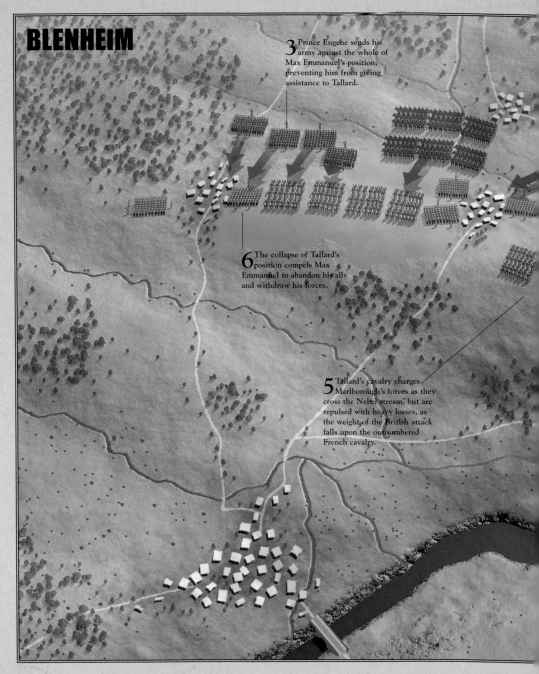

BLENHEIM

3 Prince Eugene sends his army against the whole of Max Emmanuel's position, preventing him from giving assistance to Tallard.

6 The collapse of Tallard's position compels Max Emmanuel to abandon his ally and withdraw his forces.

5 Tallard's cavalry charges Marlborough's forces as they cross the Nebel stream, but are repulsed with heavy losses, as the weight of the British attack falls upon the outnumbered French cavalry.

2 Holstein-Beck's German battalions attack Oberglau. The Germans manage to wrest the town on the second try.

4 Marlborough's main attack falls on Tallard's center. The French marshal deployed two ranks of cavalry with few infantry in reserve.

1 Marlborough attacks Blenheim with 20 battalions, pinning much of Tallard's infantry deployed in and around the town.

KEY

← ALLIED ARMY

← FRANCO-BAVARIAN ARMY

SARATOGA 1777

In the fall of 1777, the British Major General John Burgoyne moved his army southward through the rebellious colony of New York, toward Albany, in the main thrust of a three-pronged offensive. Rather than victory, Burgoyne found frustration, hardship, and eventually surrender following a series of battles, which ended at Saratoga.

With the colonial rebellion in its third year, the Continental Army under General George Washington (1732–99) had accomplished precious little against the stalwart British. The redcoats occupied the city of New York and had seized the initiative. Only the minor victories at Trenton and Princeton the previous December lifted the rebel spirits, countering the memories of repeated reverses on the battlefield and a harsh winter encampment at Morristown, New Jersey. What the British could not destroy from without, rivalry and jealousy among the American commanders threatened to destroy from within. The Revolutionary leader John Adams (1735–1826) called 1777 the "year of the hangman" because its

SARATOGA FACTS

Who: The British General John Burgoyne (1722–92) and a force of British regulars, Indians and German mercenaries numbering 8,000 faced 7,000 Continental soldiers and frontier riflemen under the command of General Horatio Gates (1727–93) and subordinates Benedict Arnold (1741–1801) and Daniel Morgan (1736–1802).

What: In the climax of his ill-fated campaign, Burgoyne was compelled to surrender the remnants of his army at Saratoga following crushing defeats at the battles of Freeman's Farm and Bemis Heights.

Where: Eastern New York in the valley of the Hudson River north of Albany.

When: October 17, 1777.

Why: The British determined a grand strategy to split New England, the hotbed of revolutionary ardor, from the remaining colonies.

Outcome: The turning point of the American war for independence, the surrender of an entire British army in the field at Saratoga convinced France to enter the conflict on the side of the Americans.

MARKSMAN IN ACTION: *while soldiers of other military units look on, a buckskin-clad member of Morgan's Riflemen demonstrates his marksmanship skills during a training exercise.*

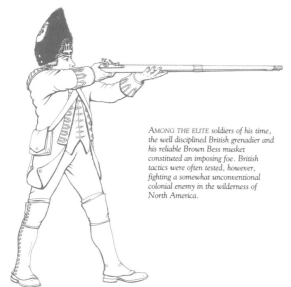

AMONG THE ELITE soldiers of his time, the well disciplined British grenadier and his reliable Brown Bess musket constituted an imposing foe. British tactics were often tested, however, fighting a somewhat unconventional colonial enemy in the wilderness of North America.

appearance resembled three gallows. Nevertheless, as long as there were rebel armies in the field the struggle for independence remained alive. From the British perspective, the opportunity seemed ripe for a decisive campaign to divide the colonies and ultimately conquer.

GRAND STRATEGY

For some time, British strategists, both political and military, had advocated a bold stroke from supply bases in Canada and into the Hudson River Valley of New York. A successful effort would isolate New England from the rest of the colonies and hasten the defeat of the "upstart" colonials. Major General John Burgoyne, a card-playing social climber who owed much of the rank and privilege he enjoyed to having married well, offered a tactical scenario for such an undertaking. Burgoyne proposed a coordinated offensive from three directions.

He intended to take personal command of a force, which included more than 4,000 British regulars, 3,000 German mercenaries, and several hundred French-Canadian militiamen and Indians. Because suitable roads were virtually nonexistent along his intended line of advance, Burgoyne would take his army by boat from the vicinity of Montreal down Lake Champlain and then overland to the town of Albany. A second British force, numbering 800 redcoats and Canadians commanded by Colonel   Barry St. Leger, was to advance southwest up the St. Lawrence River, cross Lake Ontario, and march up the valley of the

Mohawk River to rendezvous with Burgoyne at Albany. The third British thrust would be undertaken by General William Howe (1729–1814) and a portion of the 16,000 troops in garrison at New York City. Howe was to advance northward along the Hudson and tie up any American troops that might be detached to oppose Burgoyne. Howe was not expected to cover the entire distance to Albany, roughly 200 miles (320km) away.

FORT TICONDEROGA

On June 13, 1777, Burgoyne set off on his expedition down Lake Champlain. Three weeks later, his combined force reached the first significant barrier to the advance. Fort Ticonderoga had been built by the French in 1755, and earthworks raised for additional defenses during previous wars dotted the surrounding landscape. In the spring of 1775, Americans under the command of Ethan Allen and Benedict Arnold had captured the fort, and now a garrison of 2,500 under General Arthur St. Clair opposed the British offensive.

Although Fort Ticonderoga itself provided a formidable obstacle, it was evident to commanders on both sides that the position was vulnerable to artillery bombardment from surrounding hills, which commanded the approaches to the fort. St Clair's force was too small in number to adequately defend Ticonderoga, much less the surrounding hills. As Burgoyne issued orders for artillery to be dragged up nearby Mount Defiance, St. Clair had no option except to evacuate.

LOAD AND FIRE

The cartridge and musket were introduced widely in the latter decades of the seventeenth century. The paper cartridge contained both the powder and ball. The musketeer tore open the cartridge with his teeth, poured the powder into the barrel, followed by the ball, and finally the paper for wadding.

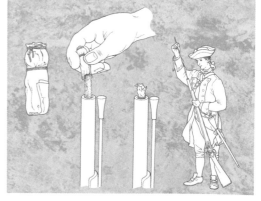

AMERICAN INFANTRYMEN

Infantrymen of the fledgling Continental Army, inexperienced and often ill equipped, demonstrated a remarkable resolve when under capable leadership. Enduring tremendous hardship, their eventual victory was bolstered by militia, irregular units, and the intervention of the French military.

On July 6, Fort Ticonderoga fell virtually without a shot being fired. The following day, three regiments of St. Clair's rearguard, commanded by Colonel Seth Warner, were surprised by British units under General Simon Fraser at Hubbardton, southeast of Ticonderoga. One American regiment was overwhelmed while preparing breakfast. The remaining colonials rallied and fought in small groups from the cover of the forest. When Fraser ordered a flanking movement, it became apparent that the Americans might become trapped, and Warner instructed his men to flee the area and make their way to Manchester individually.

Burgoyne continued his southward march, first along Wood Creek to Fort Ann, and then through a tangle of brambles and thickets to Fort Edward on the Hudson. The hit-and-run tactics of the colonials harassed the British every step of the way, and nearly four weeks passed along the trail.

BENNINGTON

By the time they emerged from the wilderness at Fort Edward, Burgoyne's exhausted troops were short of food and supplies. Lieutenant Colonel Friedrich Baum, who commanded the Brunswick Dragoons, a mercenary unit, proposed a foraging expedition into an area called the New Hampshire Grants. Although Burgoyne expected Baum's force of 800 men to encounter little opposition, Colonel John Stark had assembled a rebel army of about 1,500 men at Bennington during the first week of August.

When Baum became aware of Stark's presence, he ordered his troops to dig in and urgently requested reinforcements. The American commander was intent on attacking and developed a complicated plan for double envelopment of the enemy position. On August 16, Stark ordered attacks against both British flanks, stirring his soldiers by shouting, "There they are! We'll beat them before night, or Molly Stark will be a widow!"

With more than 1,000 men, Stark charged the British entrenchments head-on. The attack developed flawlessly and both British flanks were driven back. The center, however, where the dragoons were posted, held firm, the cavalrymen wielding sabers when their ammunition ran out. But when an American musket ball felled Baum, his men became disorganized and gave way. Burgoyne had detached another 600 German soldiers to reinforce Baum, but they arrived too late to save their shattered comrades. Nevertheless, the Americans had become confused themselves during the pursuit of their fleeing enemy, and the relief force nearly succeeded in turning the tables on Stark.

At an opportune moment, Warner appeared on the field with 300 colonials, and the Americans renewed their assault. The Germans broke and fled in panic, leaving 200 dead and up to 700 prisoners. American casualties were only 30 dead and 40 wounded. Burgoyne was shocked by the defeat at Bennington, but his entire plan was beginning to unravel.

REDOUBTS OF THE PERIOD were constructed from sloped earthen works, supported by wooden pillsades and fronted by jagged, cut-down trees and thorns from nearby woods.

ORISKANY

While Burgoyne was trudging through the wilds of the New York countryside, St. Leger embarked from Fort Oswego on July 25. Eight days later, his troops came upon Fort Stanwix, situated at the site of modern-day Rome, New York. Recently reinforced, Fort Stanwix also had provisions that could last for several weeks. The American commander, Colonel Peter Gansevoort, refused a British demand for surrender, and St. Leger settled in for a siege.

Two American relief columns advanced toward Fort Stanwix, one consisting of 900 soldiers under Benedict Arnold, and the other of 800 colonial militia raised in the surrounding area and commanded by Colonel Nicolas Herkimer. When St. Leger realized that he was in for a fight, he dispatched 400 Indians and loyalists to ambush Herkimer in a wooded ravine about six miles from Fort Stanwix. Meanwhile, Gansevoort sent a raiding party from the fort to attack the British encampment.

On the morning of August 6, the Indians and loyalists surrounded and fell upon Herkimer. For an hour, they held the upper hand. Then heavy showers intervened, and the Americans regrouped and counterattacked. Under the weight of their enemy's greater numbers, the Indians and loyalists retreated. Both sides had suffered more than 150 killed in what is now remembered as the battle of Oriskany.

When Gansevoort had dispatched his raiding party, many of the British troops in St. Leger's command were busy hacking away brush from the banks of Wood Creek in an attempt to establish a solid line of communication with Fort Oswego. The raiders destroyed much of the British camp,

PERCHED IN A TREE, *a colonial militiaman fells a British regular with a single shot from his Kentucky long rifle. American militiamen were among the first sharpshooters to employ successful sniper tactics against a regular army.*

particularly damaging that of the Indians, who decided to withdraw. St. Leger's strength was greatly diminished, and he was also aware of Arnold's approach to Fort Stanwix. Therefore, his only alternative was to lift the siege and retrace his steps to Fort Oswego. One prong of the British offensive had been decisively broken.

Back in New York City, Sir William Howe was under no obligation to follow Burgoyne's plan to the letter. Rather than advancing up the Hudson Valley, Howe decided to move against George Washington's army near Philadelphia. His reasons for doing this remain the subject of conjecture to this day. Howe's subordinate, Sir Henry Clinton (1738–95), did send a message to Burgoyne offering to move up the Hudson with a relatively small force.

Clinton proceeded to capture two American forts on the Hudson, sliced through a barrier of chains and logs the colonials had placed across the river, and forced the rebels to burn a small fleet they had assembled upstream. When a third fort fell to the British, Clinton had played his last card. The obstacle of distance proved to be one which he could not overcome. It was October, and Burgoyne was still more than 100 miles (160km) away.

FREEMAN'S FARM

Along with the battle of Bemis Heights, fought on October 7, the action at Freeman's Farm on September 19, 1777 was the decisive action of the Saratoga campaign. In mid-August, Horatio Gates had replaced General Philip Schuyler as commander of the main American army in the north. Burgoyne had suffered serious casualties at Bennington, while Gates' number of effectives increased with the return of Benedict Arnold from Fort Stanwix and successful recruiting spurred by news of atrocities committed by Indians allied to the British.

Occupying a strong position at Bemis Heights, Gates became aware that Burgoyne had crossed the Hudson and marched southward in September. Gates deployed his forces with three infantry brigades and massed artillery to his right, nearest the river, 2,000 soldiers under Brigadier Ebenezer Learned in the center, and the combined forces of Benedict Arnold and Daniel Morgan, numbering about 2,000, on his left. One major concern was that the British might skirt the American left flank and occupy nearby high ground, forcing the Americans out of their position with artillery fire.

For this reason, Arnold strongly urged Gates to allow him to attack the British first. Gates, however, waited for Burgoyne to join the battle. When Burgoyne moved three divisions forward on the morning of September 19, Gates ordered Morgan's riflemen, crack shots to a man, forward. As they concentrated their fire on British officers, Morgan's men goaded the redcoats into a charge. Arnold committed his reserve force and pushed the British, under General John

FAMED ARTIST JOHN TRUMBULL captured the surrender of General John Burgoyne and British forces at Saratoga to the Continental Army under General Horatio Gates. To the left of Gates, wearing buckskin, stands General Daniel Morgan, whose command played a key role in the victory.

Hamilton, to the breaking point. When Arnold requested reinforcements, Gates refused and ordered Arnold to retire to the American lines. Arnold did not respond to the order and continued to attack. Only the arrival of 1,100 fresh troops under the command of the German General Baron von Riedesel managed to drive Arnold back. In the evening gloom, Burgoyne counted his losses at 600, twice that of the Americans, who still held the high ground.

BEMIS HEIGHTS

When Burgoyne took stock of his situation after the fight at Freeman's Farm, the tally was disconcerting. Supplies were inadequate, his strength had been reduced through combat, desertion, and disease. He was on his own. No help was forthcoming from other British armies. Still, one decisive blow against Gates might save the campaign for the British. From their positions around Freeman's Farm, the British advanced, 1,500 strong under the command of Simon Fraser, to probe the American positions around Bemis Heights. Fraser's movement was discovered, and Gates again sent Morgan forward to exact a toll on the British. Morgan hit Fraser's right at the edge of a wheatfield, while Enoch Poor's 800-man brigade hit the left. Both flanks collapsed and exposed Riedesel's Germans in the center to attack by Learned's brigade.

A growing animosity between Gates and Arnold had erupted into open contempt, and Gates replaced his unruly subordinate with General Benjamin Lincoln. During the battle of Bemis Heights, Arnold was officially without a command. He did not, however, stay out of the fight. Arnold galloped to the sound of the guns and shouted to Learned's attacking troops to follow him. Riedesel's veterans broke, and Fraser was shot dead trying to patch together a second line of defense. With Fraser's reconnaissance force shattered, Arnold exhorted his men to attack a pair of British fortifications at Freeman's Farm. The first, Balcarre's redoubt, was flanked and captured as its German defenders threw down their arms. A short time later, Breymann's redoubt also fell to the Americans. Arnold, however, had been seriously wounded in the leg during the fighting at Breymann's. It was the same leg which had suffered a wound at Quebec. Had Arnold died during the Battle of Bemis Heights, he would certainly have been remembered as one of the great heroes of the American Revolution. Instead, his betrayal of his fledgling country in a bargain with the British has made his name synonymous with treason.

When the fighting ended, the British had lost another 600 soldiers. In comparison, American casualties were relatively light at 150.

AFTERMATH

Leaving casualties behind, the British tramped toward the high ground around the village of Saratoga the following day. At first, the commander agreed with his officers that a fighting retreat to Fort Edward might be accomplished. He later reconsidered and opened negotiations for surrender. On October 17, 1777, the surrender of Burgoyne at Saratoga altered the course of the American war for independence.

SARATOGA

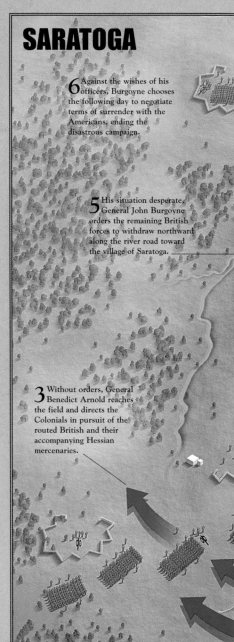

6 Against the wishes of his officers, Burgoyne chooses the following day to negotiate terms of surrender with the Americans, ending the disastrous campaign.

4 Initially repulsed, the Americans eventually capture a pair of British redoubts. While directing the effort, Arnold is seriously wounded in the leg by a musket ball.

5 His situation desperate, General John Burgoyne orders the remaining British forces to withdraw northward along the river road toward the village of Saratoga.

3 Without orders, General Benedict Arnold reaches the field and directs the Colonials in pursuit of the routed British and their accompanying Hessian mercenaries.

2 Daniel Morgan's frontier riflemen spearhead a devastating assault on the British left, while 800 more Colonials assail their exposed right flank.

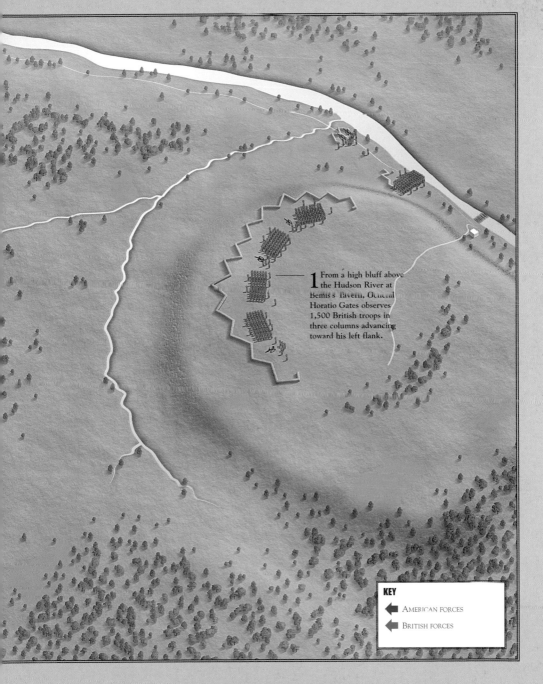

1 From a high bluff above the Hudson River at Bemis's Tavern, General Horatio Gates observes 1,500 British troops in three columns advancing toward his left flank.

KEY

← AMERICAN FORCES

← BRITISH FORCES

TRAFALGAR 1805

Nelson's victory at Trafalgar finally ended the threat of French invasion of the British Isles and secured the Royal Navy's dominance of the seas for the next 100 years. But at the moment of his greatest triumph, Britain's foremost naval hero was killed on the deck of his flagship HMS Victory.

N elson's victory at Trafalgar 200 years ago is the most famous and decisive naval battle of all times. But, often forgotten, is that it was the product of Napoleon's plans to invade Britain. By the spring of 1805 Napoleon had assembled some 2,000 gunboats and transports in the French Channel ports to ferry an army of 167,000 veteran troops to the coast of Kent. For the invasion to succeed Napoleon had to be sure the Royal Navy was safely lured out of the Channel when his ramshackle flotilla of barges and flat-bottomed boats sailed out of Boulogne and Calais.

Napoleon had a justified contempt for his own navy but this time he needed its support if he was to destroy his most dangerous foe. Unfortunately, Napoleon had a knack for appointing the wrong men to crucial posts when it came to sea warfare and

TRAFALGAR FACTS

Who: The combined Franco-Spanish fleet of 33 ships of the line under Admiral Pierre Villeneuve (1763–1806) versus a British fleet of 27 ships of the line under Vice Admiral Lord Horatio Nelson (1758–1805).

What: Nelson's head-on attack on the Franco-Spanish line broke their formation and allowed the superior gunnery of the British ships to destroy the enemy in detail.

Where: At the western entrance to the Straits of Gibraltar off Cape Trafalgar, Spain.

When: October 21, 1805.

Why: Nelson, having chased the Franco-Spanish Fleet around the world, caught up with it in the Straits of Gibraltar and

Villeneuve chose—for personal reasons—to fight rather than flee.

Outcome: The Combined Fleet, despite heroic resistance, was smashed and Britain had removed, for good, the threat of a French invasion.

THIS PRINT, after the painting, "Trafalgar" by William Overend, was published in the Illustrated Sporting and Dramatic News in 1905 with the title, "'The Hero of Trafalgar' Nelson on Board the Victory, October 21st 1805." Nelson is shown standing on the right on the deck of the Victory, facing fixedly ahead while the battle rages around him.

LORD HORATIO NELSON, as painted by Sir William Beechey (1753–1839), the English landscape and portrait painter.

when he picked Count Pierre Villeneuve he had truly excelled himself. Not only had he survived Aboukir Bay (1798), thus acquiring a life-long terror of Nelson, but Villeneuve detested Napoleon's person and politics. Villeneuve, quite rightly, did not think much of Napoleon's confused and wooly ideas when it came to naval strategy— and especially his plan to lure Nelson to the West Indies with Villeneuve's squadron that sailed out of Toulon on March 30. At that very time Nelson was sailing in the balmy Mediterranean waters between Sardinia and Sicily expecting Villeneuve to set sail for Egypt. It was only on April 18 that he knew that the French fleet was heading west into the Atlantic.

On May 12, with 10 ships of the line and three frigates Nelson headed out into the Atlantic bound for the West Indies. Four days later Villeneuve had reached Martinique where he was determined to stay until Admiral Ganteaume with his 21 sail of the line joined him from Brest. But Villeneuve had to begin sailing back to European waters to support Napoleon's landings by June 22 at the latest. On May 26 six Spanish ships of the line under command of Admiral Federico Gravina (1757–1806) joined them, bringing the Combined Fleet to 21 ships of the line.

CALDER'S ACTION

Meanwhile Nelson had again been fed faulty intelligence, so when he reached the West Indies he sailed south to Trinidad rather than north. He had missed the elusive enemy again. Nelson's colleague, the Channel Fleet commander, Admiral Sir Robert Calder (1745–1845), had more luck because he ran into the Combined Fleet at Cape Finisterre on July 22. Calder had 15 ships of the line facing Villeneuve's 21 ships of the line and seven frigates. An indecisive action, hampered by thick fog, ensued in which Calder captured two Spanish ships and damaged four others, while suffering only four ships damaged and 199 casualties among his own squadron. Both fleets sailed off in opposite directions on July 27.

Although Calder thought he had done well, the failure to destroy the Combined Fleet led to criticism at home, and Calder demanded a court-martial to clear his name. Calder's only consolation was that Villeneuve's performance was considered even worse.

Ungraciously the French commander blamed Gravina and the Spanish for the defeat at Finisterre when in fact the Spanish had fought splendidly, as Napoleon—an inveterate Hispanophobe—had to admit a month later.

DEATH FROM ABOVE could come from weapons such as this coehoorn mortar in platforms called "fighting tops." Fire from marine marksman and blasts of shot could clear the upper decks of an enemy warship, rendering her immobile, or "decapitate" a foe by selective fire at officers.

NELSON AT CADIZ

Nelson had nothing to celebrate either as he returned one last time to England on August 19. He had expected boos and catcalls but he was feted and praised on all sides. Even the stone-faced Premier, William Pitt, gave him his full backing. The same day that Nelson returned to take command of the British blockading squadron at Cadiz—September 29—the Admiral celebrated his 47th birthday. He looked, with his almost white hair, sunken face, and small, maimed body at least a decade older.

Old-looking he may have been but Nelson was his usual fighting self. He perked up when Pitt's promise of aid was quite unexpectedly fulfilled—by October 15 Nelson had some 27 ships of the line and five frigates. The frigates were under the command of Captain Sir Henry Blackwood (1770–1832), standing off some 3 miles (4.8km) from shore to keep an eye on the Combined Fleet in Cadiz. The Combined Fleet numbered 2,600 sailors and 33 ships of the line to Nelson's 27 ships and 2,100 sailors. (Most of Nelson's ships, despite the supposed ubiquity of the press gangs, were undermanned compared to the enemy.)

Nelson planned that, once the Combined Fleet sailed out of Cadiz, he would attack the enemy in two columns at right angles to their line, thus breaking it up and then isolating and destroying the rearmost part before the vanguard could support it. Nelson may have thought this was a "secret" plan but Villeneuve—who had studied Nelson closely—realized immediately that this was what Nelson was going to do. Villeneuve may have been a timid and uninspiring commander of men, but he was no fool, and his actions on October 21 proved he was no coward either.

DISPOSITIONS

The Combined Fleet began to sail out of Cadiz during the early hours of Saturday October 19 but they had only reached the entrance of the Straits of Gibraltar two days later. The Franco-Spanish battle line, if one could call it that, was a straggling and scattered confusion of ships 9 miles (14.4km) long. This morning, Monday October 21, would be fateful for both sides as a growing groundswell gave indication of an Atlantic storm coming their way.

Originally heading into the Mediterranean, Villeneuve gave orders for the entire fleet to reverse course because he was determined to die in battle and not have to face the odious Corsican's wrath should he escape to Naples. By 10 A.M. his fleet—in the shape of an irregular crescent with wide spaces between the vessels—had finally changed direction. Admiral Le Pelley's Division now formed the vanguard while Gravina's tough Spaniards—who should have been in the lead—became the rearguard. An hour later Villeneuve observed how Nelson's fleet bore down on them in two separate columns readying themselves for battle.

GUN DECK

Three-tiered gundecks marked the "First Rate" capital ships of the Age of Fighting Sail. On the top deck the loaded cannon is run out on its truck through the open gun port, ready to fire upon the approaching enemy. The middle deck depicts a fired cannon rolling back into ship from the recoil of its shot, where it will be cleaned and reloaded by the gun crew. The lowest deck shows a gun secured against the closed gun port for sea worthiness. A "loose cannon" was more than metaphorically dangerous in a ship rolling and pitching in heavy weather.

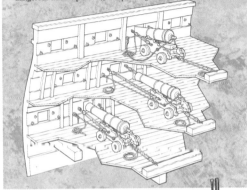

As for the British they had readied themselves for battle since 6 A.M. Nelson was determined to give chase and catch up with the fleeing Combined Fleet in order to destroy Napoleon's naval arm. To his and the other British commanders' utter astonishment the enemy, at 8:40 A.M. reversed direction, and headed back west—straight at them! As usual, Nelson was determined to take the lead with HMS *Victory* (his 100-gun flagship) but his commanders warned him that this would make him a sitting target for the enemy's fire. Nelson brushed aside the idea that he should let

ALL NAVIES *of the period used onboard marines to pour musket fire on the crews of enemy ships from the rigging. It is a French marine from the Redoutable that is thought to have killed Nelson when the two ships were engaged in a point-blank exchange of fire.*

ABOVE: *THREE TIERS OF GUNS protrude from the side of HMS Victory. First laid down in 1759, HMS Victory was a first-rate ship of the line with 100 guns and a complement of more than 850 men. In July 1803, she became Admiral Nelson's flagship, and he is said to have only spent 25 days off the ship from that time until his death.*

his deputy Admiral Collingwood's squadron take the lead. The winds were west-north-west, favoring the British and the clouds were gray and compact as the distance between the enemy fleets shrank with alarming rapidity. At 11 A.M. Nelson hoisted a unique but morale-boosting, if patently obvious, signal to his Fleet: "England expects that every man will do his duty." There was an almighty roar of approval from officers and men across the British fleet as the signal was read and understood.

THE BATTLE

Forty-five minutes later the first hesitant firing began as Villeneuve, on his flagship *Bucentaure* (80 guns), gingerly hoisted his pennant. Nelson, by contrast, was on the poop deck of the *Victory*, as he made—at 11:50 A.M.—his last signal for the Fleet to "Engage the enemy more closely." By 12:04 P.M. *Victory*'s massive oak sides were being showered with shot from *Bucentaure* (concentrating her fire against *Victory*'s port quarter), *Redoutable*, *Héros*, and the Spanish behemoth—the 136-gun *Santissíma Trinidad*, the flagship of Admiral Baltazar de Cisneros.

While these fired broadsides against *Victory* the French and Spanish sharpshooters on the decks and in the masts swept *Victory*'s decks with musket fire. *Victory*'s wheel was smashed, forcing her to be steered from below deck, Nelson's secretary John Scott was killed, the mizzen topmast was shot away, and all the other masts were damaged. *Victory* finally passed under the stern of the *Bucentaure*, and unleashed a devastating double-shotted raking broadside through her stern galleries, dismounting 20 guns and killing dozens of her crew. The rest of the fleet followed, breaking the Franco-Spanish line just as Nelson had planned and the battle became a mêlée of individual ship-to-ship actions where superior British gunnery would dominate.

By 1:10 P.M. *Victory* was entangled with the French *Redoutable* commanded by Captain Jean-Jacques Lucas—a firebrand Provençal—who inspired his crew to fight ferociously against their British enemy. In a matter of minutes the accurate and deadly French fire had killed 40 Marines. A sharpshooter aboard the *Redoutable* hit Nelson with a shot that penetrated the Admiral's shoulder, lung, and pierced his spine.

Now and for the next two hours the battle was at its fiercest. The *Redoubtable* was now under fire from both sides as the 98-gun HMS *Téméraire* joined the fight. At 1:40 P.M. the *Téméraire* raked the *Redoubtable*—by now a wreck—with repeated broadsides but Lucas and his brave crew refused to

CANNON OF CAST IRON mounted on rolling wooden trucks were a cheap and functional weapon for every size of warship. Broad wheels let the cannon roll over the gundecks while crews checked the recoil with hawsers. The corkscrew-like worm, shown left, was used to remove the burning remnants of the expended powder bag, and the sponge and bucket used to wash the gun out.

strike their colors until *Téméraire* was in as equally miserable shape as their own vessel. Finally Lucas and his men—utterly exhausted—surrendered. The *Redoutable* ship had lost 487 killed and 81 wounded including Lucas—a staggering 88 percent of its crew!

By 2:30 P.M. the *Santissíma Trinidad* too was a complete wreck but when a British boarding party stepped onto the deck a Spanish officer told them that the proud flagship had not capitulated despite being unable to fire a single gun. It would be hours until she was finally seized by the British. *Bucentaure* was also, by 4:15 P.M., out of commission with 450 casualties, hardly a crew member still standing, her three captains wounded.

Villeneuve, who had been standing completely still during the whole ordeal hoping with all his heart to be killed, did not have a scratch on him when his crippled flagship surrendered to Captain Israel Pellew of the *Conqueror*. Fifteen minutes later, at 4:30 P.M., his surgeon William Beatty being unable to do anything for him, Nelson died knowing that his beloved fleet had won a great victory. By this time Collingwood had smashed most of the Spanish squadron under Admiral Gravina, well to the southwest of

"THE DEATH OF NELSON" by Daniel Maclise (1806–70). This large painting shows Nelson after he was shot by a sniper on board the French ship Redoubtable. He must have been an easy target in his undress uniform of Vice Admiral, despite the smoke of battle.

the main battle area. The Spanish, like the French, put up a ferocious defense of their ships but were in the end defeated by the more experienced British.

AFTERMATH

At the end of the battle, 17 ships of the Combined Fleet were in British hands, and another one was a blazing wreck. Of the 15 survivors, four were taken at the battle of Cape Ortegal on November 4 and only 11 made it back to Cadiz under the badly wounded Gravina. A storm blew up after the battle, however, forcing the British to scuttle many of their hard-won prizes.

The news of Nelson's victory reached England on November 6, where rejoicing at the defeat of the enemy fleet and the end of the invasion threat was tempered by grief at the loss of the nation's greatest hero. The Battle of Trafalgar, one of the most decisive victories in naval history, was the beginning of a century of almost unrivaled dominance for the Royal Navy.

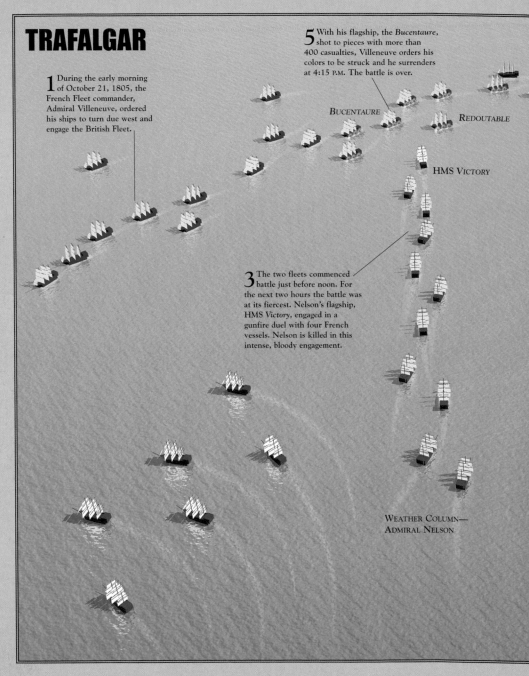

TRAFALGAR

1 During the early morning of October 21, 1805, the French Fleet commander, Admiral Villeneuve, ordered his ships to turn due west and engage the British Fleet.

5 With his flagship, the *Bucentaure*, shot to pieces with more than 400 casualties, Villeneuve orders his colors to be struck and he surrenders at 4:15 P.M. The battle is over.

BUCENTAURE

REDOUTABLE

HMS VICTORY

3 The two fleets commenced battle just before noon. For the next two hours the battle was at its fiercest. Nelson's flagship, HMS *Victory*, engaged in a gunfire duel with four French vessels. Nelson is killed in this intense, bloody engagement.

WEATHER COLUMN—
ADMIRAL NELSON

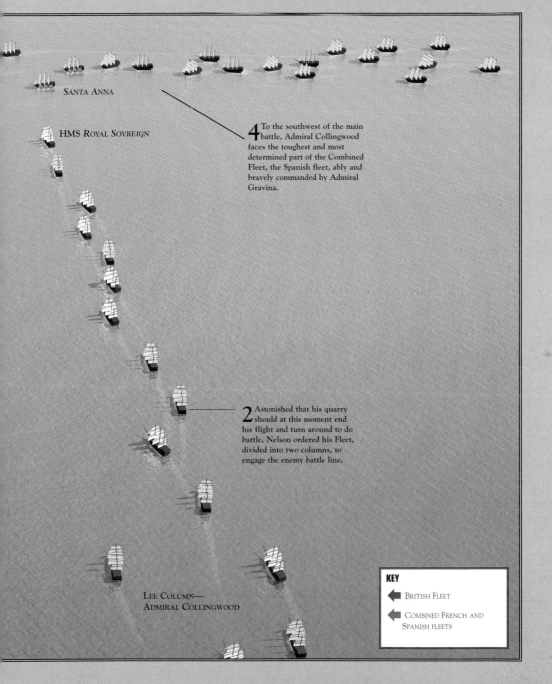

SANTA ANNA

HMS ROYAL SOVREIGN

4 To the southwest of the main battle, Admiral Collingwood faces the toughest and most determined part of the Combined Fleet, the Spanish fleet, ably and bravely commanded by Admiral Gravina.

2 Astonished that his quarry should at this moment end his flight and turn around to do battle, Nelson ordered his Fleet, divided into two columns, to engage the enemy battle line.

LEE COLUMN— ADMIRAL COLLINGWOOD

KEY

◄ BRITISH FLEET

◄ COMBINED FRENCH AND SPANISH FLEETS

AUSTERLITZ 1805

A year after his coronation as emperor, in the culmination of the greatest campaign of his career, Napoleon defeated the combined armies of Russia and Austria at Austerlitz, where he, his generals and superbly trained troops displayed their prowess on the battlefield. But for all its genius, the victory at Austerlitz did not immediately bring peace.

Napoleon's campaign against the Third Coalition powers in late 1805 must be regarded as his greatest and that the battle itself Austerlitz in Bohemia a masterpiece of Napoleonic military leadership. The Allies (Austria, Britain, Russia, Sweden, and Naples) were certain of the swift and overwhelming defeat of Napoleon's brash, postrevolutionary army and parvenu "Empire." William Pitt and Czar Alexander I, the two main architects of this the largest coalition ever created against France, were going to attack Napoleon with 400,000 troops on a broad front stretching from Naples in the Mediterranean to Hanover and Pomerania on the Baltic. Napoleon could only hope to prevail if he moved fast, struck hard and divided

AUSTERLITZ FACTS

Who: The Emperor Napoleon (1769–1821) with 73,000 men defeat the combined armies of Imperial Russia, led by Czar Alexander I (1777–1825), and Austria lead by Emperor Francis II (1768–1835) totaling 85,000 troops.

What: Napoleon provoked the Allies into launching an attack on ground of his choosing, then occupied the Prätzen Heights in the center of the battlefield, dividing the enemy and defeating them.

Where: Near the village of Austerlitz in Bohemia, 70 miles (113km) north of Vienna.

When: December 2, 1805.

Why: The new revolutionary state in France and Napoleon's usurpation of the French throne were deeply threatening to the established monarchies of Europe who suspected that Napoleon sought to establish French hegemony across the continent.

Outcome: The Allied army was shattered. The French held the field, having dealt a major blow to the Third Coalition.

IN THIS OIL PAINTING NAPOLEON is seen inspecting and encouraging his troops in their bivouacs during the night prior to the battle on December 2, 1805 (by Baron Louis Albert Bacler D'Albe [1761-1848]).

THE CAMPAIGN

On September 8, 1805 an Austrian army, led by General Karl Mack (1752–1828), invaded Bavaria whose army of 22,000 did not challenge the enemy advance, allowing Mack to occupy Munich four days later. Mack moved his army westward to Ulm and Ingolstadt to keep an eye on the Black Forest (Schwarzwald) where he was sure the French would cross into southern Germany. An attack further north was blocked, or so Mack mistakenly believed, by the Prussian enclaves of Anspach and Bayreuth. Surely Napoleon would not dare to anger Prussia into joining the Allies by violating their territorial integrity.

his enemy before the more ponderous Austrians were ready. Napoleon had a grand total of 350,000 men under arms but it was only his Grande Armée—facing England along the Franco-Belgian Channel coast—194,000 strong, that could hope to meet and defeat the Austro-Russian army in Central Europe.

Napoleon had no such scruples. While he sent Murat's Cavalry Corps supported by Lannes V Corps through the Black Forest to keep Mack occupied. He sent the other five corps of his "Grand Armée d'Allemagne" in a huge wheel through Franconia and northern Bavaria. Murat crossed the Rhine at Strasbourg between September 25 and 27 while the rest of the Grande Armée crossed the Neckar River on October 1 aiming to reach the Danube and cut Mack's line

NAPOLEON RECEIVES NEWS of his victory at Austerlitz. An aide arrives with news that the French have broken the Allied lines and the enemy's defeated troops are retreating.

of retreat eastward. As yet Napoleon had no idea exactly where Mack's main army was and if they were—as he hoped—still at Ulm. He expected Mack to retreat toward Vienna before it was too late.

Four days later Mack had news that French troops had crossed the Anspach on their way south toward Donauwörth where, three days later, the Austrians lost 600 men trying to hold this vital position. It left Mack's main army cut off and surrounded at Ulm. Mack—made into a scapegoat by the Austrians—was not the fool that he was made out to be. He ordered his army to break through toward Bohemia cutting through the thinly held French lines and on October 11 he had a singularly successful encounter with the enemy. But the attack was not pressed home with any determination by either the officers—who detested Mack as a foreigner and reformer—and the troops who had lost faith in Mack and the other officers ability to lead them.

Mack's situation was now quite hopeless as the French noose around his army's neck was tightened with every passing day or even hour. He could see no point in further useless bloodshed and on October 25 his army, 24,000 strong, capitulated at Ulm. In all the misguided invasion of Bavaria cost the Austrians 60,000 of their best troops.

It was no wonder that the French troops, whose casualties were trifling, were astounded with their own success and how a ruthless and swift advance had spared them a pitched battle against an enemy who—as shown at Wagram four years later—should not be underestimated. Ulm, rather than Austerlitz, was the most brilliant showpiece of Napoleonic generalship in this campaign since the enemy had been outmaneuvered and forced to capitulate without any major loss of life on either side.

THE ALLIED PLAN

According to the Allies' half-baked "grand strategy" Mack should not have advanced at all before the Russians had arrived. The vanguard of the Russian expeditionary army, some 24,000 men, only reached Branau-am-Inn by the end of November when Ulm made all plans for an advance redundant. The Russian commander-in-chief, General Mikhail Kutuzov (1745–1813)—cautious, shrewd, and experienced—chose to retreat but he was only able to escape through some very fast marching and his subordinates deft handling of the rearguard. Here both General Miloradovich and the Georgian Prince, Peter Bagration, excelled in blocking, evading, and mauling the pursuing French.

On November 11 the last Austrian troops (11,000 strong) left Vienna for the concentration area in Bohemia where the Allied armies by the end of the month numbered 80,000. The following day the bands of the Grande Armée

entered this Imperial capital of 240,000 souls playing catchy marching songs. The Austrians, unlike the more determined and fanatical Russians in 1812, did not set fire to their capital and fight a guerrilla war.

Upon his arrival in Vienna—he was to occupy it again in 1809—Napoleon had good reason to review his situation. He had lost 50,000 men during this campaign and faced Archduke Charles with 85,000 men in Italy and the main Allied army in Bohemia. If they coordinated their attacks he would be crushed in the middle. There was little risk of this because Charles was determined to stay on the defensive: He distrusted the Russians more than he disliked the French and had opposed the war from the beginning. Charles' passivity ensured that there would be no Allied pincer-movement to strike Napoleon in the rear.

DISPOSITIONS

The second and main phase of the campaign had begun. Napoleon had only 53,000 men under his command by the time he reached Brünn (Brno) on November 23 and by that day the weather had suddenly turned cold. Napoleon, as was his habit, examined the ground and found the ideal battlefield around the Prätzen Heights, toward the small town of Austerlitz. Turning to his officers Napoleon said: "Gentlemen, examine this ground carefully. It is going to be a battlefield: You will have a part to play upon it".

THE FRENCH CURRASIERS were not only the most dapper cavalry in the French Army but under such dashing commanders as Murat and Marshal M. Ney (1769–1815) a deadly force on any battlefield.

It was here that Napoleon decided to trick the Allies into making a premature attack by having Soult and Lannes occupying the Prätzen Heights, Wischau, and Austerlitz. He then met Count Dolgoruki—the Czar's ADC—feigning anxiety and an uncharacteristic lack of self-confidence. All to fool the Allies into believing he was in weak position and seemingly anxious to avoid a battle with the superior Allied army. Then on November 30 Napoleon ordered Soult to withdraw his troops in some haste from Prätzen and Austerlitz itself. The Allies would then be tempted to attack.

During the following day, but without the enemy noticing, French generals Bernadotte and Davout—the latter having marched his troops nonstop from Vienna—had joined him thus evening out the numbers. By December 2, Napoleon had 73,000 men and 139 guns facing 85,400 Russian and Austrian troops with 278 guns. The Allies were still superior in numbers but with a massively reduced margain and their slight numerical superiority was more

than canceled out by the presence of Napoleon and the sheer qualitative superiority of the Grande Armée.

The Allies had decided to attack the French right with most of their army and roll up the French army while General Bagration in the north attacked along the Olmütz-Brünn road. Some 59,300 troops were to leave the Prätzen Heights, take the villages of Telnitz and Sokolnitz and then join up at Kobelnitz leaving the French Army pushed back to a line from Turas to Pantowitz. Then Kollowrath's Corps of 24,000 would strike at the hinge of the French line at Pantowitz and the French would be routed.

THE BATTLE BEGINS

The winter mist descended upon the battlefield playing havoc with the Allied plans and the Russian general, Langeron, pointed out that the Allied offensive would leave the key to the whole battlefield—the Prätzen Heights—completely undefended. Napoleon was not going to oblige the Allies, whose plan seemed amateurish and the trick of rolling up his left flank was too blunt to pass unnoticed. He had been told during the night by his spymaster, Savary, that the Allies were on the move. At 5 A.M. when he held his council of war Napoleon left Legrand and Davout with 18,600 men to hold the left while he concentrated the bulk of his army, 65,000 men, on his right.

Alexander I and Francis II had breakfast at the height of Stary Vinohrady where the Czar reprimanded Kutuzov for not getting his troops to advance more quickly. Kutuzov replied that he needed all the units to be in line before he could advance—which they finally did by 6 A.M. At the village of Telnitz the Austrian advance guard ran into heavy fire from the elite Corsican Legion—nicknamed the "Emperor's cousins." For an hour a fierce battle was fought around the small village until the French retreated.

Some 13,600 Russians, led by General Doctorov, could have realized the Allied plan had he pressed on and hit Napoleon's vulnerable and open flank. But Doctorov chose to await Langeron's Corps, which was delayed by a confusion of troop movements atop the Prätzen Heights. The delay in the Allied attack to 7 A.M. allowed the French to reform and during the morning hours 10,000 French troops held up the advance of 50,000 Russians and Austrians.

THE PRÄTZEN HEIGHTS

Napoleon had set up his field HQ on the nearby Zarlan Heights and at 8:45 A.M. he observed through his telescope how the Allies marched south, abandoning the crucial Prätzen Heights—a hillock that dominated the entire battlefield. Napoleon asked how long it would take for Soult's men—concealed at the bottom of the hill—to march up and seize the heights. Soult replied that it would take only 20 minutes. So Napoleon waited until the very last

AUSTRIAN DRAGOON

To match Napoleon's Cuirassiers, the Austrians had the elite dragoon, who were similarly attired and equipped as their feared French enemy. However, the Austrain dragoons lacked the fiersome reputation of their oponents. Heavy cavalry of this type were used as shock troops on the battlefield—either to force the issue through a massed frontal assault, or by turning a battle by quickly exploiting weaknesses or gaps in the enemy's lines.

THE FRENCH ARTILLERY arm were the best of their time. The attention, resources, and confidence that Napoleon devoted to his artillery often paid off in battle and showed clearly that the Emperor had been an artillery officer in his youth.

Allied troops had left Prätzen before he ordered Soult to advance.

Despite the French observing almost complete silence as they carefully advanced up the slope, their movement was observed and reported by a Russian officer to Kutuzov. The general ordered his firebrand deputy Miloradovich to retake the heights but it was too late, although the Russians made valiant efforts to dislodge Soult's force from the village of Prätzen. By 11 A.M. the height was held by Soult despite several failed attempts by the Russians to take it back. Both Kutuzov and the Czar were almost killed by the heavy French artillery fire.

Growing ever more desperate the Czar sent his brother, Grand Duke Constantine, and his 8,500 Imperial Guards—which had been kept in reserve—into the fray. These tall, handpicked troops advanced on the Prätzen Heights and broke through the first French line but the heavy musket and artillery fire proved too much. The attack did have an effect because many of the French troops broke and fled at the Russian onslaught. In their stampede this mass of fleeing humanity almost engulfed Napoleon's HQ.

By 2 P.M. there was nothing left of the Russian army's central position and Allied resistance was now disjointed and disorganized. In the streets of the village of Sokolnitz and around its venerable old castle dead, dying, and wounded lay in heaps. Davout, in an order that sullied his good reputation, gave orders for his troops to spare no Allied prisoners or wounded. However, large numbers of Allied troops escaped the French onslaught unscathed across the frozen ground and marshes.

AFTERMATH

As it began to snow the battle came to an end, with the French too exhausted to pursue the fleeing Allied troops. Napoleon had dealt a massive and fatal blow to the Third Coalition that left Austria crushed, Russia humiliated, and Britain shorn of its continental allies. The French had lost 9,000 men—a mere 12 percent of their numbers—while the Allies had lost almost one-third of their army, some 27,000 troops. Napoleon's army was also left in possession of the battlefield. Austerlitz was the zenith of French military power but it did not lead to peace on Napoleon's terms. It was only after two years of savage fighting against Prussia and Russia that these powers were, finally, in July 1807, forced to sue for peace with France at Tilsit.

THIS CANVAS by Antoine-Jean Gros (1771–1835) shows Napoleon and Austrian Emperor Francis II discussing peace terms following the battle.

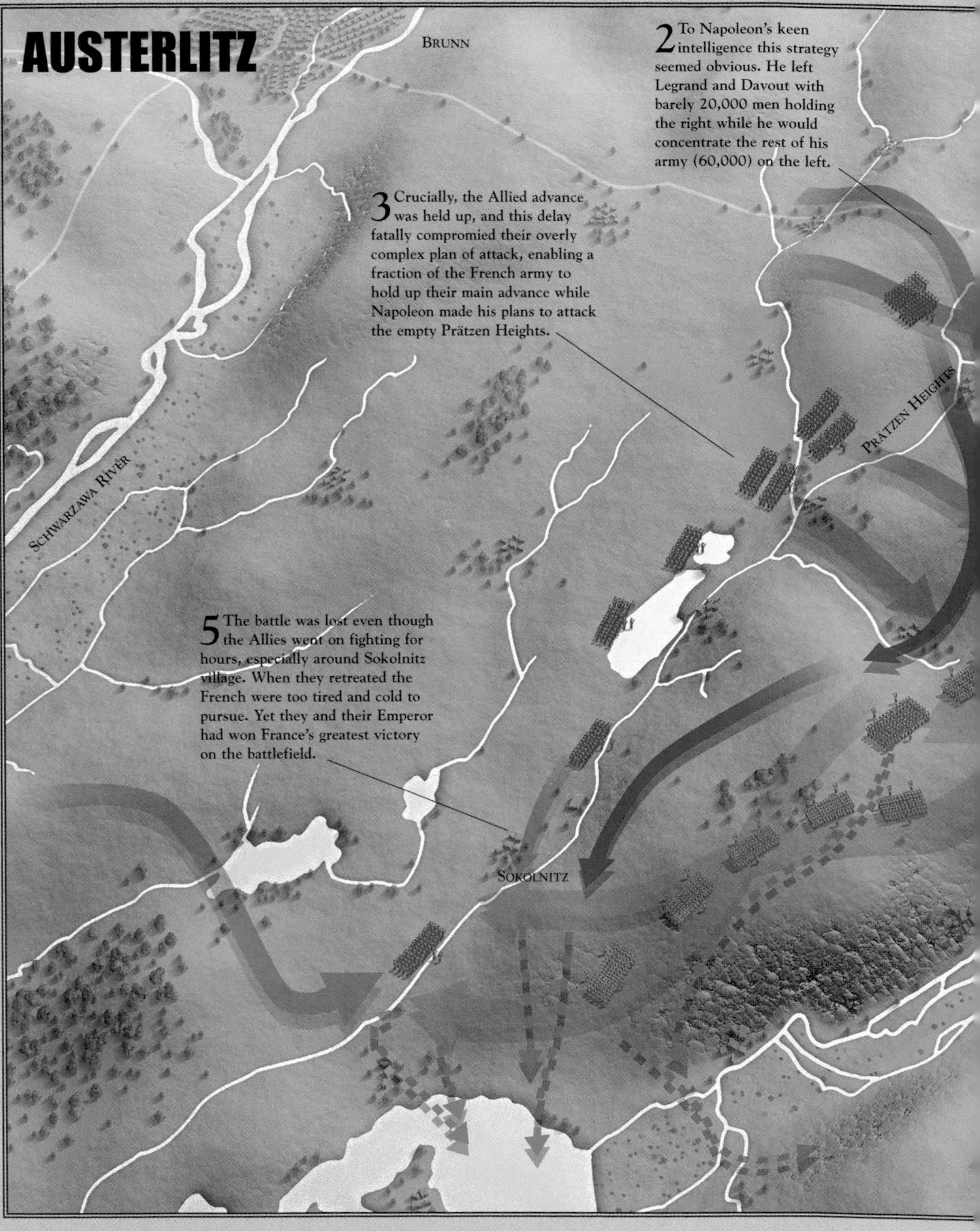

AUSTERLITZ

BRUNN

2 To Napoleon's keen intelligence this strategy seemed obvious. He left Legrand and Davout with barely 20,000 men holding the right while he would concentrate the rest of his army (60,000) on the left.

3 Crucially, the Allied advance was held up, and this delay fatally compromised their overly complex plan of attack, enabling a fraction of the French army to hold up their main advance while Napoleon made his plans to attack the empty Prätzen Heights.

5 The battle was lost even though the Allies went on fighting for hours, especially around Sokolnitz village. When they retreated the French were too tired and cold to pursue. Yet they and their Emperor had won France's greatest victory on the battlefield.

SCHWARZAWA RIVER

SOKOLNITZ

4 Soult's Corps marched up the heights and before the Allies realized what had happened seized this crucial position at the center of the battlefield. Too late, Kutuzov, sent General Miloradovich to retake the heights but repeated assaults failed to dislodge the stubborn French defenders.

AUSTERLITZ

1 The Allied grand strategy was simple and effective—at least on paper. While Bagration in the north diverted Napoleon's attentions, the bulk of the Russo-Austrian army would attack from the Pratzen Heights and link up behind Napoleon's lines with Kollowrath's Corps.

KEY

FRENCH ARMY

RUSSIAN & AUSTRIAN FORCES

WATERLOO 1815

The final battle of the Napoleonic Wars saw the French Emperor's ambitions crushed once and for all. Despite flashes of his former brilliance in the campaign, Napoleon was unable to break up the Allied armies, and his fate was sealed by the Prussians marching to Wellington's aid on June 18 rather than falling back after their reverse at Ligny.

Revolutionary, then Napoleonic, France had been fighting Britain and her allies for 20 years when, finally, Napoleon abdicated in April 1814 and was exiled to the island of Elba. But discontent in France with the Bourbon King, Louis XVIII, led to Napoleon risking a passage from the island with 1,000 men for France, where he landed on March 1, 1815. Louis was forced to flee to Belgium while the Allies began to mobilize their armies. Napoleon sincerely wished for peace but the other European powers could never permit him to threaten peace again and he was therefore obliged to mobilize eight corps. Tired of war and bloodshed the French were reluctant to pay taxes and place recruits at the Emperor's disposal. The troops were

WATERLOO FACTS

Who: The Emperor Napoleon (1769–1821) with 72,000 men of the French Armée du Nord attacked an Anglo-Netherlandish army of 60,000 men under the Duke of Wellington (1769–1852), who was joined by Prince Gebhard von Blücher's Prussian army that evening.

What: In a superb defensive battle, Wellington's army was able, with great difficulty, to hold off Napoleon's disjointed attacks until the Prussian army arrived.

Where: The ridge of Mont St. Jean, near the village of Waterloo, 10 miles (16km) south of Brussels in Belgium.

When: June 18, 1815.

Why: Napoleon's escape from Elba and restoration of the Empire could not be tolerated by the Allies, who sought to crush this threat to European peace.

Outcome: Defeat at Waterloo forced Napoleon's second abdication, after which he was finally exiled to St. Helena in the South Atlantic.

A CLASSICAL PAINTING of Marshal Ney's cuirassiers with foaming horses and waving black plumes riding with death-defying courage against the indomitable squares of red-coated infantry.

weary as were the officers and even Napoleon's own marshals—most of whom owed their rank and wealth to his patronage—were reluctant to fight. This was especially true of Ney who disliked Napoleon as a tyrant who would plunge France into new and dangerous adventures. Ney, who had first promised Louis to bring back Napoleon in an iron cage before going over to him, felt deep down that Napoleon was a spent force and that France, facing a hostile European coalition, could not prevail. Unfortunately for Napoleon his irreplaceable Chief of Staff from the old days, Marshal Berthier, had died in a accident and his replacement Marshal Soult was not so talented. The combination of Napoleon's physical and mental decline, coupled with the bungling of his subordinates Soult and Ney would lead to defeat at Waterloo.

THE ALLIED ARMIES

On the opposite side Wellington was not having a smooth run either. His Peninsular veterans were dispersed across the world or had been demobilized. As a consequence Wellington was reduced to fighting Napoleon with a motley army of Dutch, Belgian, German mercenaries (Hessians and Nassauers), and a small force of British troops—many of whom were raw recruits. He had 68,800 infantry and 14,500 cavalry making a grand total of 92,300 troops divided into three infantry corps

95TH RIFLES

In the British Army and the British expeditionary army in Belgium of 1815, the 95th Rifles stood out for two glaringly simple reasons. Firstly, its infantrymen were equipped with rifles, rather than the rest of the Army's trusted Brown Bess muskets. Secondly, when the rest of the army, irrespective of arm, wore the King's vivid scarlet uniforms the 95th clothed, for reason of camouflage, in dark-hued green. They were formed during the Peninsula War (1808–14) for a dual purpose—to fight as regular infantry and also as skirmishers and snipers ahead of the main army.

commanded by himself, General Hill, and the Dutch Prince of Orange. The cavalry was under the command of the Earl of Uxbridge who doubled as Wellington's second-in-command. Relations between the two men were frosty—Uxbridge had eloped with Wellington's sister-in-law—and had been appointed against Wellington's express wishes.

The Allies were therefore relying on the Prussians with 130,000 men to stem Napoleon. Their legendary commander, Field Marshal Prince Gebhard von Blücher (1742–1819) may never have been the greatest of strategists given his troops' nickname for him—Alte Forwärts ("Old Forwards"), but he could be relied upon to fight the French and come to the aid of Wellington who expected Napoleon to attempt to drive a wedge between their separate armies.

QUATRE BRAS AND LIGNY

On June 15 Napoleon crossed the frontier into Belgium with 123,000 men in his Armée du Nord at Charleroi—exactly where Wellington had not expected him to strike. "Napoleon has humbugged me, by God" was Wellington's comment as he rushed to assist his troops holding Marshal Ney at the crossroads of Quatre Bras. Ney had showed uncharacteristic lethargy by failing to occupy this vital position, compounding this error by only opening the battle in the afternoon and then using 4,000 cuirassiers to charge the British infantry squares. Obviously Ney had, three days later at Waterloo, a complete loss of memory as he repeated that mistake—charging unbroken infantry formations without infantry support.

That same day, June 16, the main battle took place at Ligny between Napoleon's main army of 71,000 men and Blücher's 84,000 Prussians. The Prussians had chosen to overextend themselves across marshy ground but Napoleon was not at his tactical best either. He delayed the battle until the afternoon when he was obliged to simply sledgehammer the Prussian lines into submission. For almost two hours savage fighting went on, often hand-to-hand with bayonets and firing at point-blank range. Prussian losses amounted to 19,000 and while Blücher quit the field Napoleon had sustained heavy losses—some 14,000 men—that he could ill afford. Napoleon sent Marshal Grouchy in pursuit of the Prussians with 30,000 men, but Grouchy failed to press the enemy closely, and far from retreating back to Germany as Napoleon had expected, Blücher marched west to support Wellington as he had promised.

Having beaten the Prussians Napoleon rushed to Quatre Bras where he found the British, having held off Ney's attacks, withdrawing from the battlefield in an orderly fashion, without any effort on the part of the French to pursue or harass them. Ney and his staff were sitting down for supper instead. Napoleon could not believe his eyes and gave his officers a violent dressing down that while it was deserved did nothing to raise Ney's morale. Fatally, Ney would remember this latest humiliation at Waterloo and acting upon his own initiative show that he was as dynamic as ever.

MONT ST. JEAN

There was a much-needed lull the following day as Wellington's army numbering 74,300 troops in total took up position around the farm of Mont St. Jean and the village of Waterloo where Wellington set up his headquarters. Wellington faced a French army of 74,500 men that had set up camp south of the road to Brussels while Napoleon, in spite of his superstitious frame of mind, had set up his headquarters at the inn of "La Belle Alliance."

The two armies may have been almost exactly and evenly matched numerically. This, however, took no account for the vitally qualitative differences between the two armies. Napoleon's troops were seasoned veterans where most of Wellington's men were recently recruited troops and only 28,000 of these were British—they too in great part newly recruited men. Furthermore the French had not only more cavalry and artillery but what they had was of far greater quality than Wellington's. Not only did the French 12-pounder have a superior range to the British 9-pounder but the crews handling them were more experienced and better led. Perhaps this was a due to the simple fact that Napoleon, now an emperor, had once been a young artillery officer whose handling of the French guns at Toulon in 1793 had, quite literally, shot him to fame? Wellington was, by contrast, an infantry commander.

DISPOSITIONS

As battlefields go, that of Waterloo, compared to Borodino (1812) in Russia, was a very compact and dense one where there was to be a lot of action in a compressed space in the course of a single day. A day, June 18, that was to change the course of European history forever.

Wellington had drawn up his army based on divisions divided into three corps. His extreme left flank was secured by the German division of the Prince of Saxe-Weimar backed by Uxbridge's cavalry to their rear. On the opposite side—on the extreme right—the Prince of Orange's Dutch-Belgian division, then came

ON THE LEFT A BROODING, slouched Napoleon contrasts in a second oil painting with the determined look and fit frame of Wellington. The reality was that they were two of best generals of their era, both determined to win.

Clinton's division (behind the Braine l'Allend road), Cooke's division, at the junction of the Brussels road Alten's division (facing the farm of La Haie) with Wellington's Reserve Corps and finally, strung out along the Ohain road, General Picton's division—the finest, with Clinton's, in the

IN THEIR CHARACTERISTIC bearskin caps, florid whiskers, and sideburns, the veterans of the Old Guard was Napoleon's last reserve—one that he threw away at Waterloo.

THIS WELL EQUIPPED British private belonged to Wellington's finest infantry unit, the elite Coldstream Guards, who fought hard to hold the farm house of Hougoumont.

whole Allied army. Napoleon's army was strung out along a parallel line to that of Wellington's perpendicular to the Charleroi to Brussels road with the left flank at the Nivelles road. Piré's cavalry was on the extreme left with Kellerman's III Cavalry Corps and the Cavalry of the Guard under Guyot at the rear, while Prince Jérôme Bonaparte's infantry faced the walled estate of Hougoumont. The center was made up of the divisions of General Count J.B. d'Erlon's I Corps with Milhaud's cavalry at the rear. The right flank was anchored on the position of La Haie.

Facing the prospect that Blücher might intervene at any moment, Napoleon had to make the first move and secure a swift and decisive victory over Wellington before he had to turn and face the Prussians. Should the two enemy armies actually link up it would spell doom for not only his army but his restored Empire as well. Everything depended upon this roll of the iron dice of war. Interestingly enough Napoleon's plan, as at Borodino in 1812, was unimaginative and depended upon using brute force in a frontal assault instead of trying to outflank or outmaneuver the Allied army. Napoleon aimed simply to break Wellington's line through the farm of La Haie Sainte in the center and occupy the crossroads behind, drive on and occupy Mont St. Jean farm.

THE BATTLE BEGINS

Napoleon had prepared to attack at 10:30 A.M. but there had been a downpour overnight that made the ground too soft for cavalry and artillery fire. The main assault was postponed, with fatal consequences, until 1 P.M. and the French began a preliminary artillery bombardment 10:50 A.M. against the chateau of Hougoumont on

Wellington's right held by the tough Hanoverian troops of the King's German Legion (KGL) and a detachment of Nassau troops.

To draw away Wellington's attention from his left flank—where Napoleon's main attack would be launched—Napoleon gave orders that his brother Prince Jérôme was to attack Hougoumont to draw off Wellington's reserves. But instead the Prince sent wave after wave of his infantry against the staunchly defended estate with little to show for it, tying down his own troops while Wellington only sent minimal reinforcements. He threw in all his four regiments and half of Foy's division for good measure. It was vital for Wellington to hold this crucial pivot point in the battle line at all cost so he committed his toughest troops—the Scots and Coldstream Guards—to support the German defenders.

At one in the afternoon, as Napoleon prepared to attack, came unwelcome news with a courier that General Bülow's Prussian Corps (30,000 men) was approaching from the direction of Wavre. A cautious man would have withdrawn but Napoleon gambled on Grouchy, supposedly on his way to the battlefield, taking an hour to reach him and intercept the Prussians—it took four and by that time the Prussians had helped Wellington beat Napoleon. As an additional insurance against the Prussians turning up, Napoleon ordered Count Lobau with 20,000 men to his right flank, facing east and the Prussians. Although a sensible move it also ensured that the main assault against Wellington was considerably weakened.

D'ERLON'S ATTACK

At 1:30 P.M. some 84 guns positioned at La Belle Alliance opened fire for the next half hour. These French 12-pound guns could fire roundshot some 1.1 miles (1.8km). Because of the soft, wet ground this fire proved ineffective as the shot hit the ground and sank into it, instead of ricocheting through the Allied infantry. Even if they had, Wellington had placed most of his precious troops—that he wished to spare—just beyond the ridge rather than on top of it. It was not until 2 P.M.—and every hour was precious for Napoleon before the

A BAKER RIFLE AND BAYONET, as used by rifle regiments—such as the 95th Rifles—in the Hundred Days' War. First produced in 1800, the Baker rifle was the first standard-issue, British-made rifle accepted for the British armed forces.

Prussians arrived—that Napoleon unleashed d'Erlon's I Corps. D'Erlon, hoping to break through the Allied lines by sheer weight of numbers, formed his divisions into three massive columns of battalions deployed one behind the other. Although very vulnerable to Allied artillery and musket fire in this formation, the avalanche of blue-clad infantry proved almost irresistible once I Corps' assault got underway sweeping van Biljandt's exposed 1st Netherland (Dutch-Belgian) Brigade aside. Wellington's left-center position buckled under this huge wave of attacking infantry forcing him to commit all the units he could spare. The best he had was Sir Thomas Picton's 5th Infantry Division (6,745 men) made up of British (8th and 9th Brigades) and Hanoverian troops (5th Brigade).

Picton's ferocious counterattacks, backed by Uxbridge's cavalry, including Sir William Ponsonby's 2nd (Union) Brigade, held the French—only just though and only at an enormous cost. Both Picton and Ponsonby died, Uxbridge lost a leg from a cannon shot while some 40 percent of his men were either dead, captured, or wounded. But their sacrifices were worth it since the French attack ground to a halt. They began to retreat, finally fleeing, leaving some 3,000 prisoners for the British to pick up. An hour later (by 3 P.M.) the British had defeated the first French assault.

NEY'S CAVALRY ATTACKS

At 3.30 P.M. Napoleon ordered his artillery to pound La Haie Sainte and for Ney to prepare for a new assault that he would lead in person. But without informing Napoleon Ney ordered 5,000 of his cavalry to attack what he thought were retreating enemy troops, but Wellington was simply bringing some of his units out of the range of fire and redeploying the rest. Lacking infantry or artillery support, Ney's cavalry stormed in the finest French style of mad bravado up the slope to be met by a hail of artillery and massed musket fire at point-blank range. Hundreds of cavalrymen met their death with extreme courage while the British infantry (formed in squares for defence) repelled wave after wave of the cuirassiers, dragoons, and lancers coming at them.

Ney retreated, reformed, and charged again, and again without breaking the British. At 5 P.M. General François Kellerman joined the attack with his III Cavalry Corps. Neither Ney nor Kellerman had thought of getting Napoleon's permission before they set after the "retreating" Allied troops. The intensity of the fighting was such that Ney had four horses shot from underneath him while some of the British squares were close to breaking point as Kellerman joined in. Yet it all proved to be in vain and by 6 P.M. even Ney had had enough and simply walked back, his last horse having been shot, to the French lines.

Napoleon could not believe what Ney had done or that Wellington's "mongrel" troops had been able to stand up to this onslaught. To atone for his rash stupidity Ney did eventually take La Haie Sainte held to the last by the KGL. Having lost the 2nd Regiment and its commander, Baron Ompteda, they had had enough and retreated with the broken 1st Hanoverian Brigade. Wellington's center was in a state of near collapse, which threatened to undo his entire army.

THE FINAL ATTACK

The Prussians had begun to appear at the edge of the battlefield (the Bois de Paris) by 4 P.M. and an hour later Napoleon was forced to shore up Lobau's VI Corps—now reduced to only 7,000 men—by sending 4,000 men of the Young Guard. By 7 P.M. von Zeithen's I Corps had arrived to back up Bülow's men. In a last attempt to break through Wellington's center Napoleon ordered the Old Guard—his final reserve and troops who had never been beaten—to attack in two column 75 men abreast.

Yet again, British troops concealed behind the ridge were able to surprise the columns before they could deploy into line and shattered them with close-range musketry. As the Old Guard fell back, the French army's morale finally cracked and they broke and fled, shouting "Sauve qui peut!"—"Every man for himself!" and "Trahison!"—"Treachery!" Napoleon fled in a coach and at 8:30 P.M. Wellington met his savior (of the eleventh hour) Blücher at La Belle Alliance.

AFTERMATH

The French had lost some 30,000 men. Wellington had lost 15,000 and the Prussians 6,700. By 5 A.M. the following day Napoleon was back at Charleroi heading toward Paris. On June 22, he abdicated for a second time, fled Paris, and on July 15 boarded HMS *Bellerophon* at Plymouth. Exactly four months later he stepped ashore on the island of St. Helena, his "home" until his death.

THE FINEST and noblest of the British cavalry, the Scots Greys, launched their legendary attack against the artillery and infantry of the French center with catastrophic result.

WATERLOO

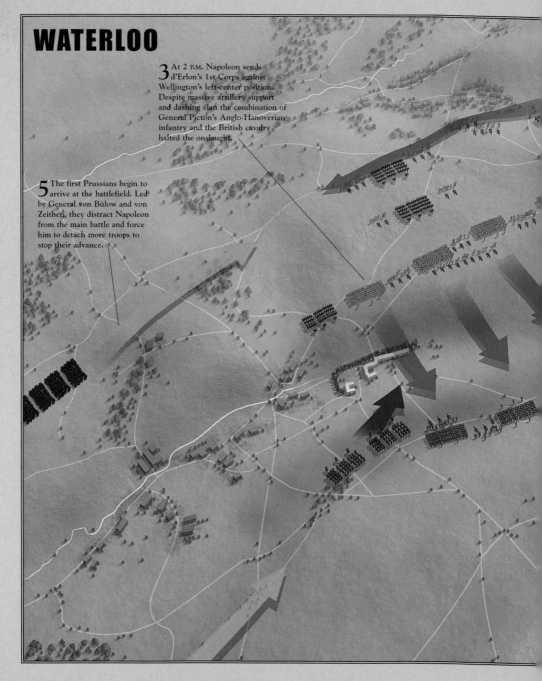

3 At 2 P.M. Napoleon sends d'Erlon's 1st Corps against Wellington's left-center position. Despite massive artillery support and dashing élan the combination of General Picton's Anglo-Hanoverian infantry and the British cavalry halted the onslaught.

5 The first Prussians begin to arrive at the battlefield. Led by General von Bülow and von Zeithen, they distract Napoleon from the main battle and force him to detach more troops to stop their advance.

6 As evening closes in, with Prussian pressure increasing, Napoleon sends his precious veterans of the Imperial Guards against Wellington. Their attack is repelled and ends in a massacre—the battle is lost for the French and the Allies are united by 8:30 P.M.

2 After an artillery barrage, Prince Jérôme Bonaparte attacked the pivotal farmhouse of Hougoumont with four regiments of infantry as news arrived that the Prussians had been spotted nearby. Napoleon detached troops under Count Lobau to block their advance.

HOUGOUMONT

LA HAIE SAINTE

4 Ney charges with his cavalry up the slope against Wellington's massed infantry in squares, meeting a hail of fire in return. For two hours, supported by General Kellerman's reinforcements, Ney launched wave after wave of attacks and almost breaks the squares.

MONT ST JEAN

1 Napoleon hoped to defeat Wellington before Blücher's Prussians could come to the rescue by attacking the Allied army's frontline at La Haie Sainte, occupying the crossroads behind that position, and then driving the Allied army back to Mont Saint-Jean village.

KEY

ANGLO-DUTCH FORCES

FRENCH IMPERIAL FORCES

PRUSSIAN FORCES

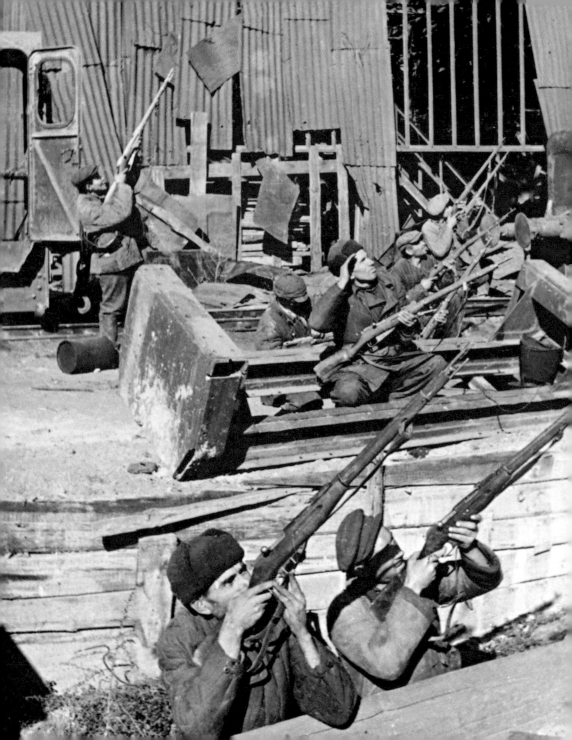

THE AGE OF THE RIFLE

By the middle of the nineteenth century the musket had been outclassed by the modern rifle, which remained the infantryman's main weapon for another century. This was first made obvious by the bloody encounters of the American Civil War, where massed infantry were cut to pieces by deadly-accurate cannon and rifle fire.

The invention of machine guns and the development of modern artillery at the end of the nineteenth century brought infantry tactics to a standstill, leading to the protracted, attritional warfare of World War I. However, with the introduction of aircraft, tank, and mechanized warfare in World War II, massed infantry armies were revitalized as war became more fluid and the flexibility of the infantry again became paramount.

Yet despite the advent of space-age precision bombing and fast-moving mechanized tactics, recent conflicts such as the Vietnam War and Iraq show that the "poor, bloody infantry" is still needed to hold ground and win victories.

MEN OF A SOVIET WORKERS' MILITIA *supposedly aim their rifles at Luftwaffe aircraft above the besieged city of Stalingrad in this posed propaganda photograph. Although individual rounds might not be lethal, massed small arms fire was proved to be effective against enemy aircraft.*

ANTIETAM 1862

In the countryside of western Maryland, the bloodiest single day of warfare in American history ended with a tactical draw but a strategic victory for the Union as the Confederate invasion of the North was thwarted. Issued after the battle, the Emancipation Proclamation transformed the American Civil War into a crusade for human rights.

The summer of 1862 was one of frustration in Washington, D.C. Sixteen months after the first shot of the American Civil War had been fired at Fort Sumter, the Union was still without a major victory in the Eastern theater. The Peninsula Campaign, its objective the Confederate capital at Richmond, Virginia, had been repulsed during the Seven Days' Battles in June and July. A humiliating defeat at Second Manassas (Bull Run) followed at the end of August. Desperate to restore order and morale among the dispirited troops, President Abraham Lincoln reinstated General George B. McClellan to overall command. A superb organizer, McClellan was the architect of the Army of the Potomac, but he was also cautious and devoid

ANTIETAM FACTS

Who: The 55,000-man Confederate Army of Northern Virginia, commanded by General Robert E. Lee (1807–70), confronted General George B. McClellan (1826–85) and the Union Army of the Potomac, which numbered more than 85,000.

What: From dawn to dusk, Union and Confederate troops fought to a tactical draw in a three-phase battle ranging north to south from a cornfield to a sunken road and a stone bridge.

Where: Western Maryland near the town of Sharpsburg and along the banks of Antietam Creek.

When: September 17, 1862.

Why: The Confederate Army of Northern Virginia invaded Maryland, carrying the American Civil War into Northern territory.

Outcome: Lee was forced to abandon the offensive, President Abraham Lincoln changed the character of the war with the issuance of the Emancipation Proclamation, and the chance of European intervention on behalf of the Confederacy was eliminated.

IN THIS ROMANTICIZED artist's conception of the Battle of Antietam, Union and Confederate troops are locked in combat at close quarters along the banks of Antietam Creek in western Maryland. In the background, their banner unfurled, Union soldiers and their mounted officers charge across the Lower Bridge spanning the stream and into a hail of Confederate rifle fire.

of initiative on the battlefield. On the other hand, the Confederate Army of Northern Virginia, always hungry, often without shoes, nevertheless displayed the spirit and dash that only victory could bring. Its commander, General Robert E. Lee, had displayed tactical brilliance and defeated the enemy at nearly every turn. Only a week after Second Manassas, he crossed the Potomac River and invaded the North.

LEE'S AUDACIOUS GAMBLE

Lee reckoned that an expedition into Maryland and Pennsylvania could accomplish a great deal, both militarily and politically, for the beleaguered South. It was believed that Southern sympathizers in Maryland would rally to the rebel army, providing food, supplies, and new recruits. The Confederates could also live off the rich farmland of southern Pennsylvania, destroy the railroad bridge across the Susquehanna River and threaten the state capital at Harrisburg. A victory on Northern soil would allow Lee to menace Philadelphia, Baltimore, and Washington, D.C. Perhaps most important of all, such a victory might bring formal recognition and much-needed assistance from the governments of Great Britain and France. Lee further realized that the capacity of the Union to wage war was virtually limitless. The Confederacy had seized the initiative. Now, it had to utilize that initiative to its fullest.

Following the abortive Peninsula Campaign, McClellan had been demoted in favor of General John Pope (1822–92), who had established and quite probably embellished his reputation as an Indian fighter in the West. During the campaign of Second Manassas, Pope may have been willing to fight, but Lee and his capable subordinates James Longstreet (1821–1904) and Thomas J. "Stonewall" Jackson (1824–63) made him appear a rank amateur. Confederate cavalry raided Pope's headquarters at Manassas, stealing his dress coat and $350,000 in cash. Then Longstreet and Jackson completed the rout on the old battlefield of Bull Run. When Lincoln swallowed his pride and recalled McClellan, the soldiers of the Army of the Potomac gave a mighty cheer. To a man, they loved "Little Mac." This time, though, McClellan did not march his troops into Virginia. He headed northwest into Maryland to intercept the invading rebels.

THE CAMPAIGN

As the Confederates advanced toward the town of Frederick, Maryland, the Federal arsenal at Harpers Ferry lay between Lee and his supply base at Winchester, Virginia. It might also sever his line of communication with Richmond via the Shenandoah Valley.

Discounting one of the principles of command, Lee divided his army in the face of an enemy of superior strength

THE USE OF ARTILLERY played a significant role in the Battle of Antietam, particularly the rifled cannon used by Union units. Rifled artillery proved much more accurate than the smooth-bore cannon of the Confederates.

and sent Jackson to capture Harpers Ferry. Lee counted on McClellan's caution, confident that Jackson could complete his task and rejoin the main army before Union troops arrived in overwhelming numbers. By September 12, the entire Army of Northern Virginia could concentrate at Hagerstown, Maryland, and continue into Pennsylvania.

While Jackson dealt with Harpers Ferry, Longstreet's corps headed for Hagerstown on September 10. Three days later, as the bulk of McClellan's army reached Frederick, a private from an Indiana regiment noticed an envelope lying on the ground. Inside were three cigars and a copy of Special Order 191, which Lee had issued on September 9. The order detailed the dispositions of Confederate troops, and it was soon in McClellan's possession.

Lee's entire army was now in great peril. If McClellan moved swiftly eastward through the passes in South Mountain, he might interpose his army between Longstreet at Hagerstown and Jackson at Harpers Ferry. His larger force could then crush these separate elements one at a time.

Unaware that Special Order 191 had fallen into McClellan's hands, Lee had already begun to worry that the capture of Harpers Ferry was taking too long. He knew that McClellan was at Frederick, and the movement of the Union force, although ponderously slow, still proceeded at a disturbing pace. Even with the knowledge of Lee's predicament, McClellan wasted several precious hours and did not start toward the South Mountain passes in earnest until the morning of the 14th.

Events now seemed to be developing rapidly, and Lee could feel his control of the situation slipping away. He ordered Longstreet to send troops from Hagerstown to defend Turner's and Fox's Gaps and Jackson to dispatch a force from Harpers Ferry to guard Crampton's Gap further south. Their delaying actions could buy precious time for Lee to gather his scattered forces. Inevitably, though, McClellan would force his way through the gaps, and Lee issued orders on the night of the 14th to abandon the Harpers Ferry positions in preparation for a general withdrawal to the safety of Virginia.

In the early hours of the next day, as Union troops marched ever closer, Lee finally received some good news. A message from Jackson stated that Harpers Ferry would fall on the morning of the 15th. Lee canceled his original order and instructed his forces to concentrate near the town of Sharpsburg. Longstreet moved, and Jackson rapidly departed Harpers Ferry, leaving General A.P. Hill's Light Division to deal with captured booty and nearly 12,000 Union prisoners.

DISPOSITIONS

Believing he might yet salvage his campaign, Lee chose to make a stand along a low ridge which overlooked Antietam Creek. General J.E.B. Stuart's cavalry screened the left flank of the Confederate line, which was anchored by General John Bell Hood's division on a forested area called the West Woods and around a whitewashed Dunker Church, which stood adjacent to the Hagerstown Turnpike. General D.H. Hill placed five brigades in the rebel center, across the Boonsborough Pike. The division of General D.R. Jones held a mile of the Confederate line, which ended along high bluffs on the west side of Antietam Creek above the lower bridge, one of three stone spans which crossed the stream. By the evening of the 16th, most of Jackson's troops had arrived from Harpers Ferry and doubled the size of Lee's force to about 36,000.

At midday on the 15th, McClellan had assembled 75,000 troops east of the Antietam. Both sides had placed artillery on the surrounding high ground, and sporadic firing

CONFEDERATE DEAD, probably from the Louisiana brigade of General Harry T. Hays, lie sprawled beside a rail fence along the Hagerstown Turnpike at Antietam. These soldiers had been locked in combat with elements of the Union Iron Brigade, commanded by General John Gibbon.

UNION INFANTRY

Ranks of well equipped Union infantrymen march toward the sound of the guns. Although the Union Army of the Potomac consisted of some units from the standing United States Army, a large number of the soldiers were volunteers and draftees. Many of these were farmers and woodsmen from the primarily agricultural areas of the North and Midwest or European immigrants, predominantly Irish and German, from the crowded urban areas of major Northern cities.

occurred on the 16th, while McClellan refined his plan of attack. Two army corps, under Generals Joseph Hooker and Joseph K.F. Mansfield were placed on the Union right and ordered to make the initial assault, with the corps of Generals William B. Franklin and Edwin V. Sumner available to exploit any significant gains. General Fitz-John Porter's corps took up positions in the Union center along the Boonsborough Pike, and the corps of General Ambrose Burnside was positioned on the left near the lower bridge. McClellan's plan was simple. If Hooker and Mansfield made

significant gains, Burnside would attack the Confederate right flank and perhaps push on into the town of Sharpsburg. Finally, Porter's troops would assault the Confederate center in support of either flank attack. In typical fashion, McClellan had squandered opportunities to attack the much smaller Confederate army on the afternoon of the 15th and again in the 16th. When battle was finally joined on the 17th, Lee was able to utilize his interior lines. Shuffling reinforcements to areas of heavy fighting, he stymied several Union breakthroughs. McClellan failed to coordinate his attacks and committed reserves in a piecemeal manner, negating his numerical superiority.

THE BATTLE

At first light, Hooker's Federals advanced down the Hagerstown Turnpike toward the Dunker Church. Artillery fire tore great gaps in the ranks of the defending

UNION SOLDIERS move about their encampment. Often, army camps included "followers" such as merchants, family members, and, in the case of the Union Army, freed slaves. The close quarters of army encampments were also environments that fostered the spread of communicable diseases. During the Civil War, many more soldiers died of disease than as a result of combat.

Confederates, and the focus of the savage fighting became a 30-acre field of head-high corn owned by a farmer named David Miller. Relieved during the night by two brigades under General Alexander Lawton, Hood's Texans were cooking breakfast when the fighting began. A desperate Lawton called for help, and Hood's shock troops sent Hooker's spearhead reeling back more than 400 yards (365m). Both sides committed additional reinforcements, and the dead and wounded began to pile up. Some accounts relate that the bloody cornfield changed hands up to 15 times.

More than 90 minutes after Hooker's opening attacks, Mansfield assaulted the Confederates over the same ground. As his right was torn apart by Confederate artillery, Mansfield was mortally wounded. One Union division, commanded by General George Greene, managed to reach the rocky ground before the Dunker Church, but no other units appeared to take advantage of the gain, and Greene's men were isolated and pinned down.

At approximately 9 A.M., Sumner himself led two divisions from the vicinity of the East Woods, about half a mile from the ragged Confederate line. In response, Jackson deployed reserves, some just off the march from Harpers Ferry and others transferred from the rebel right near the stone bridge, to spring a trap along the edge of the West Woods. During the march, the second Union division, under William French, lost contact with Sumner and veered away. A single division of 5,000 men, commanded by General John Sedgwick, continued, stumbling into the trap set by Jackson. The crossfire of nearly 10,000

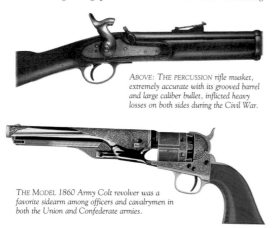

ABOVE: THE PERCUSSION rifle musket, extremely accurate with its grooved barrel and large caliber bullet, inflicted heavy losses on both sides during the Civil War.

THE MODEL 1860 Army Colt revolver was a favorite sidearm among officers and cavalrymen in both the Union and Confederate armies.

Confederate muskets cut down half of Sedgwick's strength in a mere 20 minutes. Jackson counterattacked but was repulsed by Sedgwick's artillery. The third Union attack of the morning had gained nothing, and scores of dead and wounded littered the ground around the cornfield, the Hagerstown Pike and the Dunker Church. By 10 A.M., the Confederate left had held, battered but unbroken.

The fighting now shifted southward, where D.H. Hill had taken advantage of a sunken road, which had been worn down by years of wagon traffic and now offered a natural defensive position. When French's division had marched away from Sedgwick, it had become engaged with troops from three brigades of Hill's division, which had pulled back from the fighting around the Dunker Church. A spirited battle erupted on the left of the sunken road. The famed Irish Brigade assaulted the Confederates, many of whom were from North Carolina and Alabama, in the sunken road around 10:30 A.M., suffering 540 dead and wounded before falling back. Still, the Union attacks continued. Exhausted, the Confederates began to falter when a pair of New York regiments managed to flank the sunken road and pour deadly fire down the length of the trench and a misunderstood order resulted in an entire rebel brigade abandoning its positions.

Confederate bodies were heaped two and three deep in the sunken road, which came to be known to history as "Bloody Lane." Once again, the Union army stood on the brink of a decisive victory. A patchwork defense slowed the Union tide, which had reached up to 600 yards (548m) beyond the sunken road. One more push with fresh troops from his ample reserve might win the day for McClellan, but the commander hesitated and then ordered his troops to hold their positions.

From morning until mid-afternoon, Union troops further south had been attempting to take the lower bridge across Antietam Creek. While some of his troops found places where the stream could easily be forded, the corps commander, General Ambrose Burnside, was determined to take the bridge that would eventually bear his name. It was defended by only 400 Confederate riflemen from Georgia and South Carolina. After four hours of fruitless attempts to capture the bridge, Federal troops from New York and Pennsylvania charged across and gained the west bank.

Throughout the morning, Lee had stripped his right of troops to support those hard-pressed areas on his left and center. Now, in spite of his slow progress, Burnside was in position to sweep the woefully inadequate Confederate defenders aside, capture Sharpsburg, and cut off the entire rebel army's avenue of retreat. He waited, however, for two precious hours, consolidating his hold on the west side of the creek. When Burnside finally got moving around 3 P.M., he made sluggish progress. An hour later, he was only

0.5 mile (0.8km) from the town. At the precise moment when he was needed the most, A.P. Hill and his Light Division appeared in a cloud of dust, bowling down the road from Harpers Ferry. His footsore soldiers had covered the 17 miles (27.3km) to the scene of the fighting in seven hours, and many had fallen out of the ranks due to exhaustion. The charge of the Light Division stopped Burnside's advance cold, and he retired toward the creek. By 6 P.M., the Battle of Antietam was over. Lee was too battered to take the offensive.

The casualties from America's bloodiest day were appalling. The Army of the Potomac counted 12,410 dead, wounded, or missing, while the Army of Northern Virginia had lost 10,700. Throughout the day on September 18, Lee stood his ground. McClellan declined to renew the fight and did not pursue the Confederate columns when they withdrew across the Potomac.

AFTERMATH

In the wake of the Battle of Antietam, President Lincoln became convinced that the outcome was enough of a victory to issue the Emancipation Proclamation, which freed the slaves in territory then in rebellion against the United States. The document transformed the war from an effort to save the Union to one of liberation and the perpetuation of freedom. European governments, which had abolished slavery themselves, were dissuaded from supporting the Confederate cause.

CONFEDERATE CAVALRYMAN

Armed with his trusty Colt revolver and wearing a jaunty uniform complete with a plumed slouch hat, the Confederate cavalryman was considered among the elite of his army.

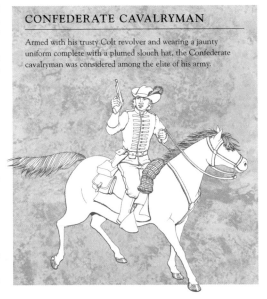

ANTIETAM

UPPER BRIDGE

1 At dawn, Hooker's corps attacks Jackson on Lee's left flank. Thrust and counterthrust leave the cornfield and the Dunker Church grounds strewn with dead and wounded.

2 Mansfield assaults the Confederate left, making only limited progress, while Sedgwick's charging division of Sumner's corps plunges into Jackson's trap and is decimated.

DUNKER CHURCH

POTOMAC RIVER

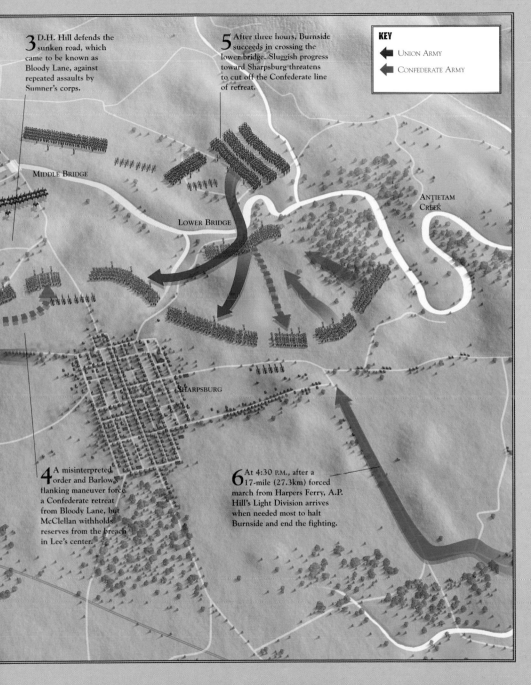

3 D.H. Hill defends the sunken road, which came to be known as Bloody Lane, against repeated assaults by Sumner's corps.

5 After three hours, Burnside succeeds in crossing the lower bridge. Sluggish progress toward Sharpsburg threatens to cut off the Confederate line of retreat.

KEY

UNION ARMY

CONFEDERATE ARMY

MIDDLE BRIDGE

ANTIETAM CREEK

LOWER BRIDGE

SHARPSBURG

4 A misinterpreted order and Barlow's flanking maneuver force a Confederate retreat from Bloody Lane, but McClellan withholds reserves from the breach in Lee's center.

6 At 4:30 P.M., after a 17-mile (27.3km) forced march from Harpers Ferry, A.P. Hill's Light Division arrives when needed most to halt Burnside and end the fighting.

GETTYSBURG 1863

In an epic three-day battle, the brief history of the Confederacy reached its zenith as General Robert E. Lee's second invasion of the North was repulsed in southern Pennsylvania. After Gettysburg, the outcome of the American Civil War appeared inevitable as Union armies maintained an offensive posture on all fronts.

For General Robert E. Lee, the stunning Confederate victory at Chancellorsville in May 1863, provided both his crowning achievement and his darkest moment of battlefield command. Although the Union army under General Joseph Hooker had been routed, Lee's most capable lieutenant, General Thomas J. "Stonewall" Jackson, had been mortally wounded by friendly fire. Although the loss of Jackson was a severe blow, Lee nevertheless felt compelled to follow up the victory at Chancellorsville. He reorganized the Army of Northern Virginia into three corps, commanded by generals James Longstreet, A.P. Hill, and Richard S. Ewell. The Confederate army was flush with victory and stood at the height of its strength;

GETTYSBURG FACTS

Who: General Robert E. Lee (1807–70) and 75,000 soldiers of the Confederate Army of Northern Virginia opposed 97,000 troops of the Union Army of the Potomac, commanded by General George G. Meade (1815–72).

What: During three days of fighting, Confederate forces failed to penetrate Union defenses along a 3-mile (4.8km), fish-hook shaped line from Culp's Hill and Cemetery Hill southward along Cemetery Ridge to Little Round Top.

Where: South of the town of Gettysburg, in Southern Pennsylvania.

When: July 1–3, 1863.

Why: For the second time in the American Civil War, the Confederate Army launched an invasion of Northern territory.

Outcome: Lee's invasion was repulsed, and the military might of the Confederacy suffered irreplaceable losses in what was rapidly becoming a war of attrition. President Abraham Lincoln issued one of the enduring documents of American freedom with the Gettysburg Address.

IN THIS SECTION OF THE GETTYSBURG CYCLORAMA, *painted in 1883 by French artist Paul Philippoteaux, the 19th Massachusetts and 42nd New York regiments rush forward to bolster the Union line at the height of Pickett's Charge. During the high tide of Confederate military strength, a handful of the attackers breached the Union position on Cemetery Ridge, but only briefly.*

A CONFEDERATE INFANTRYMAN of the 1st Texas Brigade lunges forward with his bayonet-tipped musket. Troops of the 1st Texas were heavily engaged in the capture of Devil's Den on July 2, 1863, at Gettysburg.

therefore, its commander looked to the north for a second time. Lee's aims were similar to those that had precipitated the invasion of the North, which had ended nine months earlier with the battle of Antietam. Destroying the Pennsylvania Railroad bridge over the Susquehanna River would disrupt enemy communications, and Confederate troops could sustain themselves with supplies procured from Northern farms. Lee might capture Harrisburg, the Pennsylvania state capital, and threaten Baltimore, Philadelphia, or Washington, D.C. Perhaps most important, the population of the North was becoming war-weary. The presence of victorious Confederate forces in Union territory might bring about peace overtures and secure Southern independence.

THE CAMPAIGN

On June 3, 1863, the Army of Northern Virginia began streaming steadily to the northwest, across the mountains of the Blue Ridge, and then northward through the Shenandoah Valley. For three weeks, the Confederates operated virtually at will against only token resistance. With Ewell's corps in the van, the Confederates were spread across miles of the Pennsylvania countryside. By the end of the month, Ewell was menacing Harrisburg, General Jubal Early's division had occupied the town of York, and Robert Rodes' division was miles to the north at Carlisle.

Hooker's Army of the Potomac became alerted to the Confederate offensive on June 25, during a heavy clash between Rebel cavalry under General J.E.B. Stuart and Federal horsemen commanded by General Alfred Pleasonton at Brandy Station, Virginia. Hooker set his army in motion to intercept the Confederates and requested that the arsenal at Harpers Ferry be abandoned and its garrison of 10,000 men added to the field army's ranks. When President Lincoln and the Union army's general-in-chief, Henry W.

Halleck, declined, Hooker asked to be relieved of command. On June 28, a mere four days before the battle of Gettysburg, General George G. Meade was placed in command of the Army of the Potomac.

The rapid northward movement of the Union army caused Stuart to initiate a lengthy ride around Meade and out of contact with Lee. Thus, during a critical period of the campaign, the Confederate commander was deprived of his eyes and ears. Lee, warned by a Southern sympathizer, knew for certain only that the Army of the Potomac was on the march. Without intelligence from Stuart, he had no choice but to concentrate his forces. Reluctantly, Lee ordered Ewell to abandon his planned attack on Harrisburg and join the corps of Hill and Longstreet at Gettysburg.

IN SEARCH OF SHOES

On the morning of July 1, Lee was with Longstreet's Corps at Chambersburg, 25 miles (40km) west of Gettysburg. Hill's Corps was 8 miles (12.8km) west of Gettysburg at Cashtown. Neither Lee nor Meade intended to fight at Gettysburg, which held virtually no strategic value. Lee, in fact, had admonished his subordinate commanders not to bring on a general engagement until the army could be concentrated on favorable ground. Events, however, soon began to develop beyond the control of either senior commander.

Early had already passed through Gettysburg on June 26 during his division's march to York. He sent a note to Hill, informing him that a cache of shoes might be found in the town. Four days later, the leading division of Hill's corps, under General Henry Heth, reached Cashtown. Heth sent a brigade down the Chambersburg Pike to Gettysburg in

GENERAL GEORGE MEADE

General George Gordon Meade, a Pennsylvanian known for his volatile temper, commanded an effective defense at Gettysburg, holding critical high ground and utilizing interior lines. Criticized for not vigorously pursuing Lee into Virginia, Meade commanded the Army of the Potomac for the duration of the war but was subordinate to General in Chief Ulysses S. Grant, who traveled with the campaigning army. He died in Philadelphia in 1872.

search of the shoes. The brigade commander, General James Pettigrew, withdrew from the Gettysburg area when he spotted a large force of Union cavalry moving up from the south. On July 1, Hill ordered two full divisions, those of Heth and General Dorsey Pender, to Gettysburg to determine the strength of the Union force. Probing eastward, the Confederates found two brigades of General John Buford's cavalry, screening the advance of the left wing of the Army of the Potomac. Buford had ordered his troopers to dismount and take up defensive positions west of the town and waited for the Rebels to return.

The decisive battle of the American Civil War was taking shape while the bulk of both armies and both senior commanders were not present on the field. Buford's decision to stand and fight combined with Hill's decision to send a force much greater than necessary on a reconnaissance mission precipitated an engagement from which neither side could readily extricate itself.

THE FIRST DAY

Buford's dismounted cavalrymen fought like lions against ever-increasing numbers of Confederate infantrymen. For two hours, they stood firm before infantry of General John F Reynolds' I Corps rolled in from the south. As he urged the famed Iron Brigade forward, Reynolds was killed in the saddle by a Confederate sharpshooter. Both sides committed fresh troops to the fray, and the fighting intensified. Union troops from New York and Wisconsin captured more than 200 Rebel soldiers, who had been trapped in the cut of an unfinished railroad. Hard pressed, other Union troops fought desperately to prevent their left flank from being turned.

From about 4 miles (6.4km) away, Ewell and Rodes, on the march from Carlisle, could hear Hill's artillery firing. By now, elements of the Union XI Corps, under General Oliver O. Howard, were shuffling through the streets of Gettysburg toward the fighting. The Confederate generals, however, recognized an opportunity to hit the exposed Union right flank. Eventually, the combined weight of Rodes' assaults, the renewed effort of Heth's division, and advances by three of Pender's brigades threatened to overwhelm the Union I Corps on Seminary Ridge.

It was, however, the XI Corps on the Union right that gave way first. Raising a cloud of dust on the Harrisburg

SOLDIERS OF THE 114th Pennsylvania Zouaves, their colorful uniforms patterned after those of French military units, were heavily engaged with Confederate troops from Georgia and Mississippi at the Peach Orchard and the Wheatfield on July 2, 1863.

Road, Early's division appeared from the north and routed a Union division, which had taken up positions on a small knoll. Georgia, Louisiana, and North Carolina troops stunned the Union right, and successive units of the XI Corps faltered, broke, and ran through the town to the relative safety of Cemetery Hill.

Its flank fully exposed, the patchwork battle line of the Union I Corps on Seminary Ridge collapsed. Streaming back through Gettysburg, more and more Union troops reached Cemetery Hill, where General Winfield Scott Hancock, commander of the II Corps, had become the fifth general of the day to command the Union forces. Meade would not reach Gettysburg from Taneytown, Maryland until after midnight. Lee had arrived on the field at 1:30 P.M. but was largely a bystander during most of the fighting.

As the Union troops scrambled to consolidate their position on Cemetery Hill, Lee grasped the significance of his opportunity to win a decisive victory. He forwarded a

THE SEVEN-SHOT SPENCER CARBINE was the most effective shoulder arm of the Civil War. A breechloader rather than a more cumbersome muzzle loader, the Spencer, it was said, "could be loaded on Sunday and fired all week." The shorter stock of the carbine and its rapid firepower made it a popular choice among Union cavalry troops.

UNION CAVALRY OFFICER

His saber drawn, a Union cavalry officer leads a charge. Much maligned early in the war, Union cavalry units continued to improve, holding their own and eventually getting the better of the vaunted Confederate cavalry in several fights.

cryptic verbal order to Ewell, which said in effect that it was only necessary to "press those people" in order to take possession of the heights and to capture Cemetery Hill, nearby Culp's Hill or both "if practicable."

The fight, however, had gone out of Ewell. The enemy beyond Cemetery Hill was of undetermined strength. Hill's corps was spent. Longstreet would not reach Gettysburg for hours. Under protest from subordinates, Ewell declined to continue his attack. During the night, Union reinforcements continued to arrive, Culp's Hill was occupied in force, and a defensive line was established across Cemetery Ridge to Little Round Top. Ewell's decision remains, to this day, one of the most controversial of the Civil War.

THE SECOND DAY

In the early hours of July 2, both sides held councils of war. Meade determined to stand fast, although the entire Union army had not yet reached Gettysburg. Lee, against the advice of Longstreet, decided that an attack on the Union left combined with a renewed effort against Cemetery Hill and Culp's Hill might negate Meade's advantage of interior lines and roll up the entire Union position.

Longstreet took pains to conceal his march to his designated jump-off position and was not ready to attack until about 3:30 P.M. Confederate artillery fired on the positions of the exposed Union division commanded by General Daniel Sickles in the Peach Orchard as infantrymen from Alabama and Texas marched to the east and turned northward toward Little Round Top and a jumble of huge boulders known locally as Devil's Den. Major General Gouverneur K. Warren, the chief engineer of the Army of

the Potomac, rode to the summit of Little Round Top as the Confederates massed for their assault. He recognized that if the Confederates captured this key hill an enfilading fire would render the entire Union line untenable. Warren searched frantically for troops to defend the position. His plea for help was answered by two brigades of General George Sykes' V Corps. These troops from Pennsylvania, New York, and Maine scrambled into position moments before the attacking Confederates started up the slope.

While the desperate defenders of Little Round Top, scavenging ammunition from their own dead and wounded, beat back multiple attacks, fighting raged nearby. Successive Confederate assaults shattered Sickles' salient in the Peach Orchard, and the Wheatfield became a scene of tremendous carnage. At the end of the day, Longstreet had overrun Devil's Den and his troops controlled the Peach Orchard. However, thanks to Warren's initiative, Little Round Top was in Union hands.

At Culp's Hill and Cemetery Hill, Ewell sent troops from the divisions of Early and General Edward Johnson forward in the fading light. Fighting continued for several hours as the Confederates made headway. Some of Early's troops reached the crest of Culp's Hill and engaged in hand-to-hand fighting with the defenders. While the rest of his line was unmolested, Hancock was able reinforce the threatened area, and by 10 P.M. the fighting had petered out.

PHOTOGRAPHER TIMOTHY O'SULLIVAN recorded this grisly scene of Union dead in a meadow near the Peach Orchard. These soldiers were probably killed on July 2, 1863, defending the advanced positions of the Union III Corps.

THE THIRD DAY

The climactic day at Gettysburg began on the Union right at Culp's Hill and Spangler's Spring, where Confederate forces still held earthworks dug by the Federals on the night of July 1. At daylight, further Confederate attacks against the strong entrenchments on Culp's Hill proved fruitless. Two Union divisions under Generals Thomas Ruger and John Geary rooted elements of Johnson's division out of their hard-won but meager lodgment. Before noon, the Federals had regained their lost earthworks, and the fighting had ebbed. A strange silence now hung over the field. It was a deceptive quiet, for the final act of the Gettysburg drama was to unfold in a few short hours.

Lee apparently reasoned that Meade had left his center vulnerable to attack by reinforcing his flanks. Therefore, a concentrated blow against the Union centre on Cemetery Ridge might break through the line. Longstreet strongly dissented. The attacking troops would be obliged to cross more than a mile of open ground and traverse a picket fence along the Emmitsburg Road, all the while exposed to artillery fire from massed guns on Cemetery Ridge and the heights at either end of the Union line.

Most of Lee's army had been heavily engaged on July 2, and the only substantial force available to mount such an assault was the division of General George Pickett, which had guarded Confederate supply wagons for the previous two days. Pickett commanded three brigades, led by generals Richard B. Garnett, James L. Kemper, and Lewis A. Armistead. These would be supported by the divisions of Joseph Pettigrew and Isaac Trimble, who had assumed command for the wounded Heth and Pender respectively. The attacking force would number roughly 15,000 men.

At 1 P.M., nearly 150 Confederate guns opened a cannonade against the Union center. Soon, approximately 80 Union cannon replied from Cemetery Ridge. The artillery duel continued for two hours. Then, at 3 P.M., Pickett shouted, "Up men and to your posts! Don't forget today that you are from Old Virginia!"

Pickett's troops stepped off to the northeast, wheeled with parade-ground precision to the east, and headed toward the Union center. Their objective was a large copse of trees on the crest of Cemetery Ridge. As they crossed the open fields, Union artillery began to tear large gaps in the Confederate ranks. Then, as the Rebels came closer, Union infantry opened fire from the low stone wall to the front of the charging mass and against both of its flanks. Following the battle, the sharp 90-degree angle of the wall came to be known simply as The Angle.

Garnett was killed, and General Kemper fell seriously wounded. On foot, Armistead led his men through a momentary breach in the Union line, waving his hat perched atop his sword. As he lay his hand on a Union cannon, Armistead was mortally wounded. No Confederate reinforcements were available to exploit the breakthrough, and Union troops steadily closed on both flanks. At long last, the shattered remnants of the famous Pickett's Charge limped back toward their own lines, having achieved nothing but immortality. The high tide of the Confederacy had smashed itself upon the rock of the Union center.

AFTERMATH

On July 4, Lee began a long, painful retreat to Virginia, his dream of a military victory on Northern soil dashed. That same day, the Confederate city of Vicksburg, Mississippi, surrendered, and the South was split in two. These devastating defeats sealed the fate of the Confederacy. In the three-day orgy of death and destruction at Gettysburg, the Union suffered 3,149 killed and 19,661 wounded or captured. The Confederacy suffered 4,536 dead and 18,089 wounded or taken prisoner. On November 19, 1863, President Lincoln offered a short speech of slightly more than 200 words during the dedication of a new cemetery for the Union soldiers killed at Gettysburg. The Gettysburg Address still resonates more than two centuries later.

IN ONE OF THE FEW photographs taken during the dedication of the Gettysburg National Cemetery on November 19, 1863, President Abraham Lincoln is barely visible seated at the left on the crowded speakers platform. Lincoln's Gettysburg Address, consisting of slightly more than 200 words, remains one of the principal documents of American freedom.

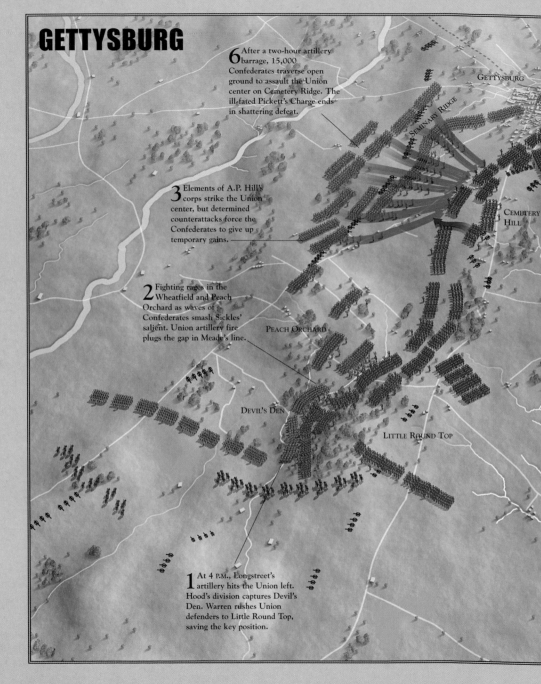

GETTYSBURG

6 After a two-hour artillery barrage, 15,000 Confederates traverse open ground to assault the Union center on Cemetery Ridge. The ill-fated Pickett's Charge ends in shattering defeat.

3 Elements of A.P. Hill's corps strike the Union center, but determined counterattacks force the Confederates to give up temporary gains.

2 Fighting rages in the Wheatfield and Peach Orchard as waves of Confederates smash Sickles' salient. Union artillery fire plugs the gap in Meade's line.

1 At 4 P.M., Longstreet's artillery hits the Union left. Hood's division captures Devil's Den. Warren rushes Union defenders to Little Round Top, saving the key position.

GETTYSBURG

SEMINARY RIDGE

CEMETERY HILL

PEACH ORCHARD

DEVIL'S DEN

LITTLE ROUND TOP

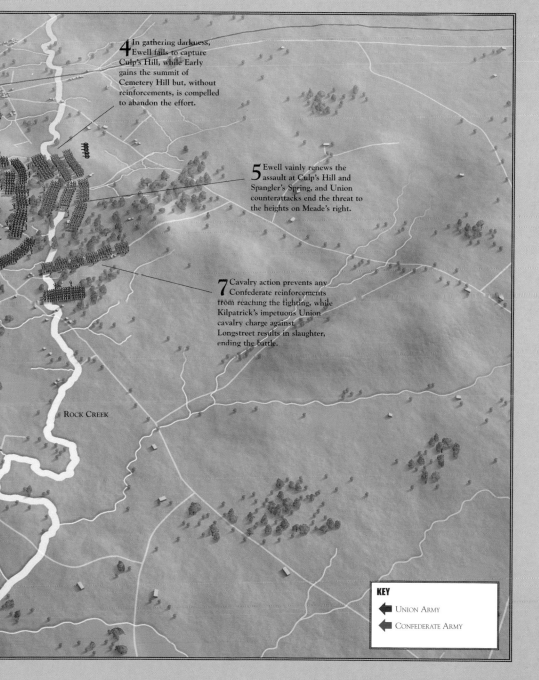

4 In gathering darkness, Ewell fails to capture Culp's Hill, while Early gains the summit of Cemetery Hill but, without reinforcements, is compelled to abandon the effort.

5 Ewell vainly renews the assault at Culp's Hill and Spangler's Spring, and Union counterattacks end the threat to the heights on Meade's right.

7 Cavalry action prevents any Confederate reinforcements from reaching the fighting, while Kilpatrick's impetuous Union cavalry charge against Longstreet results in slaughter, ending the battle.

ROCK CREEK

KEY

⬅ UNION ARMY

⬅ CONFEDERATE ARMY

VERDUN

1916

Verdun epitomizes the attritional struggle that became characteristic of the World War I on the Western Front. Intended to destroy the French reserves, the battle drew in massive numbers of German troops as well, and ended without any decisive result.

As World War I settled down into trench warfare in late 1914, it became more or less impossible to inflict a traditional victory on the enemy. Previously, victory was decided by the defeat of an army in the field or the occupation (or threat of occupation) of key areas such as capital cities. That was simply impossible now. There seemed to be no way to break through the lines and capture strategic objectives, and deep defensive positions made it virtually impossible to drive the enemy from the field. The problem in both cases was the availability of reserves, coupled with the capability to move them to a threatened point faster than a successful attack could be exploited.

Victory in the Great War would therefore be a matter of exhausting the other side, of making the cost of continuing so high that peace became essential, at

VERDUN FACTS

Who: French Second Army under General Henri Pétain (1856–1951), later replaced by General Robert Nivelle (1856–1924), versus the German Fifth Army under Crown Prince Wilhelm (1882–1951), with General Erich von Falkenhayn (1861–1922) with overall responsibility for operations as Chief of the General Staff.

What: The fortified city of Verdun was besieged and the attackers slowly ground their way in while artillery inflicted horrendous casualties. A counteroffensive eventually regained the lost ground.

Where: The city of Verdun on the Meuse River, France.

When: February 21 to December 18, 1916.

Why: The German high command wanted to draw French reserves into a "meatgrinder" and destroy them, forcing France to make peace.

Outcome: After a hideous attritional struggle all that was achieved was massive casualties on both sides.

FRENCH INFANTRY ADVANCE *through the shattered landscape, surrounded by the horrors of war. There is still something splendid about images of this kind—the reality was infinitely more dreary and squalid.*

A FRENCH 1897-VINTAGE *cannon. Designed for mobile operations in the open, weapons of this sort were less useful in the static trench warfare on the Western Front than high-trajectory howitzers and mortars.*

whatever price. The key here, once again, was reserves. So long as the opposition had sufficient manpower available to feed into the combat zone, the war could go on. The German high command therefore came up with a plan to destroy the French reserves by drawing them into a "meatgrinder." The German plan was to attack something that the French had to defend, and to destroy their army with artillery and infantry attacks. The chosen objective was the fortified city of Verdun.

A GERMAN FLAMETHROWER TEAM. *Used to dig a determined foe out of good positions, early flamethrowers posed a threat to everyone around them, not just the enemy.*

VERDUN

Verdun was an ideal target in many ways. Lying in a loop of the Meuse River, the city had poor communications. Only one road ran in and out of the city. The logistic problems of the attack were eased by the fact that there was a major German railhead just 12 miles (19.3km) away, allowing quick transportation of ammunition, supplies, and reinforcements as the attack developed. Verdun lay in a relatively quiet sector of the front, and many of the heavy guns of its forts had been sent to other sectors where they seemed to be more badly needed. It was garrisoned by three divisions, which represented fairly light defenses.

German offensive plans included the assembly of 10 divisions to make the actual attack, supported by experimental "infantry batteries" of 3in (77mm) field guns, which were supposed to advance with the infantry to provide direct support but in the event were unable to cross the shell-torn wasteland. Another new weapon also made its debut at Verdun, the flamethrower. The attack was supported by large quantities of heavy guns—more than 1,400 pieces in total. These included huge 16.5in (420mm) and 12in (305mm) weapons that had previously been used to reduce forts in Belgium. More than 500 minenwerfer were also deployed. These fired a 100lb (45.3kg) explosive shell, which could have a deadly effect if it landed in a trench. Countless lighter weapons such as trench mortars were also available.

The offensive was codenamed Operation Gericht ("Judgment"). Its aim was to force the French into a battle of attrition on unequal terms. If they failed to meet the challenge, Verdun would fall. If they stood and fought, their army would be bled white and they would ultimately be forced to sue for peace. The operation was scheduled to start on February 10, but was delayed by bad weather until the 21st. Although the preparations for the operation were spotted, there was no attempt to reinforce Verdun, and the initial artillery onslaught caught the garrison unprepared.

OPENING BARRAGE

As February 21, 1916 dawned, the frigid air was shattered by the scream of heavy shells and the "whizz-bang" of anti-personnel weapons. More than two million shells fell on the forward French positions in the next 12 hours, after which the infantry began their attack. For the first two days the German forces made relatively little headway, but on the 24th they broke through the main defensive line, taking 10,000 prisoners and capturing 65 artillery pieces. The infantry were preceded in their attacks by a rolling barrage from the immense number of guns at their disposal, which wrecked the defenses and drove the survivors under cover.

Between the awesome artillery barrage, the suddenness of the attack and the cold weather, the French were paralyzed. Some units broke and fled to the rear, leaving weak areas in the defenses through which the German assault troops advanced. The whole Verdun defense was collapsing. Something had to be done, and fast.

Verdun was supposed to be invincible—a French army commission in 1915 had confirmed this, and fired a general for saying otherwise. Yet on February 25, Fort Douaumont, a key component of the city's defenses, fell to German assault. This was a serious blow to French morale, though it could have been avoided had the garrison not been stripped to the bone. The defending infantry had broken under bombardment leaving a platoon of artillerymen as the only defenders. A nine-man German patrol found a way into the fort and discovered that it was virtually undefended. They led 300 of their fellows in and captured the keystone of the Verdun defenses almost without firing a shot.

PÉTAIN TAKES CHARGE

At the same time as Fort Douaumont was being captured by the enemy, General Pétain was arriving to take charge of the defences of Verdun. He found a desperate situation, with the only supply route into the city along a single road and a narrow-gauge railroad alongside it. This road, dubbed La Voie Sacrée, was Verdun's inadequate lifeline, and Pétain's first task was to improve it. Thousands of men worked to widen the road, allowing a less restricted flow of supplies into the city. By the time they had finished, something like 6,000 trucks could use the road every day, and over half a million troops, plus all their supplies, moved into and out of the city along it. Pétain decided that units were only to serve 15-day tours in the trenches, to allow them time to rest and recuperate, so La Voie Sacrée saw an endless stream of units rotating to and from the front line. Although Pétain had improved the desperate logistics situation, things were still bad. The fighting ebbed somewhat at the very end of February, only to be resumed on March 5.

THE ATTACK IS RENEWED

A new German offensive was thrown in along the west bank of the Meuse, straight into the teeth of a well prepared defense. Pétain had deployed his best troops to meet this assault, and they were supported by a powerful concentration of artillery. This assault marked something of a turning point in the defense of Verdun. French gunners were not only inflicting horrific casualties on the attackers, but were conducting effective counterbattery fire against their artillery. By the middle of April all the very heavy guns on the German side were out of action, and the German

artillery had suffered another serious blow when a shell landed among almost half a million heavy artillery shells stockpiled in Spincourt forest. This caused the largest single explosion of the entire war.

The attacks continued through April and into May, and threatened to indeed "bleed the French army to death." However, gains were relatively slight and when Pétain was relieved by General Robert Nivelle, the French began to recover their offensive spirit.

NIVELLE TAKES OVER

Where Pétain had been the defender of Verdun and had prevented its fall, Nivelle took the offensive. The French slogan for Verdun was "Ils ne passeront pas!" ("They shall not pass!"), but Nivelle's aim was more than barring the door —he intended to kick the Germans back out. At first Nivelle could do no more than Pétain; German attacks were still making gains and with Fort Douaumont in German hands the crux of the defense was now Fort Vaux. Vaux protected an area of high ground from which German guns would be able to fire directly into the city and, even more importantly, at the bridges over which all supplies into the city were fed. Fort Vaux became the target of German assaults, and on June 7 it fell to them. Nevertheless, the balance was shifting. Nivelle was an artillery officer, and

THE GERMAN GEWEHR 98 was a fine rifle, but like all such weapons it was cumbersome in a close action, such as a trench assault, where fighting was hand-to-hand and shooting at very short ranges.

under his command the French guns became more effective. Even as the Germans advanced toward the surviving forts, Souville and Tavannes, their casualties mounted. Things hung in the balance throughout the end of June, and despite the opening of the Somme offensive on July 1, the Germans pushed onward, creeping ever closer to the city itself. On July 11 an attack actually reached Fort Souville, but its failure marked the end of German attempts to take Verdun. Thereafter they found themselves on the defensive as French counterattacks began to retake some of the lost ground.

FRENCH COUNTERATTACKS

Nivelle's position was improved by the Somme offensive, which was launched partly to reduce the pressure on Verdun.

A REMARKABLY CLEAN and spruce German soldier poses with rifle and grenade. He wears a gas mask typical of the type issued later in the war. Early versions were hurriedly improvised and only marginally effective.

It did not succeed as an operation in its own right, but was successful in drawing in supplies and reinforcements that could otherwise be set against the defenders of Verdun. As the pressure eased, Nivelle launched counterattacks to drive the Germans out and retake the lost forts. The largest of these was on October 24, against Fort Douaumont and involved 170,000 infantry, 700 guns, and more than 150 aircraft. After this the French ground slowly forward, retaking Fort Vaux in early November. In the middle of December the German army retreated from Verdun, leaving what was left of it in French hands.

"THE MEATGRINDER"

By the end of the Verdun offensive, the Germans had indeed managed to cause vast French casualties—550,000 of them in fact. However, this was only achieved at a cost of 450,000 casualties of their own. During the summer it was obvious

FRENCH INFANTRY DIG IN *somewhere in the Verdun sector, September 1916. The lot of the infantry was hard, living in wet and unsanitary conditions. This, combined with the horrendous casualties of the Verdun campaign, led to low morale and widespread rebellion among French troops in 1917.*

that the cost was going to be very high, but the decision was taken to continue the offensive. One German casualty was the career of General Falkenhayn. On August 29 he was reassigned to command forces fighting against the Romanian army, which had joined the Allies the day before. This reassignment effectively represented a demotion. Falkenhayn was replaced by Hindenburg with Ludendorff as Quartermaster-General. Blaming Falkenhayn for the situation was perhaps unfair—he had realized as early as March that casualties were going to be too high, and pushed for an end to the operation. However, Crown Prince Wilhelm insisted on continuing.

The original German plan was reasonably sound—to attack something the enemy had to defend and drain his resources by artillery bombardment followed by infantry occupation of the devastated territory. However, the German army fell victim to "mission creep," and at some point the capture of Verdun became the objective of the operation. This was not the plan originally —the idea was to destroy the French army, not to seize a city —and Verdun was not worth half a million troops.

However, as the battle went on the objective shifted until the German army was being ground down in order to take a city it did not want or need. Winning the battle had become more important than the strategic objectives that inspired it. This led to losses that could not be sustained and were wholly unnecessary.

AFTERMATH

Virtually every French division on the Western Front passed through the Verdun meatgrinder. Rather fewer, but still large, numbers of German formations were rotated into the offensive. Massive casualties on both sides reduced the fighting power and the morale of both forces, and arguably it was the plight of Verdun that forced the Allies to make their costly Somme offensive, which in turn cost both sides vast numbers of lives. In the end, what was a workable plan did not succeed and the battle was inconclusive. The German failure to take Verdun was a boost to morale on the Allied side, and although the Somme offensive failed to achieve anything significant either, the German army did pull back to the Hindenburg Line in 1917.

The vast casualties at Verdun and the Somme were partly to blame for the collapse of French morale in 1917, the increasing cynicism and mistrust of commanders among the British troops, and the decline of the German army, which lost the best of its junior leaders in the bitter fighting of 1916. Verdun was perhaps a situation where failure to win in an operational context paved the way for defeat at the grand strategic level.

FRENCH INFANTRY SERGEANT

There were no great differences between the equipment used by troops on both sides in World War I; this French sergeant's equipment is similar to that used by his German foes. A metal helmet offers some protection against overhead shell bursts and he is armed with a rifle and a bayonet. He may have a grenade or two available.

Although heavy artillery hurled tons of shells across the trench lines and specialist weapons gradually emerged including aircraft and armored vehicles most of the great battles of the war were decided by infantrymen who doggedly clung to their positions or struggled to prise one another out of them.

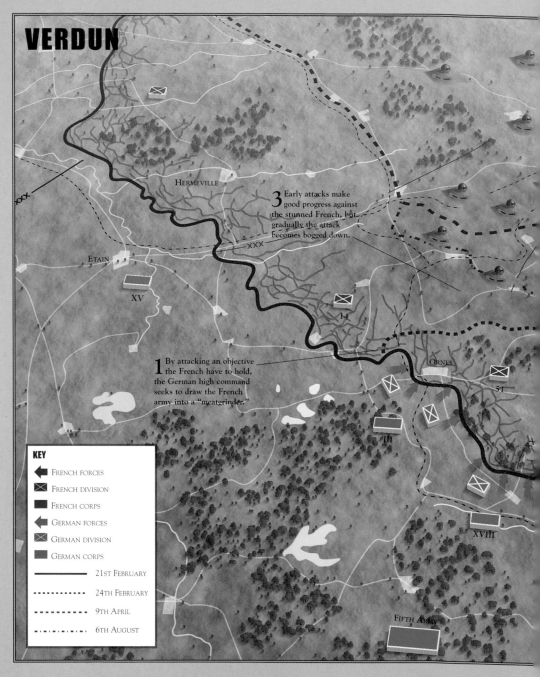

VERDUN

HERMEVILLE

3 Early attacks make good progress against the stunned French, but gradually the attack becomes bogged down.

ETAIN

XV

14

1 By attacking an objective the French have to hold, the German high command seeks to draw the French army into a "meatgrinder."

ORNES

51

III

XVIII

FIFTH ARMY

KEY

◄ FRENCH FORCES

✕ FRENCH DIVISION

▬ FRENCH CORPS

◄ GERMAN FORCES

✕ GERMAN DIVISION

▬ GERMAN CORPS

──────── 21ST FEBRUARY

•••••••• 24TH FEBRUARY

▬ ▬ ▬ ▬ 9TH APRIL

▬ • ▬ • ▬ 6TH AUGUST

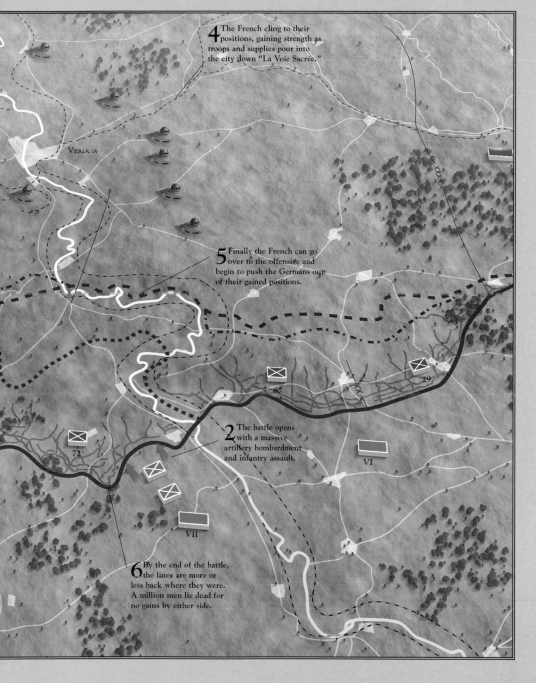

4 The French cling to their positions, gaining strength as troops and supplies pour into the city down "La Voie Sacrée."

VERDUN

5 Finally the French can go over to the offensive and begin to push the Germans out of their gained positions.

67

29

2 The battle opens with a massive artillery bombardment and infantry assault.

72

VI

VII

6 By the end of the battle, the lines are more or less back where they were. A million men lie dead for no gains by either side.

THE SOMME 1916

The battle of the Somme is today synonymous with military folly and pointless bloodshed, but in truth there were good reasons to attempt the massive assault. The military balance at the time favored the defender, but there seemed to be no other way to break the deadlock.

At the outset of World War I, military thinkers expected a war of maneuver in which cavalry would play its traditional role as a striking arm. At first, something like this actually did happen, and in some areas of the Eastern Front the war retained a nineteenth-century character, complete with the odd saber mêlée between opposing cavalry brigades.

In the West, however, it quickly became obvious that the defender had a huge advantage over the attacker. Things had been heading this way for some time. During the American Civil War and the Franco-Prussian War, the long-range accurate firepower of infantry rifles made assault by infantry or cavalry a hazardous business. Machine guns tipped the balance further, though they were heavy and unable to redeploy quickly. The war on the Western Front took on many of the characteristics

THE SOMME FACTS

Who: British Fourth Army with support from British Third Army and French Sixth Army, attacking German Second Army.

What: After massive artillery preparation the British and French forces attacked well defended German positions and gradually ground their way in, forcing costly counterattacks to regain lost ground.

Where: Between the Somme and Ancre rivers on the Western Front in France.

When: July 1 to November 18, 1916.

Why: With the war deadlocked and enemy troops entrenched on Allied soil, it was necessary to regain the offensive and break the German lines. The need to relieve

pressure on Russia and the French at Verdun also played a part.

Outcome: After bloody fighting and massive casualties on both sides, little was immediately gained. However, the German army lost much of its best manpower and later withdrew to the Hindenburg Line.

COUNTERSNIPING IN THE TRENCHES. *As a fellow soldier (background) holds aloft a helmet in the hope of attracting a shot, a British sniper waits for his German counterpart to reveal his position by firing.*

of a siege, with heavily entrenched forces on both sides fighting from behind barbed-wire obstacles.

Between the big offensives, the war became one of raid and counter-raid, usually at night, with artillery pounding away at the opposing trenches. Infantry holding the forward positions were subjected to horrible conditions, huddling in their muddy dugouts and enduring bombardment while being unable to reply. Being under fire and unable to fight back is one of the most morally draining experiences men can suffer and morale was, unsurprisingly, a problem.

Something had to be done, for several reasons. The presence of German troops on Allied soil meant it was not politically viable to sit on the defensive and hope that the naval blockade of Germany would eventually strangle her into submission. The French fortress of Verdun was at that time under pressure too. In short, the German army had to be attacked and defeated. It would be an expensive undertaking in terms of material and casualties, but in January 1916 when the plan was formulated the Allies believed it could be done.

THE PLAN

The primary exponent of the plan was the French commander, Marshal Joseph Joffre (1852–1931). He wanted an offensive in the Somme area for the reasons listed above, and the British commander, General Sir Douglas Haig (1861–1928), was willing to consider it. Haig preferred the idea of an attack somewhere else, such as Flanders, where the terrain was better and there were more strategic objectives.

A BRITISH 4.7-IN (11.75CM) BREECH-LOADING GUN. In the American Civil War, just 50 years previously, most artillery units were still armed with short-ranged smoothbore cannon. The increase in artillery killing power contributed to a static war.

He also wanted to wait for the reinforcements that the new conscription system would provide, and for fresh troops from around the Empire to arrive. There was also the possibility that the new secret weapon, code-named "tanks," might be some help. However, Joffre could not wait.

Haig proposed an assault in the middle of August, but Joffre was adamant that the French army would not exist by then. He had originally proposed to use two French armies in the Somme offensive, but the Verdun meatgrinder reduced the French capabilities, and the original offer of 40 divisions was amended to 16. The remainder would have to come from the British. Nevertheless, the attack seemed to be practicable, and it was vital that something was done, so Haig agreed. The opening date for the offensive was set at July 1, 1916, and a force comprising 21 divisions was allocated to the initial offensive, with three infantry and five cavalry divisions in reserve to follow up a victory.

HEAVY DEFENSES

Although the Somme sector had been fairly quiet for some time, German defensive preparations had been continuous. The trenches were backed by strongpoints and dugouts in an impressive defensive complex, which also included medical facilities, kitchens, laundries, and electrical generating stations. Many of these installations were concealed by woods or villages, and their existence was not obvious to observers on the Allied side.

The Allies would have to cross low ground and fight their way uphill into the first line of German positions, which was overlooked by the second, and so forth. The defenders enjoyed an excellent view of the battlefield, making concealed preparations and maneuvers very difficult. The defenders also had vast reserves of ammunition, and

plenty of heavy weapons. Their high position also had psychological advantages whereas the Allied troops would be slogging uphill into the teeth of heavy resistance.

The Allied preparations for the offensive were not only observed from the enemy positions. Operational security was poor, and comments by British and French officers found their way into German intelligence reports. By the time the Allies opened up with their massive artillery bombardment on June 24, the Germans already knew something was up. They had even guessed the date of the intended assault.

Although 1.75 million artillery shells were fired at German positions in a six-day preparatory bombardment, the defenses were not seriously disrupted. Artillery fire was supposed to cut enemy wire, but all it tended to do was move it around and tangle it up even more. Muddy shell craters were tough going, and just to add to the misery heavy rain turned the whole area into a quagmire.

Although conscription had been introduced in Britain, most of the troops waiting to go over the top were in volunteer units from Kitchener's New Army. Among the attackers were several notable names—future military commanders Montgomery and Wavell, as well as Siegfried Sassoon and John Masefield.

On the German side the troops, who included an Austrian volunteer corporal named Adolf Hitler, were ready to receive and repel an assault. Casualties were taken, and a six-day bombardment, even ridden out in deep bunkers, is no joke. Overall, though, the defenders knew they were in good shape to deal with the coming attack. Their artillery was registered by map grid on the entire battlefield, and fire could be called down quickly on any enemy concentration.

The defenders could see the ground in front of their positions clearly, and were aware of choke points and obvious routes that attackers would be channeled into. Their machine guns were ready to sweep these areas as the enemy passed through them. If, somehow, the first trench line were taken, the defenders could fall back to secondary positions and carry on the fight from there.

THE FIRST DAY

The offensive began at 7:30 A.M. on July 1, much as the Germans had predicted. All along the line, the attacking units lurched into motion, and the defenders began firing at them. The British forces went into action in long lines, proceeding at a walk across difficult terrain and stopping to struggle past tangles of wire. Initial reports to Haig were rather optimistic. At 8 A.M. he was to record that everything was going well and the first enemy positions had been

THE BRITISH "TOMMY"

At the battle of the Somme, each British soldier, or "Tommy" as they were known, was covered in mud that dried in the sun and carried a formidable burden. Every soldier was carrying at least 60lb (27kg) of equipment including a rifle with 220 rounds of ammunition, two hand grenades, and a couple of (empty) sandbags to fortify captured enemy positions against counterattack. In addition to this not inconsiderable load, many men carried other burdens. Everything that might be needed had to be transported forward by the assaulting troops. This included carrier pigeons, field telephones and their cables, digging equipment, and extra ammunition. All of this had to be carried through mud and wire, uphill, under machine-gun fire.

overrun. This was somewhat inaccurate. The reality was that British troops were being cut down in their thousands, often just beyond their trenches or in gaps in the wire that were becoming choked with bodies. Meanwhile, the French forces were also struggling. Their soldiers were less heavily burdened that the British and used more flexible tactics, rushing from position to position while others covered the advance with rifle fire. Although their casualties were lighter (on account of not presenting such a

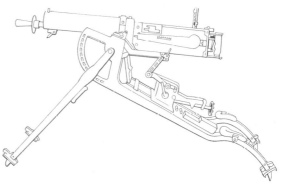

THE GERMAN MAXIM 08 could spit death at a rate of 450 rounds per minute at a range of 6,560ft (2000m). Its effectiveness as a defensive weapon was amply demonstrated at the Somme, when just a few guns were able to mow down whole British batallions in a matter of minutes.

JULY 1, 1916: Preparing for the assault. Canadian troops fix bayonets as they await the order to go "over the top."

wonderful target perhaps), the French force under General Fayolle did not have the numbers needed to smash a hole in the German lines.

HORRIFIC CASUALTIES

The first day of the Somme offensive resulted in some 57,470 British casualties, of whom almost 20,000 were killed. Only 585 were captured, mainly because few of the British troops got close enough to the German lines. Some units, such as the Canadian 1st Newfoundland Regiment, had been effectively wiped out. This horrific slaughter was made worse by the ponderous linear formation used by attacking units, although with such inexperienced troops there may have been no alternative.

The British had attacked with 200 battalions in 17 divisions of about 100,000 men. Of these, only five divisions got any men into the enemy positions at all. The rest were halted in no-man's land. It was not for lack of trying, but the

defenders were simply too strong. The Tyneside Irish Regiment, numbering about 3,000 men, suffered nearly 100 percent casualties. The regiment began its advance behind the main start line, in support of the initial attack. Despite the fact that this formation was not an immediate threat to the defenders, it came under such withering fire as it moved up that it never crossed the start line. A total of 500 men were killed or wounded in one battalion and 600 in another. Casualties might have been even higher, but for the fact that many defenders became so sickened by the slaughter that they ceased fire once the attackers in their sector stalled, and allowed the survivors to retreat unmolested.

ATTRITIONAL STRUGGLE

Despite the fact that fully 20 percent of the attacking force had been killed, the Allies kept on attacking. Perhaps they had no alternative. Pressure had to be taken off Russia and Verdun somehow, and there was no time to build up for an offensive elsewhere. Logistics took too long, and the Allies needed to act now. Men could be fed in, but supplies and ammunition stocks took time to assemble. The Allies had to succeed on the Somme or at least pull in enough German reinforcements to reduce the pressure elsewhere.

At first the slaughter was very much one-sided as the Allies threw in new assaults and these were chewed up by the machine guns and artillery, or stalled on the wire. It may have seemed that the Allies were simply throwing away lives, and at first this may have been the case. For example, one German regiment took 180 casualties on the first day of the Somme whereas the British force facing it lost more than 25 times as many men.

For two weeks little was achieved. Then, on July 14 a force of French and British troops managed to make some gains along the flanks of the Somme River. Minor gains followed, but the cost was immense, and fresh troops were fed into the battle on a regular basis as shattered formations had to be pulled out. Through July and August the slaughter went on, though now it was less one-sided. Forty-two German divisions were deployed to the Somme sector in those two months, and the necessity of counterattacking Allied gains resulted in heavy casualties. At the end of July, casualties reached 200,000 for the Allies and 160,000 among German troops. The Allies had advanced 3 miles (4.8km), and little had changed at the end of August.

NEW IDEAS

Tactics had been evolving during the long struggle, and the raw British troops had learned from their more experienced French counterparts. Techniques like predawn attacks had achieved some successes. The Allies were becoming more flexible and inventive. It was time to try something new. The main problems facing the Allies were wire and machine guns,

BARBED WIRE came in many different varieties, including the coiled "Dannert" wire (far left), the virtually impenetrable high wire entanglements (center left), and the apron fence, both square and pyramid shaped (right and far right). All sides sent out wiring parties at night to repair damage.

and now they, potentially, had a means to deal with both. Created specifically as a machine-gun destroyer, the monstrous armored fighting machine known as a "tank" made its appearance. Tanks came in two types. "Male" tanks mounted a main armament of 6-pounder guns derived from naval weapons, while "female" tanks carried only machine guns. Both types were slow, prone to mechanical breakdown, and required a large crew to operate. The could cross trenches, crush wire, and, usually, shrug off small-arms and machine-gun fire, which gave them a fighting chance.

Thirty-six tanks were deployed for a renewed assault, despite the fact that their crews were not fully trained. Only 18 went into action because the rest had broken down, but their appearance shocked the defenders into a panic. The Allies gained 3,500 yards (3,200m) for relatively slight cost, easily the biggest success of the offensive to date. However, it was not possible to exploit the breakthrough and several tanks were lost to artillery fire. The rest broke down or got stuck.

Tanks were not a decisive weapon on the Somme, mainly because they were committed in difficult terrain and in small numbers. Their success prompted further experiments, which were locally useful but achieved little on a strategic scale. That would change with the massed tank action at Cambrai in 1917, but for now the tank was simply another factor in a desperate struggle.

THE OFFENSIVE WINDS DOWN

As the weather worsened through October and November, the Allies attacked again and again, battering at the German positions until November 19, when the operation was ceased. At that point the Allies had advanced no more than 7 miles (11.2km) along a 20-mile (32.2km) front. In the middle of November, the casualty figures came to 419,654 for the British and 194,541 for the French, and this while the slaughter at Verdun was ongoing. These immense losses—just short of 615,000—were sustained in failing to break through the Somme positions. However, the German army took 650,000 casualties in repelling the assault, and this had serious repercussions. The German army in 1914 was a splendid military instrument built on Prussian military traditions and

victories in France and Austria. As 1917 began it was a tired and dispirited force, whose best men had fallen in the struggles on the Somme. So many good young officers and NCOs had fallen that the German army never really recovered.

AFTERMATH

The Battle of the Somme shook the confidence of the British army in its commanders and political leaders. It finished Joffre's military career, though Haig was promoted to Field Marshal at the end of the year. The battle is remembered as the worst slaughter in British military history, but in some ways it did manage to achieve its aims. The German army was badly battered and perhaps dismayed at the doggedness of the attackers. Whatever the reason, the German army fell back to the more easily defended Hindenburg Line in February 1917.

"TANK TERROR" is the term used to describe the psychological effect of an armored vehicle on infantry. Rifles and grenades were unlikely to halt even an early tank.

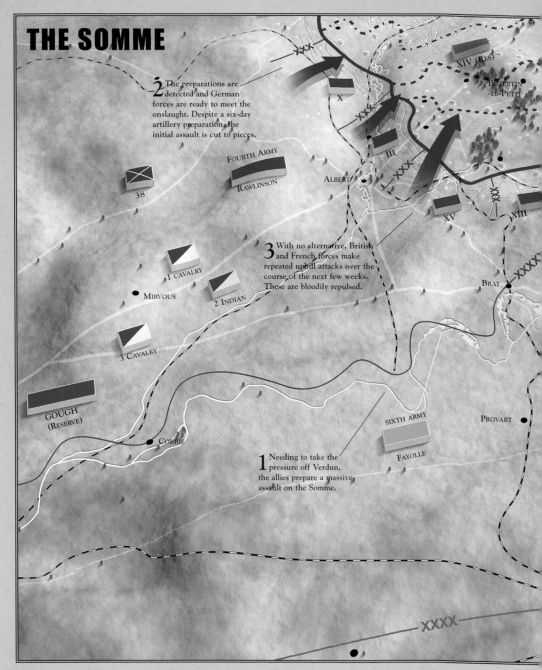

THE SOMME

2 The preparations are detected and German forces are ready to meet the onslaught. Despite a six-day artillery preparation, the initial assault is cut to pieces.

XIV (RES)

BOZERTIN -LE-PETIT

X

III

FOURTH ARMY

RAWLINSON

38

ALBERT

XV

XIII

3 With no alternative, British and French forces make repeated uphill attacks over the course of the next few weeks. These are bloodily repulsed.

1 CAVALRY

MIRVOUS

2 INDIAN

BRAY

3 CAVALRY

GOUGH
(RESERVE)

CORBIE

SIXTH ARMY

PROVART

FAYOLLE

1 Needing to take the pressure off Verdun, the allies prepare a massive assault on the Somme.

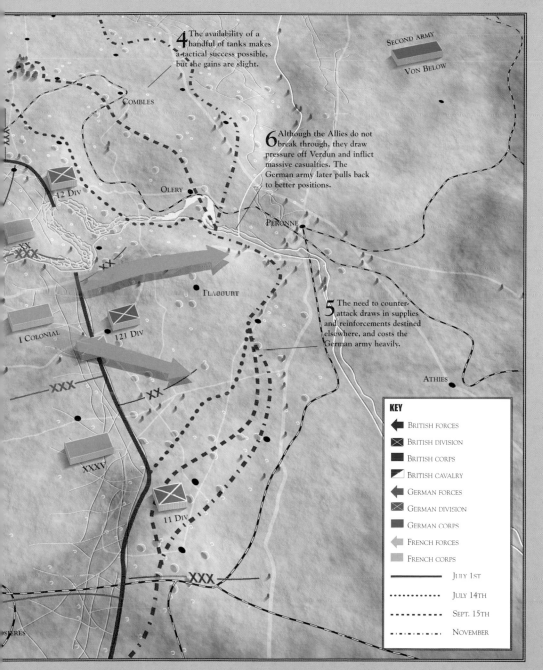

4 The availability of a handful of tanks makes a tactical success possible, but the gains are slight.

SECOND ARMY

VON BELOW

COMBLES

6 Although the Allies do not break through, they draw pressure off Verdun and inflict massive casualties. The German army later pulls back to better positions.

12 DIV

OLERY

XXX

PERONNE

XX

FLAUCOURT

5 The need to counter-attack draws in supplies and reinforcements destined elsewhere, and costs the German army heavily.

I COLONIAL

121 DIV

XXX

XX

ATHIES

XXXV

11 DIV

XXX

KEY

◄ BRITISH FORCES

☒ BRITISH DIVISION

■ BRITISH CORPS

◪ BRITISH CAVALRY

◄ GERMAN FORCES

☒ GERMAN DIVISION

■ GERMAN CORPS

◄ FRENCH FORCES

■ FRENCH CORPS

——————— JULY 1ST

· · · · · · · · · JULY 14TH

- - - - - - - SEPT. 15TH

·—·—·—·— NOVEMBER

THE BATTLE OF BRITAIN

1940

In the summer of 1940, Britain was isolated on the fringe of a hostile continent. Only a narrow strip of water stood between British cities and the panzer divisions. Crossing "the world's biggest antitank ditch" required air superiority, which ultimately the Luftwaffe failed to secure.

Some historians present the two World Wars as a single conflict with a 20-year ceasefire in between, and with hindsight it is not difficult to see how the roots of the second conflict lay in the first. In the 1920s, as a disarmed and humiliated Germany struggled with economic and social troubles, the rest of the world tried to come to terms with the cost of the recent Great War. Treaties were signed to limit naval construction and avoid a costly arms race, and the general feeling was that another war must be avoided at almost any cost.

THE BATTLE OF BRITAIN FACTS

Who: The German Luftwaffe versus the British Royal Air Force, augmented by foreign volunteers.

What: The German's attempts to destroy the RAF resulted in fierce air battles, which ultimately the Luftwaffe failed to win.

Where: British airspace, mainly over the southern and eastern counties.

When: Summer 1940.

Why: Hitler's Nazi Germany wanted to invade and subdue Britain, and needed air superiority to do so.

Outcome: A desperate struggle brought the RAF to the brink of defeat but ultimately it managed to hold on long enough to prevent invasion.

PILOTS OF NO. 92 SQUADRON *Royal Air Force scramble for their fighters early on in 1941. The squadron took part in the final stages of the Battle of Britain, but by this time they had switched to offensive operations over France.*

VICTIMS OF GERMAN BOMBERS are pulled from their homes in the East End of London by rescue workers during the Blitz.

As a consequence, Britain and her allies were completely unprepared to fight a second World War. The Royal Navy was substantial but was hampered by treaty limitations, while the army was small and underequipped. In particular, armored forces had not been developed with any real enthusiasm, despite the fact that the British invented armored warfare.

THE ROYAL AIR FORCE

The Royal Air Force of the 1930s was something of a social institution, a private club for well-off young gentlemen who flew obsolescent aircraft and cut a dash at parties. Equipment was outdated, though entirely serviceable. Design and acquisition of new aircraft was of low priority. This could very well have cost Britain the war.

The Gloster Gladiator, the RAF's front-line fighter in 1937, was a very good aircraft in some ways—it was pilot-friendly, very maneuverable, and had no vices—but it was a biplane fighter armed with four machine guns. The first production Messerschmitt Bf 109s were in service two years later, and had they met Gladiators over southern Britain the result would have been a massacre. Fortunately, a move in the late 1930s to develop a decent low-wing monoplane fighter for the RAF paid dividends, and just in time. The Gladiator was designed in the early 1930s, before air power

was really appreciated. Once it was realized that aircraft would play a major rule in any future war, new projects began to emerge.

The Hawker Hurricane was considered radical by many—"eight machine guns is going a bit far" one critic claimed—but this was the armament carried by the Hurricane I, which first entered service in December 1937, and by September 1939 equipped 18 squadrons. The more famous Supermarine Spitfire entered service in August 1938, though in smaller numbers than the Hurricane. The Spitfire was originally also armed with eight 0.303in (7.6mm) machine guns, but a small number received 0.788in (20mm) cannon in place of four of the machine guns.

The decision to arm fighters with cannon or machine guns was influenced largely by their intended role. Multiple machine guns were considered best for defeating fighters: A lot of bullets were required to obtain hits, and fighters were relatively fragile. Cannon were better for destroying bombers. Their heavier shells were more likely to cause serious damage to a large aircraft that could fly quite happily with a scattering of small holes in the fuselage. Many fighters adopted a hybrid armament of cannon and machine guns.

THE BOMBER THREAT

In Germany, which had created its air force from scratch in defiance of treaties forbidding it, there was no obsolete "legacy" equipment to rely on, so modern aircraft had to be acquired from the outset. Thus German fighters and fighter-bombers were somewhat ahead of the competition. The disparity in equipment was not all that great, but there was a general feeling that the Hurricane was outmatched by the Bf 109 whereas the Spitfire was more or less its equal.

Air power had been very much in its infancy during World War I, but it had achieved very promising results. In the 1930s, it was thought that "the bomber will always get through" and that bombing could achieve decisive results. Experience in the Spanish Civil War seemed to bear this out, and the effects of air raids on towns and cities were likely to be horrible. If a country were not to collapse and surrender due to civilian casualties, the bomber had to be stopped. Guns on the ground could do so much, but it was fighter interception that was the big hope in the fight against the bomber.

BRITISH PREPARATIONS

RAF Fighter Command fought hard during the Battle of Britain, of that there can be no question. However, it might not have prevailed but for the sophisticated detection and coordination system that supported it.

During the 1920s, the assumption in Britain was that the next great threat would come from the traditional enemy rather than a thoroughly defeated and demilitarized

Germany. In order to defeat the half-expected horde of French bombers, an early-warning system was set up in southern England. This consisted of acoustic detectors, effectively great stone mirrors that focussed sound at a single point and allowed aircraft to be heard at great distances—if they approached from the right direction.

The detectors themselves played no part in the Battle of Britain. However, the command and control system set up to feed their data to the fighter stations was still in place when war with Germany broke out in 1939. Its information came not from acoustic detectors but from the "Chain Home" radar stations recently installed on the south coast. These stations provided early warning, which allowed a response to be planned and fitted to the circumstances. Had the fighters had to scramble when their pilots saw enemies overhead, the battle could not have been won.

THE OUTBREAK OF WAR

Things did not look good at the outbreak of war. After several months of "phoney war" or "Sitzkrieg," German forces advanced into France and overran its defenses. The British were forced to refuse French requests for more Hurricane squadrons, effectively admitting that they did not think France could be saved.

The decision not to send fighters to reinforce defeat was a morally courageous one, and it played a part in the eventual salvation of all Europe from Nazism. The RAF was stretched thin enough as it was. Had more of its strength been sacrificed in a political gesture, Britain too might have been lost. Although the French, aided by British forces, put up a fight, they were simply unprepared for the armored onslaught they faced, and France was quickly knocked out of the war. Though much of the British army was evacuated and managed to reach home, it left behind most of its heavy equipment and needed time to reorganize and re-equip.

If Germany could launch the invasion of Britain (codenamed Operation "Sealion") in the near future, the prospects of preventing it were slim. Various measures were put in place. Crash programs to expand the army, backed up by a major fortification project and the formation of what became the Home Guard, offered a chance to resist an invasion. The navy declared it could prevent an invasion for a time but not indefinitely. Its cruisers and

THIS LUFTWAFFE Heinkel He111 bomber pilot is wearing the one-piece canvas flying suit designed for summer use. He is also kitted out with a lifejacket, in case of the very real possibility of having to ditch his aircraft over the English Channel.

battleships could certainly shatter an invasion flotilla, but to do so they would have to operate in restricted waters under very hostile skies. The fleet was prepared to do what it could, but if the Germans had air supremacy then that amounted to going down fighting to buy time for the land forces.

Air supremacy was the key. With it, the German invasion would ultimately be unstoppable. Without it, the chances of success were much slimmer and so the Luftwaffe set out to secure control of the skies. Its commander, Reichsmarshall Hermann Göring (1893–1946), believed that the small and unprepared Royal Air Force would crumble quickly. He claimed that RAF Fighter Command could be put out of actions in four days, and after four weeks there would be nothing left of the British aircraft

MESSERSCHMITT BF 109

The Bf 109 was one of the best aircraft of its era, and its pilots accordingly held high status. Better than a Hurricane and only just matched by the Spitfire, the Bf 109 was a dangerous foe. Later in the war, it found itself outmatched by developed versions of existing Allied fighters and by aircraft designed specifically to beat it, but in the summer of 1940 the Bf 109 pilot was lord of the air and his machine almost without parallel. At various times the Bf 109 served as an air superiority fighter, an escort fighter, an interceptor, a ground-attack aircraft, and a reconnaissance aircraft. The Bf 109 was produced in greater quantities than any other fighter aircraft in history, with more than 31,000 units built.

THE MESSERSCHMITT BF 110 was a "heavy fighter" intended to be able to escort bombers. It was outmatched by single-engined British fighters and was so badly mauled that the bomber escorts were sometimes given an escort of single-seaters.

until, on August 13, a major air offensive was launched against RAF airfields in the south of England. Alder Tag, "Eagle Day," was a desperate time for Fighter Command. Aircraft that survived the fighting in the air might return to a bomb-cratered runway or be destroyed on the ground while rearming. Fighter Command was stretched to the limit, but it did not break. As ground crews rearmed and refueled the undamaged planes, and did their best to return

industry to produce replacement aircraft. This claim turned out to be somewhat optimistic.

THE BATTLE OPENS

Göring's plan was to draw out the RAF's fighter strength and destroy it by attacking targets such as coastal convoys, airfields, and radar stations, as well as reducing Britain's capability to replace aircraft by bombing factories. The fighting began on June 30, 1940. The raids were stepped up

ONE OF THE FINEST FIGHTERS of all time, the Supermarine Spitfire served in 40 different versions. It was slightly faster and much more maneuverable than the Bf 109, but it could be out-climbed by its foe.

even badly shot-up ones to some semblance of serviceability, work parties filled in the runway craters while nearby soldiers manned machine guns and anti-aircraft guns to defend the embattled airfields.

Information came in from central command, directing the tired pilots to new battles as they took off again and again to intercept new raids. Particularly hit hard was 11 Group, which covered Kent and Sussex, but somehow they managed to go on fighting through "Eagle Day" and the terrible weeks that followed.

The projected four days were long gone, and yet the RAF was still in the fight. At times reeling like a punch-drunk boxer who just will not go down, Fighter Command fought back with everything at its disposal, and each raid bled the Luftwaffe.

The British enjoyed a number of advantages over the attackers, though it might not have seemed like it at the time. British aircraft entered battle close to home, benefiting from the traditional advantage of "interior lines" over an enemy who had to travel to the battlefield. Thus fighters could be switched from one target to another as long as they had fuel and ammunition, and as long as their pilots could stand it. Fighting at a distance from its airfields took its toll on the Luftwaffe. Pilots were required to spend more time in unproductive travel to and from the battle area, which wasted fuel, increased maintenance requirements per minute of combat time, tired out pilots, and also took aircraft out of the fight for much longer than their British equivalents, which were often fighting over their own bases.

Of course, this did mean that German pilots had less combat time per day while RAF men were flung from one action to the next with a corresponding psychological effect. The RAF was also reinforced throughout the battle by foreign volunteers and newly trained pilots. The foreigners included Free Polish, French, and Scandinavian pilots plus New Zealanders, South Africans, Canadians, and even American citizens who had come to fight alongside the British even though their nation was not yet at war with Germany.

All the same, "The Few" were getting fewer and the battle was far from won. The decision to commit fresh squadrons from less heavily beset northern sectors resulted in a massacre. These green pilots were flung into intense battle against an enemy with far more experience. Those who survived learned fast and were soon giving as good as they got.

SWITCHING TARGETS

From the German perspective, the failure of the RAF to roll over and die was inexplicable. Surely nobody could stand such horrific combat for so long and keep fighting? Göring was very jealous of the prestige of his Luftwaffe, and had staked its reputation on beating the RAF. So why wouldn't the RAF give up? In fact, Fighter Command was at the end of its tether. There were times when every flyable aircraft was in the air, and even then there were too few of them.

Perhaps not realizing that the RAF was, indeed, being ground down, Göring ordered a change in strategy. A German bomber had missed its industrial target and hit a residential area of London, and RAF Bomber Command had retaliated with a raid on Berlin. Hitler was incensed, and so deliberate attacks on London and other cities were ordered. Fighter Command had to respond to the bombing raids, but the RAF was no longer the main target. Now that its airfields were no longer under direct attack, the strain lessened slightly and hopes began to rise. Fighter Command began to grow in strength and in time gained the upper hand. It had come very close to extinction but clung on long enough to ensure victory.

VICTORY

Unlike a land battle, it is hard to determine a clear point where one side had won and the other lost in the Battle of Britain. Things certainly looked bleak for Britain on September 15, but on the 17th Hitler decided that the invasion of Britain was not possible and canceled Operation "Sealion." It can be reasonably claimed that the Battle of Britain was not so won as such by the British; it was more that the Luftwaffe failed to achieve victory.

This nonetheless represented a strategic victory for the British—the Battle of Britain was fought to prevent an invasion by German forces—even though there was no clear moment where tactical victory was achieved. While there is some doubt that the invasion would have been

successful, the fact remains that it was canceled because the RAF was still holding out despite everything the Luftwaffe could do to it. Churchill referred to the pilots of RAF Fighter Command as "The Few," and rightly commented that a very great deal was owed to these heroes. But let us not forget the other architects of victory. Those who pushed for good, modern fighter aircraft just in time, those who repaired, refueled, and rearmed the fighters, who filled in the craters and defended the airbases while they themselves were under attack, and the unsung coordinators who gathered radar data and turned it into successful interceptions. Victory in the Battle of Britain was a team effort. It was won by tenacity in the face of tremendous odds, and it most likely changed the course of the war.

AFTERMATH

The battle to destroy the RAF cost the Luftwaffe 1,733 aircraft. The RAF lost 915. Some British pilots were shot down several times. There are documented cases of men crashing near their base, running to the nearest aircraft, and going up again. Against such fighting spirit it is not hard to see how the Luftwaffe failed to win.

There was no sudden end to the air attacks, which continued throughout the war. London and other cities were bombed many times and there were plenty of smaller raids on factories and shipping to which Fighter Command responded. But starting from September 17, 1940 onward the threat of invasion receded. In 1941 Hitler sealed his fate by ignoring a bloody, battered but undefeated Britain on his flank and invading the Soviet Union. Later that year the USA entered the war. On June 6, 1944 British, U.S., and Canadian troops landed in France to begin the liberation of Europe. They landed from the south of England, from territory kept free of enemies by the courage and skill of a few fighter pilots.

AN RAF PILOT MID-SCRAMBLE. Initially commissioned officer-pilots and enlisted sergeant-pilots were segregated and had different messes although they fought together. The Battle of Britain did much to bring equality among "The Few."

THE BATTLE OF BRITAIN

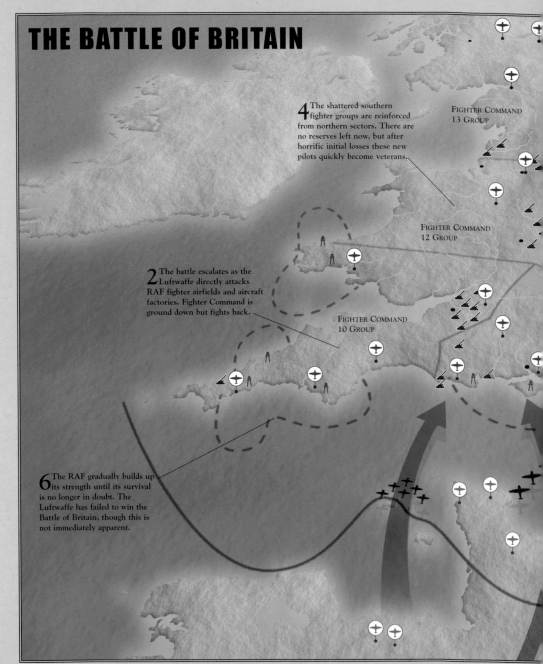

4 The shattered southern fighter groups are reinforced from northern sectors. There are no reserves left now, but after horrific initial losses these new pilots quickly become veterans.

FIGHTER COMMAND
13 GROUP

FIGHTER COMMAND
12 GROUP

2 The battle escalates as the Luftwaffe directly attacks RAF fighter airfields and aircraft factories. Fighter Command is ground down but fights back.

FIGHTER COMMAND
10 GROUP

6 The RAF gradually builds up its strength until its survival is no longer in doubt. The Luftwaffe has failed to win the Battle of Britain, though this is not immediately apparent.

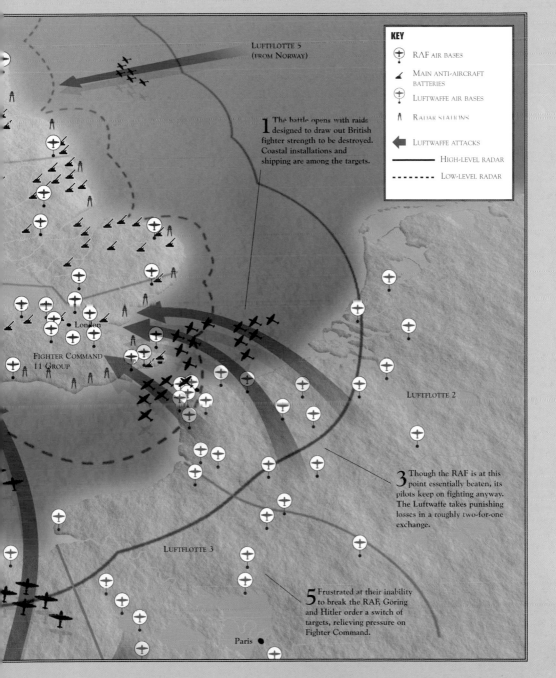

LUFTFLOTTE 5
(FROM NORWAY)

KEY

RAF AIR BASES

MAIN ANTI-AIRCRAFT
BATTERIES

LUFTWAFFE AIR BASES

RADAR STATIONS

LUFTWAFFE ATTACKS

HIGH-LEVEL RADAR

LOW-LEVEL RADAR

1 The battle opens with raids designed to draw out British fighter strength to be destroyed. Coastal installations and shipping are among the targets.

London

FIGHTER COMMAND
11 GROUP

LUFTFLOTTE 2

3 Though the RAF is at this point essentially beaten, its pilots keep on fighting anyway. The Luftwaffe takes punishing losses in a roughly two-for-one exchange.

LUFTFLOTTE 3

5 Frustrated at their inability to break the RAF, Göring and Hitler order a switch of targets, relieving pressure on Fighter Command.

Paris

STALINGRAD 1942

The turning point of World War II, the Battle of Stalingrad was a savage and bitter urban conflict in which tens of thousands of German and Soviet troops were killed. It was here that the Red Army proved it could not only hold off the Wehrmacht in a defensive battle, but also take the offensive and defeat the seemingly invincible German war machine.

O peration "Barbarossa," the German invasion of the Soviet Union, was the largest land invasion in history, pitting 3.6 million German troops and their allies against some three million Soviet troops in the western Soviet Union. Tactically and doctrinally superior, the Germans advanced further and faster than any other modern army, capturing some three million prisoners in the process. Yet the Soviet Union did not collapse as Hitler had so confidently predicted. Unclear strategic goals, logistical overstretch, unexpectedly tough Soviet resistance, and the terrible Russian winter meant the Germans failed to defeat their enemy decisively in 1941. Indeed the Red Army was able to launch a counteroffensive at Moscow on December 5–6, which

STALINGRAD FACTS

Who: The German Sixth Army under General Friedrich Paulus (1890–1957) against the Soviet Sixty-Second Army under General Vasily Chuikov (1900–82).

What: The Germans, bogged down in urban fighting where their superior mobile tactics were useless, were unable to take the city and were subsequently trapped by the Soviet counteroffensive and the Sixth Army surrendered.

Where: The city of Stalingrad on the Volga River, in the southern Soviet Union.

When: September 14, 1942 to February 2, 1943.

Why: The Germans sought to take

Stalingrad to deal both a material and psychological blow to further Soviet resistance.

Outcome: Stalingrad was the turning point in the war on the Eastern Front, when the Soviets won their first major victory.

A GERMAN MORTAR DETACHMENT *prepares to move in the factory district of the city. Some of the fiercest fighting occurred around the factories, and the Red October factory was never captured in its entirety, despite numerous attacks.*

and the oil fields, which supplied 90 percent of Soviet fuel. In the short term this would deny the Soviets fuel and in the long term provide resources for a drawn-out war against Britain and the USA. He set out this view in Führer Directive No. 41 on April 5, 1942, stating that: "All available forces will be concentrated on the main operations in the Southern sector, with the aim of destroying the enemy before the Don, in order to secure the Caucasian oil fields and the passes through the Caucasian Mountains themselves."

OPERATION "BLUE"

Operation "Blue," as the plan was code-named, was undertaken by Army Group South consisting of one million German and 300,000 allied troops, supported by *Luftflotte* 4 with 1,500 aircraft. There were two main axes of advance; Army Group A would drive for the Caucasus, while Army Group B would secure the northeastern flank of the advance along the Don and Volga rivers. "Blue" opened on June 28, 1942 and initially the Germans made rapid advances. Although they managed to inflict a number of telling defeats on the Soviets, Stalin had given permission to the Red Army to trade space for time and the retreat was made in reasonably good order.

Army Group A reached the oil fields at Maikop on August 9, but the advance slowed thereafter as resources were switched to Army Group B. Its main formation was Sixth Army led by Colonel-General Friedrich Paulus, which was pushing toward the city of Stalingrad, which sat on the major crossing point of the Volga River. On July 23, Hitler ordered that the city be taken. Militarily there were some sound reasons for capturing Stalingrad, because it would secure the flank of Army Group South and block an obvious launching point for a Soviet counterattack. However, the main motivations were political and psychological. The capture of the city that bore Stalin's name would be of huge value to the morale of both Germany and its allies.

STALINGRAD

Stalin also understood the importance of the city. On July 12 he established the Stalingrad Front made up of the Sixty-Second, Sixty-Third, and Sixty-Fourth Armies. A week later the city itself was put on an immediate war footing, but there was to be no mass evacuation of the population as Stalin believed that the troops would fight better for a "living city." On July 23 he issued Order No. 227 that the Red Army would take "Not a step back." German commanders noticed a definite stiffening of Soviet resistance, but they were able to batter their way through Sixty-Fourth Army and cross the Don on August 23.

The same day *Luftflotte* 4 launched a massive air raid on Stalingrad causing 30,000 casualties. The first German

GERMAN INFANTRY MANHANDLE *a light infantry gun into position during the fighting in the north of Stalingrad. Light guns were often used against defended infantry positions.*

caught the overextended, exhausted Germans unawares, pushing them back more than 100 miles (160km) in places before the line stabilized.

"Barbarossa" had cost the German army 1.1 million casualties. Only eight of the Eastern Army's 162 divisions were at full strength. Losses of vehicles were similarly high. By the spring of 1942 there was no question of resuming the offensive along the whole front, rather the Germans only had the resources for a single thrust. Stalin and the Soviet High Command anticipated that the Germans would resume their assault on Moscow and therefore massed their reserves in the area.

However, with the entry of the USA into the war in December 1941, Germany was now faced with the prospect of the opening of a Second Front and a long war of attrition. Thus Hitler decided to drive south toward the Transcaucasus

spearheads reached the Volga at Rynok and entered Stalingrad's northern suburbs. However, the advance on the city slowed in the face of poor terrain and desperate Soviet resistance. Thus the bulk of Paulus' army only reached the outskirts of central Stalingrad in early September. Herman Hoth's Fourth Panzer Army suffered similar difficulties in reaching the southern suburbs around about the same time.

THE OPPOSING FORCES

The Soviets estimated that about 170,000 men, 500 tanks, and 3,000 artillery pieces faced them on the 40-mile (64.3km) front around Stalingrad and its environs. They themselves could muster about 90,000 troops, 120 tanks, and 2,000 guns. A similar imbalance faced the defenders on the narrower front of the city itself, with the defending 54,000 strong Sixty-Second Army up against about 100,000 Germans. These numbers fluctuated throughout the battle due to losses and reinforcement, but the force ratios remained reasonably constant throughout. The main commanders were Paulus, an excellent staff officer and a capable solider, but probably unsuited to the bitter, attritional and messy urban battle that confronted him. Vasily Chuikov, commanding Sixty-Second Army, could not have contrasted more with the neat, fastidious Paulus. Tough, earthy, and bloody-minded, he was just the man for the grim task ahead of him and his troops.

Chuikov had also thought hard about how he was going to beat his adversary. The Soviets had chosen their ground well. In the campaigns that preceded Stalingrad, the Soviets had proved tactically and operationally inferior in the

TWO GERMAN SENIOR NCOs take a shelter in a bomb crater in the initial fighting to capture the suburbs of Stalingrad. Both men are armed with MP38s, ideal weapons for close-quarter fighting in a built-up environment.

RED ARMY SOLDIER

This Red Army rifleman is wearing the new-pattern winter uniform introduced in 1941. By late 1942, his *telogreika*, a padded khaki jacket, was in common usage throughout the Red Army. He wears the matching padded pants, *valenki* felt boots and the so-called "fish-fur" cap or *shapka-ushanka*, because the material it was manufactured from bore very little relation to real fur. He is armed with a PPSh-41 submachine gun. Ideal for urban warfare, the compact, robust PPSh-41 made up a large proportion of Soviet infantry weapons during the Battle of Stalingrad.

maneuver warfare that characterized the fighting on the wide, open spaces of the steppes. Key to German success had been the coordination of their infantry and armor and particularly close air support. They had, up to this point, eschewed urban combat in major conurbations. However, military, and particularly political, necessity meant the Germans would be fighting in an environment where their skills in maneuver were irrelevant. Even more importantly, their close air support would be considerably less effective. Conversely the Soviets' proven defensive tenacity, skill in close combat, and willingness to take losses would be a considerable advantage.

THE MAMAYEV KURGAN

The Germans' first attempt to take the city opened on September 14 with a two-pronged assault by LI Corps on the center and south, supported by a push from the extreme southern suburbs by Fourth Panzer Army. The aim was to seize the dominating heights of the Mamayev Kurgan, where Chuikov had his headquarters, and capture the central landing stage, splitting the Sixty-Second Army in two and isolating it from resupply. An artillery strike knocked out Chuikov's HQ and the Germans pushed up over the

IN AN OBVIOUSLY STAGED PROPOGANDA photograph, a group of Soviet soldiers move cautiously through the ruins of Stalingrad amid the fighting during the fall of 1942. All are armed with Soviet PPSh-41 submachine guns.

Mamayev Kurgan toward Stalingrad No. 1 railroad station and the landing stages on the Volga River. Chuikov committed his last tactical reserves and pleaded with his Front commander, Colonel-General Yeremenko, to send him Major-General Rodmitstev's elite 13th Guards Division. The division had to fight its way from the landing stage to the station and onto the southeastern slopes of the Mamayev Kurgan. The station changed hands 15 times with the German 71st Division finally securing it on September 19. By then the 13th Guards, which had entered the battle 10,000 strong, could muster just 2,700 men.

In the south of the city, the Fourth Panzer Army met intense resistance, culminating in the battle around the grain silo, where 50 naval infantry and guardsmen held up three German divisions for several days. However, by September 26 Fourth Panzer Army had reached the Volga and split Sixty-Fourth Army from Chuikov's Sixty-Second Army. The Sixth Army held the crest of Mamayev Kurgan and made substantial gains in the center. Paulus could declare that "the battle flag of the Reich flies over the Stalingrad Party building," but the battle was far from over.

THE VOLGA CROSSINGS

Although the fighting continued around Mamayev Kurgan, the main German effort shifted into the factory district on September 27. The German attacks against the Soviet positions based around the industrial complexes of the Red October, Barrikady, and the Tractor factories, were intended to capture the landing stages behind them. Controlling the Volga was the key to the battle, because it was Sixty-Second Army's vital lifeline. Despite the tactical dominance of the Luftwaffe and the best efforts of the German artillery, they never managed to stop the flow of supplies and men across the river. After a week of bitter fighting the Sixth Army managed to cut off the Tractor Factory.

There was a lull in fighting and then the Germans redoubled their efforts in the factory district, finally capturing Barrikady and most of Red October. By the end of October they held 90 percent of the city and had all the Soviet-controlled areas under fire. But this had only been achieved at a massive cost. The Sixth Army was battered and exhausted and still it was not enough. The Red Army had taken the best the Wehrmacht could throw at and still clung onto the banks of the Volga. On November 11, Paulus launched his last major assault, again in the factory district. It met with some success as German troops managed to reach the west bank of the river.

The Soviet-made Mosin Nagant M1891/30 was considered one of the best-made rifles of World War II. It was prized by both ordinary soldiers and specialists, such as snipers, who used it to great effect at Stalingrad.

ZHUKHOV'S COUNTERATTACK

To maintain momentum over the seven weeks of bitter house-to-house fighting, the German command reduced the length of front held by Sixth Army and Fourth Panzer Army, leaving the flanks covered by Italian and Romanian forces. Stalin had given General Georgi Zhukhov (1896–1974) the task of organizing a counterattack to cut off the Sixth Army in Stalingrad. He built up one million men and 900 tanks in the hinterland behind the Volga, undetected by the Germans. Zhukov launched his assault, Operation "Uranus," on November 19. Three Armies of General Vatutin's South-West Front smashed through the Third Romanian Army and a day later Yeremenko's Stalingrad Front brushed aside the Fourth Romanian Army in the south. The two fronts met at Kalach on November 23, completing a perfect encirclement, that trapped roughly 250,000 German and Axis troops in the Stalingrad pocket.

Paulus requested permission to break out, but Hitler refused. The head of the Luftwaffe, Herman Göring, pledged to supply the Sixth Army by air and Hitler ordered Field Marshal von Manstein (1887–1973) to prepare a counterattack to relieve Paulus' trapped troops. Operation "Winter Storm," which opened on December 12, needed to cover about 60 miles (97km). It was stopped 35 miles (59km) south of Stalingrad. Meanwhile Zhukov launched his offensive code-named "Little Saturn," threatening the entire German position in the south. "Winter Storm" was the Sixth Army's last hope. The Luftwaffe barely managed to land one-third of the

supplies required and from January 10 the German position was increasingly constricted by Operation "Ring," General Rokossovsky's Don Front, and his attempt to close the pocket. Despite the futility of the struggle, the Soviets were impressed by the resilience of the German defenders. Nonetheless, they took about half the pocket in a week and after the last airfield fell, Paulus asked Hitler for permission to surrender. He was refused. By January 29 the Germans had been reduced to two pockets in the city, one around the Unimag Department Store in the center, the other in the factory district. On January 31 Hitler promoted Paulus to Field Marshal. The implications were obvious; no German commander of that rank had ever been captured alive. But Paulus surrendered that day; the northern pocket held out until February 2. German casualties at Stalingrad were about 200,000, with 110,000 of the Sixth Army going into Soviet captivity. Only 5,000 ever made it home.

AFTERMATH

Stalingrad marked a decisive turn in the war against Germany. The Soviet Army had outfought and out-thought the Wehrmacht. Although Germany would maintain a tactical edge, at Stalingrad, the Soviets demonstrated a superior grasp of the operational and strategic level of war. The Red Army had drawn the Wehrmacht into an attritional battle. Yet it had also been able launch a large-scale, mobile "maneuverist" operation, which encircled and destroyed the Sixth Army. The victory at Stalingrad would be followed by many more.

The Sturmgeschütz III Assault Gun was an important part of German offensive operations at Stalingrad. These turretless armored vehicles provided the assaulting German infantry with crucial support with direct fire on point targets, such as machine-gun emplacements and heavily defended buildings.

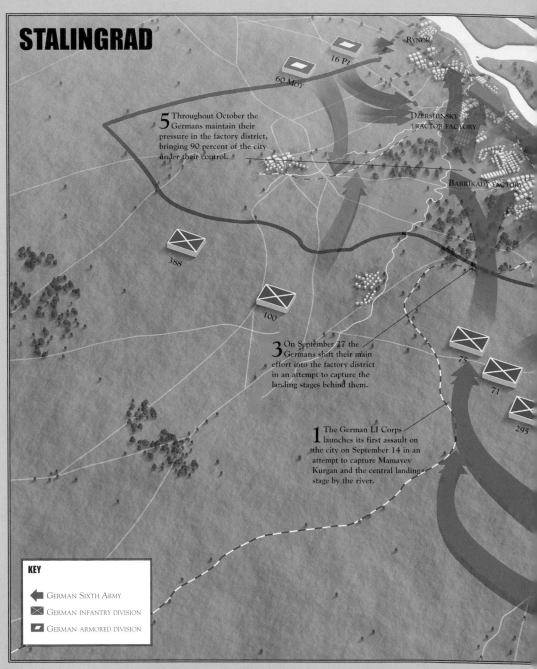

STALINGRAD

5 Throughout October the Germans maintain their pressure in the factory district, bringing 90 percent of the city under their control.

RYNOK

16 Pz

60 Mot

DZERSHINSKY TRACTOR FACTORY

BARRIKADY FACTORY

388

100

3 On September 27 the Germans shift their main effort into the factory district in an attempt to capture the landing stages behind them.

75

71

295

1 The German LI Corps launches its first assault on the city on September 14 in an attempt to capture Mamayev Kurgan and the central landing stage by the river.

KEY

◄ GERMAN SIXTH ARMY

⊠ GERMAN INFANTRY DIVISION

▱ GERMAN ARMORED DIVISION

6 The last major German attack begins on November 11. Eight days later the Soviets launch Operation "Uranus," cutting off the Sixth Army in the city.

4 The Soviets managed to maintain their supply lines across the Volga, providing the 62nd Army with just enough men and material to hang onto their foothold in the city.

RED OCTOBER FACTORY

62ND ARMY HQ

KRASNAYA SLOBODA

MAMAYEV KURGAN

PAVLOV'S HOUSE

NKVD HQ

NO. 1 RAILROAD STATION

GRAIN SILO

VOLGA RIVER

14 PZ

94

24 PZ

2 The Fourth Panzer Army attacks in support in the south of the city, but are held up by fanatical resistance around the grain silo.

29 MOT

MIDWAY 1942

The turning point of the Pacific War, the battle of Midway saw U.S. carrier aircraft destroy the Japanese carriers that had attacked Pearl Harbor. Thanks to signals intelligence and good luck, a Japanese plan to lure the American carriers into a trap instead spelled the end of Japanese naval dominance of the Pacific.

Japan's surprise strike on Pearl Harbor on December 7, 1941, had been a remarkable tactical success, but because the American aircraft carriers had been out to sea, it had been an incomplete victory. One of those aircraft carriers, the *Hornet*, took 16 B-25 bombers to attack Tokyo and Nagoya, inflicting little serious damage, but providing the Americans with a major morale boost in what became known as the "Doolittle Raid."

In May, the Americans again used their carriers to check Japanese moves toward Australia at the Battle of the Coral Sea. These two incidents led senior Japanese leaders to conclude that they had to eliminate the remaining American carriers in

MIDWAY FACTS

Who: A Japanese armada of four aircraft carriers carrying 256 aircraft, 11 battleships, and numerous smaller vessels opposed an American force that included three aircraft carriers, 234 carrier- and land-based planes, and a variety of smaller craft.

What: American carrier-based aircraft attacked and destroyed Japan's aircraft carriers, thus removing Japan's long-range strike and scouting capabilities.

Where: In the Pacific Ocean, northwest of Midway Island.

When: June 3–6, 1942.

Why: The Japanese had hoped to seize Midway Island as an advance base and as a means to lure the American fleet into a decisive battle.

Outcome: The United States destroyed Japan's aircraft carriers, giving the Americans an advantage in the Pacific War, which proved to be crucial.

PACIFIC OCEAN

JAPAN

MIDWAY ✚

Pearl Harbor

U.S. NAVY PERSONNEL *from a damaged ship are hauled out of the sea by comrades at the Battle of Midway. American losses at Midway were minor compared to the Japanese, and included one carrier, one destroyer, 150 aircraft, and 307 men.*

order to provide Japan with strategic space. Time was crucial because the United States was then in the process of converting its massive industrial potential into a military asset the Japanese knew they could not hope to match.

JAPANESE PLANS

The Japanese Admiral Isoroku Yamamoto (1884–1943), architect of the Pearl Harbor strike, sought to lure the Americans into a carrier fight, which he expected his more experienced sailors and airmen to win. A Japanese capture of Midway Island, he predicted, would force the Americans to come to battle on terms advantageous to the Japanese. Once the American fleet had been crushed, Japan could then convert Midway into a major airbase and a safe place from which to monitor American actions in Hawaii. The erroneous report of the sinking of the *Yorktown* at the Battle of the Coral Sea gave the Japanese even more confidence that they had the American fleet outgunned and outclassed. The Japanese navy spared nothing to make Midway a success, assembling approximately 200 ships, including 11

BROUGHT INTO SERVICE *the year before Midway, the Dauntless SBD Dive Bombers were critical to American victory. This photo shows the underrated American repair crews who kept the planes flying and the ships at sea.*

battleships, eight carriers, 23 cruisers, 65 destroyers, and 20 submarines. This force represented the vast majority of the Japanese fleet. The Japanese admirals confidently expected this massive armada to dispatch any American force sent out to meet it.

Partly because of his overconfidence in Japan's material (and presumably moral) superiority, Yamamoto made the fateful decision to divide his forces. He sent a diversionary force that included four battleships and two cruisers north toward the western Aleutian Islands in Alaska. These ships played no role in the battle and, as events turned out, also failed to lure any American ships into taking the bait. The main force, itself the largest armada in the history of the Pacific Ocean, was also split. Submarines moved ahead of the main Japanese forces to find the location of the American ships, report those positions, then prepare to join the battle. The van, or main strike force, commanded by the able Admiral Chuichi Nagumo (1887–1944), included four powerful aircraft carriers: the *Kaga*, carrying 30 fighters, 23 bombers, and 30 torpedo bombers; and the *Hiryu*, *Soryu*, and *Akagi*, each carrying 21 fighters, 21 bombers, and 21 torpedo bombers. The van also included battleships, cruisers, and destroyers to protect the carriers. The final part of the Japanese force was the Midway landing force of surface ships and troop transports.

AMERICAN MOVES

Two major feats by the Americans greatly undermined Japanese preparations. Lieutenant Commander James Rochefort, an eccentric cryptologist who was more comfortable in his bathrobe than in his Navy uniform, had broken enough of the Japanese naval code to guess the general lines of the Japanese plan. Rochefort had intercepted and decrypted plans for a major Japanese operation against a target codenamed "AF." Rochefort's instincts told him that "AF" had to be Midway, but American naval commander Admiral Chester W. Nimitz (1885–1966) still feared that "AF" might be Oahu. To make sure, Rochefort designed a clever ruse. He sent out an unencoded message over a frequency he knew the Japanese were monitoring, stating that Midway's fresh-water system was not working properly. A few days later, when he saw a decoded Japanese order for tanks of fresh water to accompany the "AF" operation, he had the confirmation he and Nimitz needed. Now American naval assets could be concentrated on Midway without jeopardizing the safety of Oahu.

The other great American success involved the carrier *Yorktown*. Damaged so badly at the Coral Sea that Japanese pilots reported her sunk, the *Yorktown* had limped back to Pearl Harbor, where repair crews worked furiously over the course of just three days to get her ready in time to sail toward Midway with Rear Admiral Frank Jack Fletcher's

LEFT: THE GRUMMAN F4F-3 "Wildcat" was the mainstay of the U.S. Navy's carrier aircraft in the first year of the war. Nearly 8,000 Wildcats were built over the course of the war, and they featured prominently at Pearl Harbor, Coral Sea, and Wake Island, as well as the crucial Battle of Midway.

RIGHT: THE UBIQUITOUS Mitsubishi "Zero" initially offered a shock to the Allies in the Pacific theater, outclassing all opposing Allied aircraft. This is the A6M3 model, which came into service in 1942, and could be used as a dive bomber and fighter.

Task Force 17 on May 30, 1942. The Yorktown was in a far from ideal condition, but her aircraft were unaccounted for in Japanese plans. Both Task Force 17 and Rear Admiral Raymond Spruance's Task Force 16 left Pearl Harbor before the Japanese submarines could get into position. Thus not only did the Americans have an aircraft carrier unknown to the Japanese, the Japanese had no reliable information on the whereabouts of the American ships.

Thanks in large part to Rochefort's efforts, the United States Navy did not fall for the Aleutian decoy. With the damaged but serviceable Yorktown, the Navy could count on three carriers, including the Enterprise, and the Hornet. The Americans could also count on the assistance of land-based planes on Midway Island itself. The Americans had a total of 233 carrier- and 127 land-based aircraft to meet the 248 planes of the Japanese force. The United States, still recovering from the losses at Pearl Harbor, had nothing to counter Yamamoto's seven battleships, but it was now in a position to fight the battle using carriers at long range, thus leaving the battleships isolated. As at Coral Sea, the entire battle was fought by planes from carriers; the surface ships never even saw one another, owing to the great range of the carrier aircraft.

THE FIRST STRIKE

Unbeknown to the Japanese, then, the Americans had a reasonably useful idea of what to look for and where to spot it. Just after midnight on June 4, 1942, American patrol planes spotted the Japanese van less than 600 miles (965km) from Midway Island. Although American attempts to inflict damage on the Japanese fleet from the air failed, the early warning allowed Midway to prepare its defenses and its aircraft. For his part, Admiral Nagumo was undeterred by

what he understood as a fluke American overflight of his carriers. Accordingly, he launched his air attack of 100 planes against Midway at 4:30 A.M. when his ships were still 240 miles (386km) away from Midway. The Americans, ready

JAPANESE SAILOR

The Imperial Japanese Navy (IJN) in 1942 was a powerful force with a history of big victories. Since the Russo-Japanese War of 1904–05 the Navy had seen a string of successes and a steady rise in importance. More recently, in addition to Pearl Harbor, the Japanese could look with pride on their technical abilities in the Singapore and Philippines campaigns. Its sailors were confident, disciplined, and aggressive. Service in the IJN came with great prestige; consequently, 80 percent of Japanese sailors were volunteers, a much higher percentage than Japanese soldiers. Japanese sailors especially excelled at gunnery, navigation, and night fighting. Specially trained Japanese sailors supported amphibious warfare and naval aviation, the two branches the IJN most heavily relied on during their planning for Midway.

ABOVE: A SQUADRON of Douglas SBD Dauntless are seen over USS Enterprise in late 1941, just weeks before the attack on Pearl Harbor. Despite its many shortcomings, the Dauntless played a crucial role in combatting the Japanese in the Pacific, sinking a greater tonnage of shipping than any other Allied aircraft.

for the strike, shot down 67 Japanese planes. At the same time, American planes were headed directly for Nagumo's carriers. Nagumo still had half of his planes held back in reserve, but he would have to keep his decks clear in order to recover his returning planes, which would be low on fuel. The Japanese strike did not do as much damage to Midway as was needed to ensure an easy invasion. Accordingly, the Japanese attack commander radioed back that another strike against the island was required.

THE CRUCIAL MOMENTS

Meanwhile, the American first strike had reached Nagumo's carriers. It failed, suffering heavy losses, but it revealed to Nagumo the presence of American carriers nearby. Nagumo now faced a dilemma. He had planes out to sea that he

THE SORYU was designed and laid down in 1937, the first in a new series of fleet carriers that became the mainstay of the Japanese navy during the first years of the war. With an excellent power-to-weight ratio and able to accommodate more than 60 aircraft, the Soryu was fast and agile. However, her light armor made her vulnerable to air attack.

needed to recover and he had to choose between arming his planes for a second strike on Midway Island or a strike on the American carriers whose exact location was still unknown. The former operation would require high explosive bombs, the latter operation would require torpedoes.

Nagumo first ordered his second wave to be armed with bombs for the second pass at Midway, but at 7:40 A.M. a signal came in from a Japanese cruiser reporting the American carriers east of Nagumo and closing fast. Nagumo thus had the worst possible situation, with enemy carriers nearby, but planes armed with the wrong ordnance for attacking them. He also still had airmen returning to their carrier low on fuel, with several wounded. He ordered his carriers to prepare for recovery of his first strike force, thus losing precious time.

At 9:30 A.M. and 9:40 A.M. two waves of American torpedo bombers attacked the Japanese carriers, but were annihilated by faster, more nimble Japanese fighters. The Americans lost 47 of their 51 planes. The torpedo attacks,

although ineffective, kept Nagumo from launching his planes and distracted the Japanese fighters from a more powerful wave of American SBD Dauntless dive bombers. Owing to the good luck that is the result of hard work and good guesswork, the Dauntless bombers had arrived over the Japanese carriers at the perfect time. Because of the confusion regarding the change of armament, the Japanese carriers had bombs and torpedoes stacked on the decks, instead of safely below in magazines. Because of the need to refuel the returning planes, moreover, the decks were also full of gasoline lines, and the confusion of all this activity prevented Nagumo from being able to launch his reserve fighters.

In this vulnerable position, the Japanese had to face American dive bombers launched from the Yorktown and Enterprise. At 10:22 A.M. American planes struck the Kaga, eventually hitting it four times. Within a few short minutes the Soryu and Akagi had also been hit and put out of action. Fires spread out of control and in at least one case, fire spread to the main ammunition magazines. All three carriers were later abandoned and scuttled. It was an astonishing example of chance meeting skill at just the right moment. In a matter of few minutes the entire balance of naval power in the Pacific had changed.

FINAL ACTIONS

Aircraft from the lone remaining Japanese carrier, the Hiryu, damaged the Yorktown badly enough to force Admiral Fletcher to order her to be abandoned. Already in bad shape, she had performed as well as could have been expected, and was later sunk by a Japanese submarine. Later in the day American aircraft spotted the Hiryu and scored four direct hits, causing fires that forced her crew to abandon ship. The Japanese had now lost all four of the carriers they had committed to the attack. Total Japanese losses included four carriers, two heavy cruisers, three destroyers, 229 aircraft, and 3,500 men. American losses included one carrier, one destroyer, 150 aircraft, and 307 men.

The Americans knew they had won a major victory but decided not to risk a night action against the now exposed Japanese surface vessels. They therefore withdrew to the east to the safety of the Midway Island defenses, although American cruisers and submarines continued to harass the remaining Japanese ships. The Japanese used the time to withdraw to safety. Yamamoto, for his part, knew how bad the disaster had been for Japan, commenting to his officers, "I am the only one who must apologize to His Majesty," for the defeat. Yamamoto offered his resignation, but it was declined.

THE LAST SURVIVOR of the Japanese battle fleet at Midway, Hiryu was struck by SBD Dauntless dive bombers late on June 4, 1942. Burning fiercely, the carrier was abandoned and scuttled some 12 hours later.

AFTERMATH

Japanese losses had indeed been severe. In one day they had lost four irreplaceable carriers and as many pilots as their pre-war training system had produced in a year. Japan was left with just two carriers. The Americans had also lost a carrier, but they had an industrial base that eventually produced 35 more carriers by the end of the war. In that same time period, Japan was barely able to make good the losses from Midway alone.

Midway did not, of course, win the Pacific War for the United States. It did, however, shift the strategic initiative to the United States. Without aircraft carriers, the Japanese could not hope to conduct any more long-range surprise operations. As several other events from the war also showed, surface ships, the true strength of the Japanese fleet, were vulnerable without air cover. Future Pacific naval battles bore this dictum out, because Japanese battleships could not operate with impunity as long as American carriers were nearby. Prewar American faith in the aircraft carrier had been proven justified and as American industry produced more carriers and more planes, the scales tipped increasingly in America's favor.

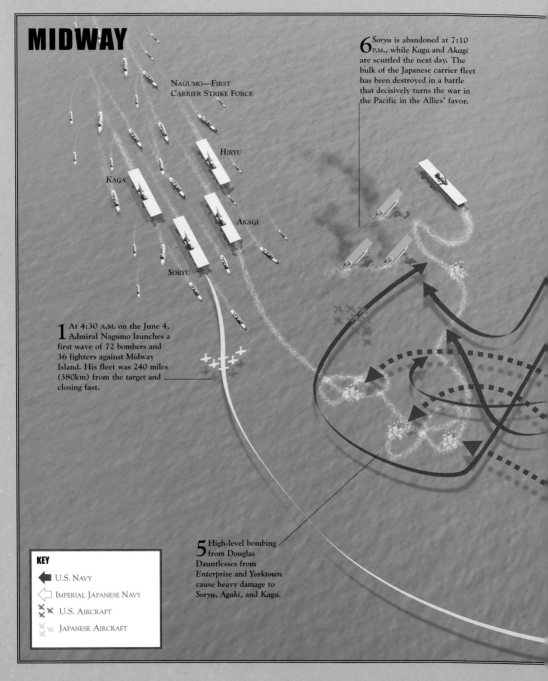

MIDWAY

NAGUMO—FIRST
CARRIER STRIKE FORCE

HIRYU

KAGA

AKAGI

SORYU

6 *Soryu* is abandoned at 7:10 P.M., while *Kaga* and *Akagi* are scuttled the next day. The bulk of the Japanese carrier fleet has been destroyed in a battle that decisively turns the war in the Pacific in the Allies' favor.

1 At 4:30 A.M. on the June 4, Admiral Nagumo launches a first wave of 72 bombers and 36 fighters against Midway Island. His fleet was 240 miles (380km) from the target and closing fast.

5 High-level bombing from Douglas Dauntlesses from *Enterprise* and *Yorktown* cause heavy damage to *Soryu*, *Agaki*, and *Kaga*.

KEY

➤ U.S. NAVY

▷ IMPERIAL JAPANESE NAVY

✕✕ U.S. AIRCRAFT

✕✕ JAPANESE AIRCRAFT

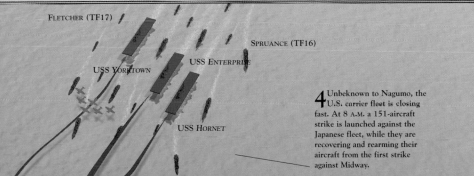

FLETCHER (TF17)

SPRUANCE (TF16)

USS YORKTOWN

USS ENTERPRISE

USS HORNET

4 Unbeknown to Nagumo, the U.S. carrier fleet is closing fast. At 8 A.M. a 151-aircraft strike is launched against the Japanese fleet, while they are recovering and rearming their aircraft from the first strike against Midway.

3 On Midway, between 7:05 A.M. and 8:10 A.M., all the base's offensive aircraft are sent to intercept the Japanese fleet in three waves. Although attacking bravely, the U.S. airplanes have little impact. However, Nagumo decides a second attack on the Midway is necessary to immobilize the airstrip and neutralize the U.S. aircraft there.

2 At 6:16 A.M., the radar station on Midway detects the incoming Japanese aircraft and U.S. aircraft are scrambled to intercept. However, the slow Grumman Wildcats and Brewster Buffalos are no match for the superior Zeros.

MIDWAY ISLAND

NORMANDY 1944

The battle for Normandy began with the spectacularly successful D-Day landings, thanks in no small part to an astounding campaign of deception that mislead the German commanders completely. However, the breakout from Normandy was more problematic, and was only achieved after hard and costly fighting.

On the USA's entry into the World War II in December 1941, the Americans and their British allies agreed on a policy of defeating Germany first, while containing the Japanese in the Pacific. It was clear that the defeat of Nazi Germany would eventually entail the landing of an Allied army on the European mainland. The British and Americans differed in how this should be achieved.

For the Americans the issue was simple. A large force should be landed in northwestern Europe to defeat the bulk of German forces and then march on Berlin. British military leaders, haunted by the slaughter of the World War I and having experienced German military prowess, were less enthusiastic. They preferred a

NORMANDY FACTS

Who: American, British, Canadian, and French forces under the supreme command of General Dwight D. Eisenhower (1890–1969) against the German armies in the West commanded by Field Marshal Gerd von Rundstedt (1875–1953).

What: After the largest amphibious landings in military history, the Allies were able to establish themselves on the Continent and break out of Normandy after harder-than-expected fighting.

Where: The Normandy peninsula in western France.

When: June 6–August 19, 1944.

Why: The Allies sought to establish a Second Front, liberate Western Europe, and drive on into Nazi Germany.

Outcome: The German Army in Normandy was effectively destroyed and the Allies advanced east toward the German border.

AMERICAN INFANTRY WADE ASHORE on Omaha Beach. *These are almost certainly part of a later wave of troops to land, because they are not encoutering the deathly fire experienced by the earlier waves. Despite the low-lying cloud apparent in this photograph, the weather cleared in the afternoon, allowing Allied airpower to dominate the battlefield.*

strategy of dispersing German strength by continuing the campaign in the Mediterranean. For a while the British policy prevailed, but at the Casablanca Conference of January 1943, the British were forced to accept American military logic and agree to a major military landing in France. In May a provisional date for the operation, now code-named "Overlord," was set for May 1, 1944.

OPERATION "OVERLORD"

The prospect of transporting enough troops across the English Channel to establish and hold a beachhead and then reinforcing them faster than the Germans could bolster their own forces was a daunting task. Eschewing the most direct route across the Straits of Dover, the planners decided to land in Normandy. This was largely because it was within the range of Allied air cover, had firm and sheltered beaches, and was close to Cherbourg, a major port. General Dwight D. Eisenhower was appointed Supreme Commander with General Bernard Montgomery (1887–1976) as the commander of the invasion's land forces. They immediately

RIGHT: GENERAL EISENHOWER gives a pep talk to members of the 101st Airborne prior to their drop on the Normandy countryside.

BELOW: A BRITISH SARGEANT smiles for the camera as infantry form up on Sword Beach, ready to support the armor that is preparing to move off. The men have canvas covers for the bolts of their rifles, to protect them from the seawater and sand as they landed.

altered the original plan, by widening the beachhead and expanding the initial amphibious assault from three divisions to five, supported by various commando and Ranger units, with three airborne divisions dropped inland to secure the flanks. They would be rapidly followed by the rest of the U.S. First Army under General Omar Bradley (1893–1981) and the British Second Army commanded by General Sir Miles Dempsey (1896–1969). By late 1943, it was clear to the Germans that an Anglo-American invasion

would come; it was just a question of when and where. Most of the German commanders, Hitler included, believed that the Allies would attempt to land on the Pas de Calais. Field Marshal von Rundstedt, the German Commander-in-Chief in the West, had 58 divisions under his command, but half of these were static, tied to stretches of coastal defenses. Key to the defeat of any Allied invasion, was his nine panzer and one panzergrenadier divisions. However, he disagreed with his subordinate Field Marshal Erwin Rommel (1891–1944), commander of Army Group B, made up of Fifteenth Army in the Pas de Calais and Seventh Army protecting Normandy, as to how that armor should be used. Von Rundstedt and General von Schweppenburg, commander of Panzer Group West, wanted the armor held back to deliver a crushing counterattack. Rommel felt this would be impossible given Allied control of the air. He believed that the Germans had to defeat the invasion on the beaches and thus he wanted the armor deployed as close to the beaches as possible. Hitler's solution was a compromise. In Normandy this meant only one panzer division, the 21st, was located close to the coast with the rest, Panzer Lehr and 12th SS Panzer, held further back. This left both commanders dissatisfied; Rommel felt his forward defences were inadequate and Von Rundstedt believed his panzer reserve was too small.

SHERMAN D-D TANK

The DD (Duplex Drive) Sherman was amphibious version of the mainstay of main Anglo-American tank. A collapsible fabric screen and inflatable pillars and two small propellers allowed the tank to "swim." Once it was ashore, the screen could be collapsed and the DD Sherman could function as a normal tank.

DECEPTION PLANS

For "Overlord" to succeed, the Allies had to train and then assemble their forces in southern England. The Air Commander-in-Chief, Air Chief Marshal Leigh-Mallory (1892–1944) had to ensure air superiority over the beaches and hamper German supply and reinforcement capabilities. The Allied air forces targeted the French transportation system, but in such a way so as not to draw attention to Normandy. An intricate deception plan, Operation "Fortitude" sought to convince the Germans that, firstly, the Pas de Calais was the intended target and, secondly, the actual invasion of Normandy was simply a diversion. This succeeded perfectly.

The Allies assembled a vast invasion fleet of nearly 7,000 warships, transports, and support vessels to escort and provide fire support or carry the 130,000 troops across the Channel. During June 5, after a 24-hour delay due to bad weather, the fleet assembled off the south coast of England and began to sail south toward the six landing beaches in Normandy, designated from west to east, "Utah," "Omaha," "Gold," "Juno,"

and "Sword." They were passed overhead by the first Allied bombers en route to attack the German defenses. These were followed from 11:30 P.M. by the transport planes taking the 17,000 airborne troops to drop zones to the east and west of the beaches.

D-DAY

The Battle of Normandy opened just after midnight on June 6 as the British 6th Airborne Division landed northeast of Caen. The first troops into action were glider-borne troops of 2nd Oxford and Buckinghamshire Light Infantry, who quickly secured the bridges over the Caen canal and the Orne River. Other units of the 6th Airborne captured several bridges over the Orne, overran the Melville Battery, and secured the invasion's left flank by holding the Ranville-Hérouvillette area. Meanwhile at about 1 A.M. the

Just 41 ft (12.5 m) in length, the LCA (landing craft assault) were some of the smaller craft used to transport troops on D-Day, carrying about 30 personnel.

American paratroops of the 82nd and 101st Airborne Divisions jumped into the marshy terrain around the westernmost landing beach "Utah." The paratroopers did much to confuse the German response, which was not helped by the fact that Rommel was on leave. "Fortitude" had also ensured that the Germans continued to expect the main invasion in the Pas de Calais even several days after D-Day and thus held back their reserves.

Two hours later 1,900 bombers began attacking the German defenses in the landing area and as dawn approached the naval bombardment opened. At 6:30 A.M. the Americans of 4th Division began their run-in at "Utah" beach; the Canadians attacking "Juno" beach would land as late as 7:45 A.M. as a result of tidal conditions. On "Utah" the Americans quickly established themselves ashore, advanced across the waterlogged terrain behind the beach and linked up with airborne forces in the area. This was achieved for the cost of just under 200 casualties.

Things went rather less well on "Omaha" beach. Allied intelligence had failed notice that the defending regiment of the 716th Division, a static formation, had been reinforced by two regiments of the veteran 352nd Division. These men largely survived the preparatory bombardment unscathed. On top of this the poor weather conditions meant that only five of the 32 DD swimming Sherman tanks and very few of the Americans' supporting combat engineers made it ashore. The assaulting troops of 1st Infantry and 29th National Guard Divisions took terrible losses to the well dug-in German troops. By the end of the day they had secured a tenuous foothold that was no deeper than 2,000 yards (1.8km) at the cost of 2,000 casualties. "Gold" was the westernmost Anglo-Canadian beach. It was assaulted by the British 50th (Northumbrian) Division.

THIS U.S. INFANTRY CAPTAIN carries an M1 Carbine. The carbine was designed for specialist troops, such as drivers and machine gunners, but such was its lightness and ease of handling it became popular with front-line troops.

Unlike the Americans, the British were supported by a variety of specialized armored fighting vehicles, such as AVRE assault tanks, to breach defenses, and Sherman Crab flail tanks, designed to clear minefields, in addition to their DD tanks. By the end of the day, 50th Division had managed to push 4 miles (6.4km) inland while 47 Commando struck westward toward the Americans on Omaha.

Meanwhile the 3rd Canadian Infantry Division landed on "Juno," the central British-Canadian beach. They met particularly strong resistance and were hampered by the loss of many landing craft to submerged obstacles. It took the Canadians an hour and a quarter of hard fighting to secure the first exits from the beach. They also managed to push about 4 miles (6.4km) inland by the end of the day.

On "Sword" the most easterly beach, effective fire support suppressed the enemy defenses and most the landing craft taking ashore the 3rd Infantry Division made the run-in undamaged. However, due to the bad weather the incoming tide was higher than expected, which meant the craft were deposited among the German submerged beach obstacles that the Allies had expected to be visible. Landing higher up the beach than expected did have the advantage of reducing the amount of ground the infantry had to cross, but in confined space of the beach armored vehicles soon became congested, hampering the British attempt to push inland. The 3rd Division was tasked with linking up with 6th Airborne on the Orne River, which 1st Special Service Brigade and 8th Brigade achieved reasonably quickly. However, the capture of Caen, which was also scheduled for the first day, proved a little more difficult. The drive on the city was disrupted by a counter-attack by 21st Panzer. The German division drove straight into the gap between "Juno" and "Sword" beaches, but faltered in the face of British anti-tank and tank gunnery.

THE BATTLE FOR CAEN

Caen had not fallen, but otherwise it had been a remarkably successful day. The Allies had achieved massive strategic surprise and landed over 130,000 men at the cost of about 6,000 U.S. and 4,300 British and Canadian casualties. The Germans had failed to drive them back into the sea and over the next few days the beachheads were linked up and resources poured into the Normandy pocket. By D-Day +6 about 330,000 men, 55,000 vehicles, and 104,000 tons of supplies had been landed. However, a rapid break-out did not follow. The Americans pushed up into the Cotentin Peninsula towards Cherbourg, while British and Canadians concentrated on the capture of Caen. Montgomery's plan for Normandy was for the British to tie down the weight of German resources, particularly their armor, to give the Americans the opportunity to break-out in the face of weaker resistance. This was a reasonable enough strategy but

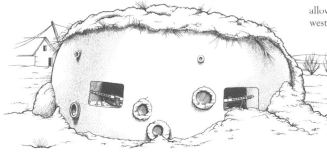

allowed Patton to shift the bulk of his forces westward. Despite the imminent collapse of the German position, Hitler insisted on a counter-offensive, which was launched against the U.S. First Army in the Mortain area on August 7, but they only succeeded in pushing their remaining armor further westward into a pocket that was rapidly closing around them. This gave Bradley the idea of pushing Patton's troops at Le Mans northward, while the Canadians drove south toward Falaise, a move that might trap an estimated 21 German divisions in the pocket. Montgomery immediately approved and although the two armies did not meet until August 19, some 10,000 Germans were killed and 50,000 captured. About 20,000 escaped. The battle for Normandy was over.

LIKE THIS MACHINE-GUN EMPLACEMENT, some of the defenses on the Atlantic Wall had been taken from the French Maginot Line and other obstacles built by the Belgians and Dutch in the late 1930s. Many of these old defenses proved very effective against the advancing Allies.

his reputation with his allies and posterity was not well served by his overconfident predictions of success for the operations to capture Caen. A Canadian push on the city on June 7 floundered in the face on the arrival of 12th SS Panzer Division, a broad outflanking maneuver was stopped at Villers-Bocage on June 12 and the carefully prepared Operation "Epsom" from June 25–30 failed in the face of desperate German counterattacks. The city finally fell on July 8. Even then the British failed to break-out toward Falaise and took massive losses, particularly in tanks, during Operation "Goodwood" from July 18–20.

THE BREAKOUT

Nonetheless these operations had had the desired effect of sucking the German armored forces into a battle of attrition on the western side of the lodgment. The German commanders had hoped to husband their panzer divisions for a counterattack that would drive the Allies into the sea, but had been forced to fritter these resources away in a desperate attempt to shore up the line in the face of constant British pressure. Meanwhile the Americans had managed to capture Cherbourg and as "Goodwood" drew in the bulk of German armor in Normandy, they prepared an offensive to capitalize on the weakened German line in front of them. This would be the crowning achievement of the campaign.

On the morning of July 25 a massive air bombardment heralded the opening of Operation "Cobra." American infantry and armor broke through the German lines and headed south for Coutances. After two days fighting it was clear that the Americans had destroyed the Germans' left flank and opened up the way into Brittany. On August 1, the U.S. Third Army under General George Patton (1885–1945) became operational and Bradley handed 1st Army over to General Hodges, stepping up to take command of Twelfth Army Group. Lack of resistance in Brittany

AFTERMATH

The Normandy Landings were an extraordinary achievement, easily the largest amphibious operation in history. The Allies had managed to establish themselves on a hostile coastline and reinforce their position faster than their enemy, who relied on the comprehensive road and rail network of northwestern Europe. Much of the success was down to an impressive logistical effort by the Allies and the importance of air power in hampering the German response. The landings did not lead to a rapid break-out and collapse of the German position in the west, but the Normandy Campaign caused losses to the Germans in terms of men and material and the establishment, at last, of Second Front meant that Germany's strategic position was now untenable.

AN MG42 MACHINE GUNNER, of the Waffen-SS "Hitler Jugend" Division. This division was brought in as reinforcements to stem the Allied advance.

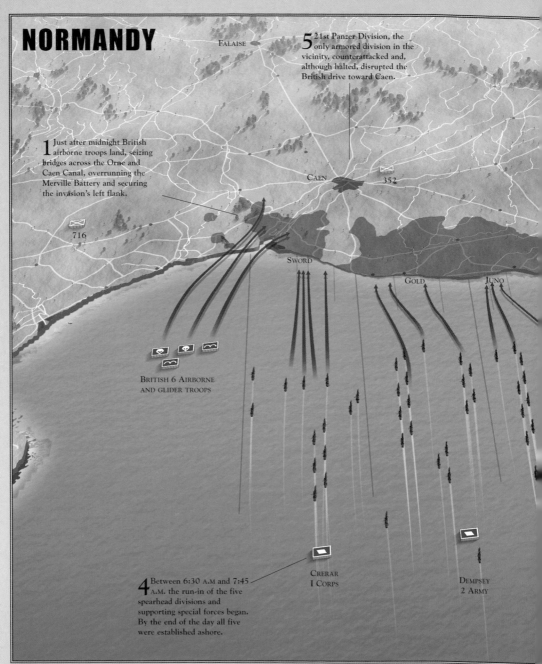

NORMANDY

FALAISE

5 21st Panzer Division, the only armored division in the vicinity, counterattacked and, although halted, disrupted the British drive toward Caen.

1 Just after midnight British airborne troops land, seizing bridges across the Orne and Caen Canal, overrunning the Merville Battery and securing the invasion's left flank.

CAEN

352

716

SWORD

GOLD

JUNO

BRITISH 6 AIRBORNE AND GLIDER TROOPS

4 Between 6:30 A.M and 7:45 A.M. the run-in of the five spearhead divisions and supporting special forces began. By the end of the day all five were established ashore.

CRERAR I CORPS

DEMPSEY 2 ARMY

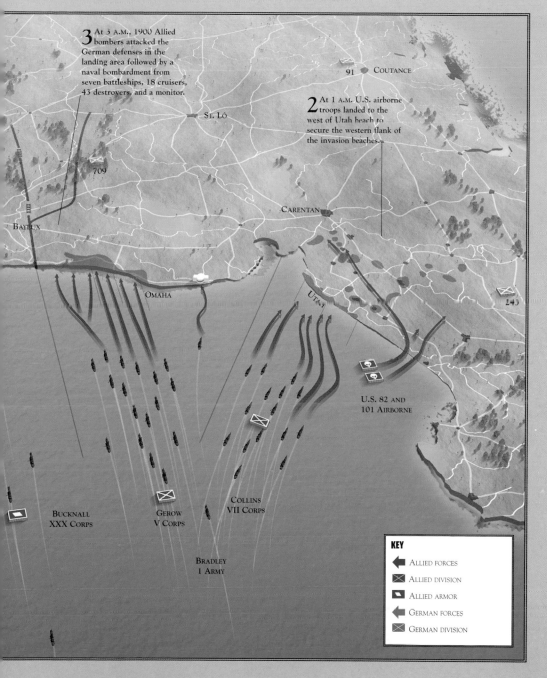

3 At 3 A.M., 1900 Allied bombers attacked the German defenses in the landing area followed by a naval bombardment from seven battleships, 18 cruisers, 43 destroyers, and a monitor.

2 At 1 A.M. U.S. airborne troops landed to the west of Utah beach to secure the western flank of the invasion beaches.

91 COUTANCE

ST. LÔ

709

CARENTAN

BAYEUX

OMAHA

UTAH

143

U.S. 82 AND 101 AIRBORNE

BUCKNALL XXX CORPS

GEROW V CORPS

COLLINS VII CORPS

BRADLEY 1 ARMY

KEY

ALLIED FORCES

ALLIED DIVISION

ALLIED ARMOR

GERMAN FORCES

GERMAN DIVISION

THE TET OFFENSIVE
1968

As 1967 drew to a close, it appeared that the United States was gaining the upper hand in the Vietnam War. The Tet Offensive of early 1968, however, began the steady decline of U.S. fortunes in Vietnam, despite an undeniable military victory.

From 1965 to the end of 1967, the principal U.S. strategy in Vietnam was "search and destroy" (S&D), an attritional form of warfare developed by General William Westmoreland (1914–2005), head of the Military Assistance Command, Vietnam (MACV), and other high-ranking U.S. staff. S&D tactics concentrated on stacking up high body counts of North Vietnamese Army (NVA) and Viet Cong (VC) personnel, utilizing the massive U.S. advantage in firepower and maneuver formations. The aim was to reach the "crossover point," where North Vietnam was simply unable to prosecute the war militarily owing to manpower losses.

THE TET OFFENSIVE FACTS

Who: The regular forces of the North Vietnamese Army (NVA) supported by the irregular Viet Cong (VC), numbering around 80,000. They took on the full might of the U.S. forces in Vietnam, plus the Army of the Republic of South Vietnam (ARVN), a combined force of over 1.5 million.

What: Communist forces launch a major offensive throughout South Vietnam, targeting urban areas and military bases.

Where: The Tet Offensive was launched along the entire length and breadth of South Vietnam, from military bases along the Demilitarized Zone (DMZ) in the north, down to the Mekong Delta in the south.

When: January 29–April 8, 1968.

Why: The North Vietnamese hoped to occupy South Vietnam's urban centers and draw out a popular uprising against the South Vietnamese government.

Outcome: Total military defeat for the NVA and VC, although the Western media focus more on the seeming escalation of the conflict rather than U.S. successes.

U.S. M113 ARMORED PERSONNEL CARRIERS (APCs) advance into Saigon to combat the Viet Cong uprising. The U.S. use of heavy firepower in urban zones, particularly of artillery and air assets, would cause great controversy in the media.

A TYPICAL U.S. MARINE in full combat gear, with a toy Christmas tree hung from his belt to add some seasonal cheer. Over his shoulder is the .3in (7.62mm) M60 machine gun, which could provide powerful suppressive fire.

By late 1967, confidence was high that S&D was paying off. There were, indeed, grounds for optimism—NVA/VC casualties were horrific and, in the long run, looked unsustainable. North of the Demilitarized Zone (DMZ), Ho Chi Minh (1890–1969) and his military commander, General Vo Nguyen Giap (b. 1911), also recognized this fact, and decided on a radical change in strategy. Instead of pursuing the slow, violent grind of revolutionary war, they would gamble on an all-out offensive in the South.

What would become the Tet Offensive was not, it should be noted, intended to defeat U.S. or Army of the Republic of Vietnam (ARVN) forces in straightforward open battle, but to elicit an uncontrollable popular uprising within the South that would destroy ARVN's capabilities, force U.S. capitulation, and establish a regime change.

To maximize the North's chances of success, Giap chose to launch the offensive during the national Vietnamese Tet Lunar New Year festival. This major cultural event, for which the Viet Cong had already declared a ceasefire to run from January 27 to February 3, would see huge numbers of ARVN troops given leave to visit families, and a general reduction in the alert status of the southern defenses. However, preparatory actions began well before the official launch of the offensive. The Tet Offensive was aimed mainly at South Vietnam's major urban centers, so preliminary NVA/VC operations looked to draw U.S./ARVN forces away into the countryside. Siege operations against the northern U.S. Marine Corps base at Khe Sanh began on January 21, 1968 (not wholly connected to Tet) and further actions around Dak To pulled manpower away from the cities. Although there was a general U.S. suspicion that an offensive was in the offing, the NVA/VC nevertheless managed to infiltrate 84,000 troops and thousands of tons of supplies along the entire length of South Vietnam, ready for the attack date.

BROAD OFFENSIVE

When the Tet Offensive was launched on January 29/30, 1968 (some assaults appear to have gone in 24 hours early, probably in error), it consisted of dozens of simultaneous actions rather than a single campaign. Thirty-six out of 44 provincial capitals, five autonomous cities, 72 district capitals, and 23 military bases came under rocket, mortar, and artillery fire, with followup attacks by either regular NVA units of battalion or divisional strength or VC assault teams. Most psychologically troubling to the U.S. government were the attacks in Saigon, conducted by a total of 35 enemy battalions. VC sappers blew their way into the U.S. embassy compound and began a six-hour small-arms engagement in the courtyard with U.S. Military Police guards. The firefight was caught live on camera, and although the VC attackers were eventually all killed (along with five U.S. soldiers) the resultant TV images profoundly disrupted the U.S. public's belief in the impregnability of their government's power.

Elsewhere across Saigon, other high-value targets came under assault, and at one point many districts fell under direct, albeit temporary, NVA/VC control. Both the MACV and ARVN headquarters buildings were attacked, as was the Presidential Palace. Other targets included U.S./South Vietnamese naval headquarters, the Korean and Filipino embassies, and the National Radio Station. During the latter operation, 15 VC managed to occupy the station, intending to broadcast revolutionary urgings across South Vietnam

A CUTAWAY OF THE AK-47 assault rifle. NVA and Vietcong forces used a Chinese-produced version of the classic Soviet assault rifle. The AK was ideally suited to insurgency use, being incredibly robust with good close-range firepower.

THE VIET CONG were lightly equipped troops compared to the U.S. and ARVN, and had excellent on-foot mobility. However, the VC were almost wiped out during Tet, crushed by U.S. firepower.

while waiting for a relief force. However, government engineers managed to cut the connection between the station and its transmitter, and the VC squad was eventually killed or committed suicide after the relief force failed to reach them.

Saigon was just one hub of NVA/VC focus during Tet. From the Mekong Delta to northern military bases at Quang Tri and Lang Vei, U.S., and ARVN forces fought desperate battles to stave off a North Vietnamese takeover. Yet the advantage inexorably swung the other way. While the initial shock and confusion of Tet were tremendous, ARVN and U.S. forces managed to snuff out the vast majority of the local attacks within three or four days. From its inept performances of the early–mid 1960s, ARVN was also emerging as a force with a new professionalism, its U.S. training being backed by a fervent desire to protect homes and districts. (Mounting evidence of NVA/VC atrocities in captured areas also inspired ARVN troops to fight to the death rather than be captured.) Furthermore, there was no sign of a popular revolt in support of the communist offensive. This kicked the supports out from under Tet, and was a bitter ideological shock to the communists.

In and around Saigon, U.S. and ARVN forces built up 10 divisions of combat troops by February 4, and launched a general counteroffensive—Operation "Tran Hung Do"—to retake the city. Using close-air support, artillery, and recoilless rifles, the allied troops smashed their way through the NVA/VC defenders with controversial excesses of firepower. By February 10, all resistance in the capital had been quashed, and it was left to South Vietnamese police to conduct a brutal hunt of VC sympathizers.

THE BATTLE FOR HUE

While the flames of the Tet offensive were being smothered in many parts of South Vietnam, in one city the battle would rage until February 25. North of Da Nang, the coastal city of Hue was one of Vietnam's most exquisite cities. It was split

U.S. MARINES RETURN FIRE against NVA forces in the southern sector of Hue, February 1968. U.S. urban warfare tactics were shown to be inadequate, and at times the U.S. wounded rate was higher than in major World War II battles.

HUE WAS AN IDEAL battleground for snipers. Here a U.S. soldier scans upper windows for snipers, with his M16 at the ready.

in two by the Perfume River, dividing the modern New City to the south from the ancient walled Citadel to the north. The Citadel's outer wall, built in 1802 under Emperor Gia Long, was 30ft (9.1m) high and 20ft (6m) thick, and was

CAPTURED NORTH VIETNAMESE Army (NVA) soldiers are taken away for questioning. In many cases NVA and VC prisoners were ultimately executed, particularly if captured by ARVN units. Some 8,000 NVA troops were killed in the Hue fighting.

bombardment. Hue's iconic beauty had kept the city apart from war's effects up until Tet, with the consequence that it was negligibly defended. Hue consequently became the only city to be fully occupied by the communists during Tet.

At first, U.S. forces around Hue responded ineffectually and with bad intelligence, sending only a handful of U.S. Marine platoons into the city. Most of these were, predictably, battered back by a division-strength NVA defense. Once the truth had dawned, the U.S. and ARVN forces began planning for a potent counteroffensive to retake the city. The allied forces divided the attack into two zones. U.S. Marine units would retake the New City, while ARVN forces would assault the Citadel. Once the Marines had cleared their tactical zone, they would then cross the Perfume River in support of the ARVN operation. In addition, the 3rd Brigade, 1st Air Cavalry (Airmobile) Division was airlanded 6 miles (9.6km) west of the city on February 2 to interdict NVA logistics and reinforcements moving between Laos and Hue.

This blocking action was to have a vital impact on the fighting. The 1st Air Cavalry soldiers, later supported by troops from the 101st Airborne Division and local ARVN

also bolstered by a brick inner wall. Such defenses, however, were irrelevant when 8,000 communist troops took over the city completely—with the notable exception of the 1st ARVN Division's headquarters at the far north of the Citadel—on January 31 following a heavy artillery

THE M60 PATTON TANK was the main U.S. MBT of the Vietnam War. Its chief role in Vietnam was infantry support rather than tank vs. tank warfare, providing heavy firepower from its 4.2in (105mm) main gun plus .50 caliber and .3in (7.62mm) machine guns.

KHE SANH

The NVA siege of the Khe Sanh Combat Base (KSCB), located amidst the jungle on a red clay hill 7 miles (11km) from the Laotian border, was a dramatic counterpoint to the Tet Offensive. The base was occupied by 6,000 U.S. Marines and ARVN troops, and by 1968 General William Westmoreland hoped that the base would attract a major NVA assault, thereby giving him the opportunity to inflict major casualties on a geographically locatable enemy. He was not disappointed. On January 20, 1968 some 40,000 NVA regulars put KSCB under siege, maintaining a constant stream of artillery fire. Although cut off from the land, KSCB was resupplied by U.S. transport aircraft, while B52s and other ground-attack aircraft blasted the surrounding jungle almost 24 hours a day. There was some heavy, even hand-to-hand fighting, around peripheral U.S. hilltop positions, but in every case the communists were battered back. Finally, on April 8, U.S. Marine and Air Cavalry units made a land link with Khe Sanh, ending a 77-day siege that cost an estimated 10,000 communist dead and 205 U.S. fatalities.

NVA soldiers take part in the bloody assault on Khe Sanh.

units, managed to stop three NVA regiments from reinforcing the communist troops in the city.

As fighting deepened in Hue itself, the U.S. and ARVN forces underwent an appalling introduction into urban warfare, something that had been neglected in many post-World War II training programs. In the New City, the 1st Battalion, 1st Marine Regiment and 2nd Battalion, 5th Marine Regiment managed to make only four blocks progress in six days of intense fighting. At first, the historic and architectural status of the city spared it U.S. heavy bombardment. Yet the bitter cost of house-to-house fighting soon changed the policy, and the destruction of Hue began. During the Hue fighting 52,000 rounds of U.S. artillery were fired into the city, along with 7,670 rounds of heavy naval artillery and 600 tons of air-dropped munitions. The consequences for the civilian population were dreadful, but by February 6 most of the major landmarks in the New City had been secured, and by the 10th its entirety was secured.

The Marines now moved across the Perfume River into the Citadel, where ARVN units had also been pushing the communists onto the back foot. Gradually ARVN troops blasted the NVA/VC from the northern parts of the Citadel. They eventually retook the airfield and, on February 24, the Imperial Palace on the Perfume River's north bank. Resistance to the allied counteroffensive held out in the far western parts of the city and in the Gia Hoi district (where the communists had slaughtered hundreds of civilians in acts of "social engineering") throughout

February, but by March 2, the whole city was back in allied hands. In terms of fatalities, the cost of Hue had been 119 U.S. troops, 363 ARVN soldiers, around 8,000 NVA regulars or VC insurgents, and some 6,000 civilians.

AFTERMATH

Hue brought the Tet Offensive effectively to a close. Although it rumbled on with the siege at Khe Sanh. When that concluded in early April it was time to assess the damage. For the North, the Tet Offensive was a catastrophic failure. Not only had it lost around 54,000 troops (against 11,000 South Vietnamese and 2,000 U.S. troops), but the Viet Cong was almost entirely wiped out as a political and military entity. Furthermore, the lack of a popular uprising destabilized the North's entire belief that the South was simply waiting for the chance to embrace communism.

The Tet Offensive was undoubtedly a military victory for the U.S., yet this was not the way it was portrayed by the Western media. The impression was given that the conflict was escalating dramatically even as politicians and commanders gave assurances that the North was on its knees. Further military requests for increases in troop levels set alarm bells ringing even among U.S. politicians, and by 1969 the policies of "Vietnamization"—transferring conduct of the war into mainly South Vietnamese hands—and progressive U.S. troop withdrawals gained dominance. In an irony not lost on governments to this day, the military victory counted for less than the media defeat.

TET OFFENSIVE—HUE

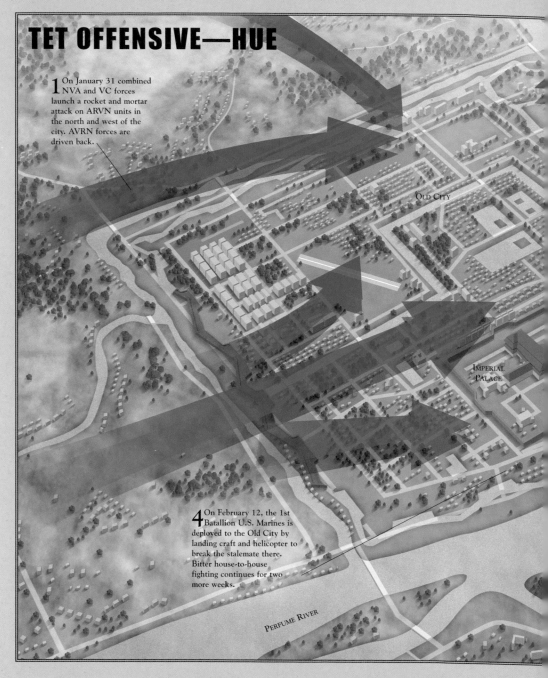

1 On January 31 combined NVA and VC forces launch a rocket and mortar attack on ARVN units in the north and west of the city. AVRN forces are driven back.

OLD CITY

IMPERIAL PALACE

4 On February 12, the 1st Batallion U.S. Marines is deployed to the Old City by landing craft and helicopter to break the stalemate there. Bitter house-to-house fighting continues for two more weeks.

PERFUME RIVER

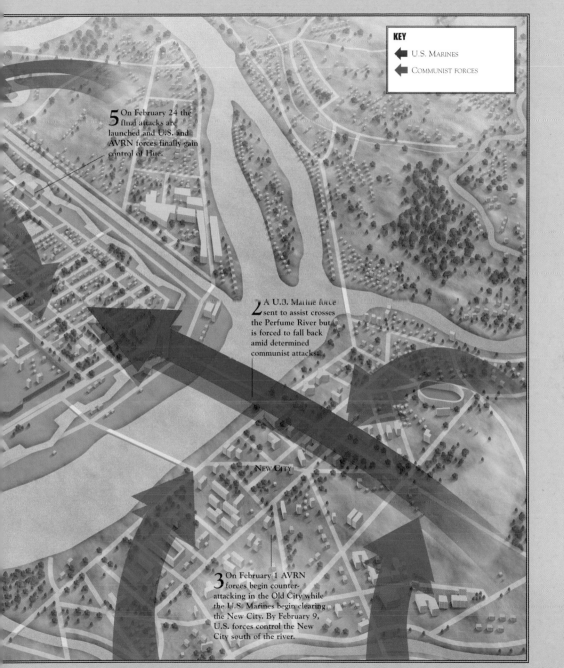

KEY

◀ U.S. MARINES

◀ COMMUNIST FORCES

5 On February 24 the final attacks are launched and U.S. and AVRN forces finally gain control of Hue.

2 A U.S. Marine force sent to assist crosses the Perfume River but is forced to fall back amid determined communist attacks.

NEW CITY

3 On February 1 AVRN forces begin counter-attacking in the Old City while the U.S. Marines begin clearing the New City. By February 9, U.S. forces control the New City south of the river.

OPERATION "IRAQI FREEDOM" 2003

Operation "Iraqi Freedom" was boldly conceived and vigorously executed. In less than 40 days U.S.-led Coalition forces crushed Iraqi military resistance, captured Baghdad, and removed the regime of Saddam Hussein.

The traumatic events in Iraq following the completion of Operation "Iraqi Freedom" have tended to cloud judgment about the sheer success of the initial military operation. "Iraqi Freedom" was arguably one of the best executed military campaigns of the last 60 years, an action in which the domination of Coalition forces was total and their casualties incredibly light. This is not to deny that there were problems in both strategy and execution, but such are the stuff of war, and the aggregate operation was a resounding triumph.

OPERATION "IRAQI FREEDOM" FACTS

Who: A U.S.-led Coalition force of more than 260,000 troops against the national defense forces of Iraq and Fedayeen irregulars.

What: The full-scale invasion of Iraq by the Coalition, with its objective as the destruction of Iraqi forces and the overthrow of Saddam Hussein's regime.

Where: The main theater of the conflict was concentrated between the Iraq-Kuwait border and Baghdad, with a separate theater in the north that was mainly in the hands of U.S.-supported Kurdish separatists.

When: March 20–May 1, 2003.

Why: "Iraqi Freedom" was part of the U.S. response to the September 11, 2001 terrorist attacks, based on claims that Iraq had broken UN sanctions, sponsored terrorist groups, and illegally possessed weapons of mass destruction (WMDs).

Outcome: Successful occupation of Iraq by Coalition forces, although the campaign ended with a dramatic rise in insurgency actions.

U.S. MISSILES *slam into key targets around Baghdad on March 21, 2003. The Iraqi forces generally expected a rerun of the 1990-91 Gulf War, when the Allies preempted the land war with a prolonged air campaign. Instead, U.S. and British land units crossed into Iraq almost immediately.*

A REPUBLICAN GUARD soldier. The Republican Guard put up the sternest resistance to Operation "Iraqi Freedom," but, suffering from low morale and a poor command structure, they were totally outmaneuvered and outgunned by U.S. armored forces.

OPPOSING FORCES

On March 17, 2003, President George W. Bush gave a clear ultimatum to the Iraqi leadership: "Saddam Hussein and his sons must leave Iraq within 48 hours. Their refusal to go will result in military conflict commenced at a time of our choosing." His threat was backed by the presence of more than 260,000 Coalition troops (214,000 U.S. and 45,000 British, the rest being small contingents from allied nations) massed in border staging areas in Kuwait. Facing them was uncertainty. Iraq's military forces had been degraded by the destruction of the 1990–1 Gulf War and the subsequent military sanctions against the country, and both morale and command initiative were poor. Yet intelligence estimates placed the number of available regular troops at more than 400,000 (including 44,000 Fedayeen Saddam paramilitaries) with up to 650,000 reserves. Even allowing for inadequacies in combat capability, that still amounted to a potent force, especially if it had taken on board combat lessons learned in the first Gulf War.

The Iraqi military, however, was expecting a rerun of the earlier conflict—with its extended air campaign prologue. They would soon be disabused. Under the overall leadership of General Tommy Franks (Commander-in-Chief, U.S. Central Command), the Coalition forces would launch an immediate land campaign, securing key positions in southern Iraq while other units drove northward to the capital Baghdad. The aim was to bypass many of Iraq's major urban centers (there was the concern that the Iraqi army would opt for urban battlefields to avoid their technological disadvantages in open-terrain warfare), pushing straight through to Baghdad and enforcing rapid regime change by crushing the top of the command structure. With no response to Bush's ultimatum, Operation "Iraqi Freedom" began on March 19.

SOUTHERN ACTIONS

The first actions of "Iraqi Freedom" were, as in 1991, an air attack. U.S. attack aircraft and Tomahawk cruise missiles made precision strikes against targets across Baghdad, hoping to take out Saddam Hussein and 55 key Iraqi leaders (this "decapitation" strike was largely unsuccessful). Shortly after, on the night

LEFT: THE U.S. M1A1 ABRAMS tank often formed the vanguard of the U.S. push up toward Baghdad. Its Rheinmetall 4.724in (120mm) smoothbore gun can hit targets at well over visual range with either depleted uranium or high-explosive anti-tank (HEAT) rounds.

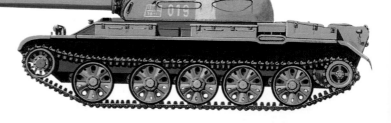

THE T-55 was one of the oldest tanks in the Iraqi arsenal by 2003. Although some models had received upgrade packages to armor, fire-control systems and main armament, they were still hopelessly outclassed by the U.S. and British tanks.

A UH-60 BLACKHAWK helicopter flies over Baghdad in May 2003. Although helicopters were ideally suited to operations over the Iraqi wilderness, they proved very vulnerable to opportunistic small-arms fire over urban zones.

of the 20th/21st, Coalition forces surged across the Iraq-Kuwait border. The attack plan for the south (operations in northern Iraq are considered in the feature box) was three-pronged. The U.S. Army V Corps, led by the 3rd Infantry Division, would drive up toward Baghdad through the desert on the western side of the Euphrates River. East of the river, the 1st Marine Expeditionary Force (MEF) would push through An Nasiriyah, cross the Euphrates, and advance on Baghdad from east of the river, thereby forming one arm of a pincer movement with the army formations. Finally, British forces, with U.S. Marine support, would operate in the far south of the country, securing the Al Faw peninsula and taking Iraq's second city, Basra.

Operation "Iraqi Freedom" got off to a brisk start. Iraqi border outposts were obliterated by artillery fire and precision attacks from U.S. Army Apache helicopters, allowing easy movement into Iraq. Late on 20 March, British and U.S. Marines stormed and secured the port of Umm Qasr (although sporadic combat would continue for the next two days), before the U.S. elements turned northward. The Al Faw peninsula was occupied by a combined arms amphibious operation, and by March 21 the British 7th Armored Brigade had reached the outskirts of Basra.

Resistance toughened here against Iraqi militia and regular forces. Fearing a horrific civilian casualty toll in an urban battle, the British stopped and waited, allowing Basra's civilians free passage out of the city. Events in southern Iraq were unfolding rapidly. The 1st Marine Division secured the Rumaila oilfields in the south of Iraq—one of the world's largest petroleum/gas reserves—before turning west toward An Nasiriyah. The task of actually securing An Nasiriyah, with its vital series of bridges over the Euphrates, fell to Task Force Tarawa, otherwise known as the 2nd Marine Expeditionary Brigade (MEB). There it would experience one of the campaign's nastier shocks.

AN NASIRIYAH AND BEYOND

The greatest challenges for the Coalition assault into Iraq were time and distance. With every hour of advance the Allied supply lines became increasingly stretched. By the end of March 22, for example, the 3rd Infantry Division was 150 miles (241km) into Iraq. This supply line had to be protected, and there remained the worrying possibility that the advance might slow down to a stop, and allow the Iraqi forces to cut up an overextended Coalition. Yet although resistance was locally fierce, so far it was not heavy enough to affect overall strategy. Iraq troops seemed more inclined to surrender than die in a hail of U.S. gunfire.

However, on March 23 events took a worrying turn around An Nasiriyah. A U.S. Army unit, the 507th Maintenance Company (part of the 3rd Infantry Division, which was also participating in actions around An Nasiriyah) was ambushed by Fedayeen fighters, who killed 11 soldiers and took seven prisoner (including the now famous Private Jessica Lynch). Marines of Task Force Tarawa moved to the rescue, but the day descended into a bloody

OPERATIONS IN NORTHERN IRAQ

The original plan for Operation "Iraqi Freedom" had involved a matching offensive down into northern Iraq from Turkey. However, the Turkish government prohibited Turkey's use as a jumping-off point for U.S. land forces (it permitted the use of air bases), so the action in the north was mainly concentrated in the hands of Kurdish Peshmerga paramilitaries acting with strong support from the U.S. 10th Special Forces Group. Furthermore, a 1,000-soldier airdrop from the 173rd Airborne Brigade secured Bashur airfield, and gave the Kurds more conventional power. Iraqi troops in the north began to retreat southward, and on March 28, U.S. and Kurdish troops took the base camp of Ansar al-Islam, an Islamic group connected with the al-Qaeda terrorist organization, after a particular violent battle code-named Operation "Viking." In a subsequent action known as the Battle of the Green Line, another Kurdish/U.S. force (operating, as usual, with good close-air support) defeated the Iraqi 13th Infantry Division, and then occupied Tikrit, securing Saddam Hussein's last possible bastion of resistance.

battle in what would become known as "ambush alley." Eighteen Marines were killed, several by the "friendly fire" of supporting A10 aircraft. It would take until the end of the month to secure An Nasiriyah, although by then the Marine advance northward had resumed. The three Regimental Combat Teams (RCTs) of 1st MEF took two lines of advance towards Baghdad: 5th RCT and 7th RCT took Route 1 directly toward the capital, while 1st RCT swung up Route 7 farther east.

The U.S. advance was becoming tougher. Out to the west, the main U.S. Army advance was facing increasing resistance from four Republican Guard divisions, and by March 25 the 3rd Infantry Division was locked in combat around An Najaf (more than 300 Iraqi troops were killed in just two days of fighting). Furthermore, a huge sandstorm across the region had reduced the Coalition advance to a

A BRITISH SNIPER serving with the 1st Battalion, Irish Guards, takes up a position close to the city of Basra, April 2003. Snipers were set up to provide protection for British Army engineers employed to put out the numerous oil-well fires started by retreating Iraqi forces.

grinding crawl, giving Iraqi irregulars a breathing space in which to redeploy and attack the supply lines.

An Najaf was steadily brought under control by U.S. forces: encircled on March 26, hammered with artillery and air bombardment, then finally stormed and controlled at the beginning of April by the 101st Airborne Division. By this point, however, the Coalition was closing on the capital.

BATTLE FOR BAGHDAD

In the far south of Iraq, battle was still raging for Basra. A large tank battle around the city on March 27 saw the Royal Scots Dragoon Guards destroy 14 Iraqi tanks. On March 30, Operation "James," a major offensive into the city, was launched by the 7th Armored Brigade, supported by the Parachute Regiment and Special Forces soldiers. Hard fighting continued for a week, but by April 6 the city was finally in British hands. However, the sudden collapse of the city's administration led to an anarchic upsurge in looting and random violence, a story that would become familiar across Iraq over the coming weeks.

While the British were fighting for Basra, the U.S. 3rd Infantry Division assaulted around the western side of Karbala, crossed the Euphrates, and closed on Baghdad. By now the resistance from Iraqi Army forces was collapsing. The Republican Guard's Medina Division on the Baghdad outskirts, for example, was obliterated on April 3–4, as was a Fedayeen counterattack. To the east, the Marines were also closing up on the city.

The U.S. commanders decided on a bold strategy to take Baghdad. On April 5, the heavily armed 2nd Brigade, 3rd Infantry, made a "thunder run" up Route 8 straight into the capital. The unit consisted of 761 men backed by tanks and Bradley armored fighting vehicles, and was essentially a reconnaissance force to test out the Baghdad resistance. Under heavy fire all the way (every vehicle was hit), the unit then swung out to reach the Saddam International Airport, already in U.S. hands.

On April 7, a second "thunder run" was made, this time plunging into the administrative heart of the capital. By nightfall Saddam's palaces were in U.S. hands, but fighting to secure the supply route was fierce, with constant firefights along the snaking streets. U.S. Marine units were now entering and securing eastern parts of the city, having forced their way across the Diyala Bridge. By April 8, the Marines had closed up to the Tigris River, effectively completing the occupation of the city. On April 9, in a highly symbolic moment, the towering statue of Saddam Hussein in Firdos Square was pulled down by an American armored vehicle.

The formal land campaign to take Iraq was effectively over. Saddam Hussein's home town of Tikrit was captured by a U.S. Marine task force on April 15, removing the last significant outpost of resistance in central Iraq, and by

An F/A-18 Hornet from the "Silver Eagles" of Marine Fighter Attack Squadron One Fifteen (VMFA-115) launches from the flight deck of USS Harry S. Truman in support of Operation "Iraqi Freedom." Coalition air superiority was essential in guaranteeing a quick victory in Iraq.

April 10, the campaign in the north had secured Kirkuk. On May 1, 2003, President Bush landed on the flight deck of the USS *Abraham Lincoln* and declared an official end to the combat operations in Iraq.

AFTERMATH

History now shows us that President Bush's dramatic declaration of the end of hostilities was deeply flawed. Poor postoperation planning fanned the flames of a spiraling insurgency in Iraq which, at the time of writing, accounts for several thousand lives in Baghdad alone every month. One of the salient features of Operation "Iraqi Freedom" was that large sections of the Iraqi public were alienated by Coalition military action. Around 30,000 Iraqi civilians were killed during the operation, and evidence suggests that a high percentage of these was caused by indiscriminate U.S. firepower rather than enemy actions. Furthermore, the fall of Saddam's regime and the inadvisable disbandment of the Iraqi army fueled an explosion of intertribal and interfaith conflicts, leading to a dreadful existence for many Iraqi people.

"Iraqi Freedom" itself was not without faults. Many commanders on the ground felt that Defense Secretary

Donald Rumsfeld's decision to limit troop numbers caused severe problems for the advance and security actions, and actions at An Nasiriyah and other places showed how effective a determined insurgency force could be. Yet war is at heart a violent, problematic encounter, and judged by the light casualties—fewer than 130 U.S. personnel and 33 British personnel killed—and the swiftness with which the objectives were achieved, it is an impressive model of a modern land campaign.

A squad of U.S. Army soldiers from the 23rd Infantry Regiment conduct an area reconnaissance mission in Baghdad, August 2006. More than three years after hostilities were declared, large numbers of Coalition troops were bogged down in anti-insurgency warfare.

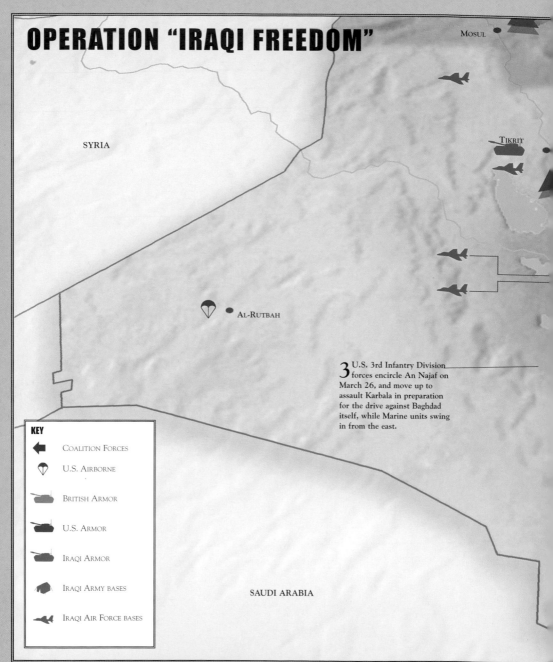

OPERATION "IRAQI FREEDOM"

MOSUL

SYRIA

TIKRIT

AL-RUTBAH

3 U.S. 3rd Infantry Division forces encircle An Najaf on March 26, and move up to assault Karbala in preparation for the drive against Baghdad itself, while Marine units swing in from the east.

KEY

COALITION FORCES

U.S. AIRBORNE

BRITISH ARMOR

U.S. ARMOR

IRAQI ARMOR

IRAQI ARMY BASES

IRAQI AIR FORCE BASES

SAUDI ARABIA

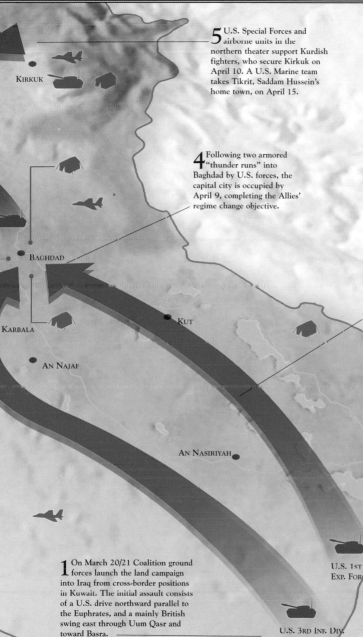

5 U.S. Special Forces and airborne units in the northern theater support Kurdish fighters, who secure Kirkuk on April 10. A U.S. Marine team takes Tikrit, Saddam Hussein's home town, on April 15.

KIRKUK

IRAN

4 Following two armored "thunder runs" into Baghdad by U.S. forces, the capital city is occupied by April 9, completing the Allies' regime change objective.

BAGHDAD

2 U.S. Marine and Army forces cross the Euphrates at An Nasiriyah, despite constant attacks, and form the eastern pincer of the drive toward Baghdad.

KARBALA

KUT

AN NAJAF

AN NASIRIYAH

BASRA

1 On March 20/21 Coalition ground forces launch the land campaign into Iraq from cross-border positions in Kuwait. The initial assault consists of a U.S. drive northward parallel to the Euphrates, and a mainly British swing east through Uum Qasr and toward Basra.

UMM QASR

U.S. 1ST MARINE EXP. FORCE

KUWAIT

U.S. 3RD INF. DIV.

UK 7TH ARMORED BDE

INDEX

Page numbers in *italics* refer to illustrations; those in **bold** type refer to map illustrations with text. Abbreviations are as follows: (B)—battle; (NB)— naval battle; (S)—siege.